KENNETH R. THOMPSON, RAMON L. BENEDETTO,
THOMAS J. WALTER *with MOLLY MEYER*

IT'S MY COMPANY TOO!

HOW ENTANGLED COMPANIES MOVE BEYOND EMPLOYEE ENGAGEMENT FOR REMARKABLE RESULTS

GREENLEAF
BOOK GROUP PRESS

Published by Greenleaf Book Group Press
Austin, Texas
www.gbgpress.com

Distributed by Greenleaf Book Group LLC

For ordering information or special discounts for bulk purchases,
please contact Greenleaf Book Group LLC at PO Box 91869,
Austin, TX 78709, 512.891.6100.

Design and composition by Greenleaf Book Group LLC
Cover design by nuphoriq

Publisher's Cataloging-In-Publication Data
(Prepared by The Donohue Group, Inc.)

It's my company, too! : how entangled companies move beyond
employee engagement
    for remarkable results / Kenneth R. Thompson ... [et al.]. -- 1st ed.

    p. : ill. ; cm.

    ISBN: 978-1-60832-396-8

    1. Employee motivation. 2. Leadership. 3. Employees--Attitudes.
4. Corporate culture. I. Thompson, Kenneth R.

HF5549.5.M63 I87 2012
658.3/14   2012942413

Part of the Tree Neutral® program, which offsets the number
of trees consumed in the production and printing of this
book by taking proactive steps, such as planting trees in direct
proportion to the number of trees used: www.treeneutral.com

TreeNeutral®

Printed in the United States of America on acid-free paper

12 13 14 15 16 17   10 9 8 7 6 5 4 3 2 1

First Edition

CONTENTS

FOREWORD

Thirty years ago Tom Peters and Robert Waterman rocked the business (and publishing) world in their "search of excellence." About twenty years later, Jim Collins had a similar impact in showing us how companies go from "good to great." Neither I nor the authors are so audacious as to claim that this book completes the trilogy and puts closure on answering the questions of what makes an organization "excellent" or "great." However, I will unequivocally state that my very close colleague and friend over the years, Ken Thompson, and his coauthors—Ray Benedetto, Tom Walter, and Molly Meyer—provide a book that triggered in me the following descriptions: evidence-based, action research; value-added; well-organized, flowing structure; engaging (or should I say entangled) writing style; and just plain entertaining and fascinating reading.

The title *It's My Company Too!* and the authors' use of the term and concept of "entanglement" led me to think, "Oh boy, what have I gotten myself into here?" Almost immediately the opening paragraphs swept aside all of my doubts; the reason for the title and the explanation of entanglement—to represent going beyond engagement—were not only clear but made theoretical and practical sense. The introductory chapter lays out the authors' purpose of asking important questions concerning what really makes (and differentiates) great employees and, in turn, great organizations. To answer these questions, the authors then spell out the very impressive, award-winning criteria they used when they selected the organizations they would study in depth through rich interviewing data and archival research.

The eight organizations selected for study are not the corporate icons that all of us know about and that Peters and Waterman and Collins touted (many of which subsequently failed). Instead, they are "out of the box" organizations such as North Lawndale Employment

Network, Sweet Beginnings, Tasty Catering, Advocate Good Samaritan Hospital, and Mike's Carwash. Although most of us would think this is a strange array of organizations to study, these organizations have three things in common: They are all multiple award-winners (including winners of the coveted Baldrige), they all have entangled employees, and they are all highly entangled organizations. Oh, and by the way, they each represent at least one of the central, integrated themes, as identified by the authors' research, that makes truly wonderful (and high-performing) employees and organizations. Specifically, these fascinating organizations have one or more of the following identifiable dimensions: extraordinary leaders, an ethical climate, utilization of all their human capital, processes to guide performance, tools to increase employees' self-efficacy, the provision of freedom and responsibility within a culture of discretionary thinking and action, and guidance in the transformation process to remarkable performance.

The book is truly a pleasure to read. The documentary-style examples from real people, with no holds barred, gives tremendous insights into some of the most challenging problems facing all organizations today. What the authors identify as entangled employees using discretionary thinking that results in entangled, award-winning, top performing organizations is not intended to be *the* answer. However, this great little book certainly makes a strong case for explaining and helping solve the complex "people" side of organizations now and into the future. I strongly recommend that students, academics, top-level organizational leaders, and middle managers read the book. They will find answers to some of the more perplexing but important "people" problems they are or will be facing. You will enjoy the read.

Fred Luthans
Distinguished Professor of Management, University of Nebraska
Former President, Academy of Management
Chair, Master Research Council, HumanEx, Inc.

FOREWORD: THE BACKSTORY

Maybe it's just the journalist in me, but I like to know the genesis of things, and so when my friend Tom Walter, the CEO of Tasty Catering, invited me to write a foreword for *It's My Company Too!,* my first question was, How did it come to be written? He proceeded to tell me a most interesting tale.

It began with a confrontation, he said. In late 2005, a couple of his most promising young employees—Tim Walter (his son) and Jamie Pritscher—told him they were going to quit unless Tom and his two brothers, who owned and ran the business, changed their ways. Although just twenty-three and twenty-two years old, respectively, at the time, Tim and Jamie had already carved out important roles for themselves in the company and were regarded by the Walter brothers as its future leaders. "It was an OMG moment," Tom says. "We could not lose them."

He asked what it was about Tasty Catering's management that had led them to contemplate leaving. They said they were fed up with having to spend at least thirty minutes a day trying to figure out what sort of mood the brothers were in. It was necessary, they said, because any one of the brothers was capable of exploding without warning and countermanding another brother's orders. These sudden outbursts disrupted the workplace, making it impossible for them and others to focus on their work. The company, in other words, was preventing them from being as productive as they wanted to be.

Tasty Catering was hardly an anomaly in that regard. To the extent that it had a management philosophy back then, it was command-and-control, whereby the boss is responsible for determining what will be done—and when, and how—and the employees' responsibility is to do as they are told. That's the way most organizations have operated since time immemorial. But Jamie and Tim wanted nothing to do with it.

"I asked them what we should do," Tom recalls. "They suggested we buy the book *Good to Great* and use it as a basis for reforming our culture."

So began the turnaround that, within a year or so, produced the extraordinary culture Tasty Catering has become famous for, as described in chapter 6. The culture, in turn, caught the attention of Ray Benedetto, a retired Air Force colonel and founder of a consulting business, who proceeded to write an award-winning doctoral dissertation on it. Benedetto and Walter then recruited Ken Thompson and Molly Meyer, and together they turned the dissertation into *It's My Company Too!*, featuring eight organizations that have rejected command-and-control in favor of transformational leadership and what the authors call "entanglement."

These remarkable companies are not the first to have looked for an alternative to traditional ways of running a business. By my reckoning, that search has been going on for at least eighty years. Along the way, it's engaged entrepreneurs, big-company executives, academics, consultants, management theorists of various sorts, and, yes, even a few journalists. They've been driven by a recognition that a command-and-control approach to managing a business, while sometimes necessary, is both inefficient from a productivity standpoint and lobotomizing from a human one. Common sense told them there must a better way. After all, if employees are encouraged to take personal responsibility for the business; if it's set up to give them both a reason and an opportunity to think and act like owners; if their hearts, souls, and minds—as well as their hands— are engaged in making the enterprise successful, isn't it bound to outperform competitors whose employees are simply doing what they're told?

But creating such a culture requires fundamental changes, not to mention a lot of hard work. In particular, it means trusting employees to act like responsible adults. That's not to say they should be left to their own devices. Transparency is crucial, and everyone needs to pay attention. Call it trust-and-track, as opposed to command-and-control.

From my perch at *Inc.* magazine—first as executive editor, then as editor-at-large—I have seen an explosion of interest in, and experimentation with, such trust-and-track initiatives over the past thirty years. Virtually all of the innovation in this area has been occurring in privately owned, small to midsize organizations like the ones in this book. The trend hasn't received the attention it deserves, mainly—I believe—because of the single-minded focus on large, publicly traded companies by both academia and the mainstream business media. Perhaps *It's My Company Too!* will help open their eyes to what they've been missing.

It should. I have no doubt that the future belongs to "entangled" companies like these. For one thing, they produce better financial results than their competitors over the long run, and what works in business tends to be imitated. Not coincidentally, they also have a distinct advantage over un-entangled companies in hiring and keeping the best people, who—like Jamie and Tim—are looking for more than a paycheck, perks, or even stock options. Any company can provide those. What the entangled companies offer are the intangible rewards of work: meaning, purpose, camaraderie, personal growth, fun. Those rewards are critical because great employees always have choices about where to land. Most of them will go with the employer that can give them something the others don't have. And, in the age of "human capital," the company with the best people usually wins.

Demography also plays a role here. It seems altogether fitting that the initial push for change at Tasty Catering came from members of the millennial generation—that is, young people born in the early years of the entrepreneurial revolution, when Ronald Reagan was president, Steve Jobs first graced the cover of *Time* magazine, and Bill Gates was on his way to becoming the richest man in the world. Millennials grew up with views of business and its possibilities that are radically different from those that baby boomers and even some gen-Xers were exposed to in their youth. By the early 1990s, dozens of new business role models had emerged, ranging from fast-growing tech start-ups to socially conscious companies like Ben & Jerry's Homemade, The Body Shop, and Patagonia. Also during this period, Tom Peters, Jim Collins, and others were breaking new ground in their studies of what makes great companies tick. And then, of course, the Internet era dawned—before most millennials had reached their tenth birthday.

Studies show that command-and-control never sat well with them, and I'm told by friends of mine who employ post-millennials—or whatever members of the next generation are called—that it's a complete non-starter with that group. (Naturally, this doesn't prevent some employers from continuing to use it and then, when it doesn't work, blaming the kids for being lazy, spoiled, unreliable, or whatever.) Meanwhile, baby boomers are leaving the workforce in droves. So the writing is on the wall: Hiring and keeping the right people will become much harder for un-entangled companies as time goes on.

That said, I believe what we don't know about entanglement far exceeds what we do. Just for starters, how many entangled companies are there? Are there different kinds, and if so, how should we categorize them? What are the strengths and vulnerabilities of the different approaches? Which practices are the most effective in the short term and the long term? How does performance vary in different economic climates? Can we not only identify but quantify the boost a business gets from becoming entangled? How can these practices be adapted to work in much larger companies? And on and on.

It's My Company Too! represents a giant step forward in our understanding of the theory and practice of entanglement. Let's hope that these authors and others will continue to delve into the topic—and then share their findings with the rest of us.

Bo Burlingham
Editor-at-large of *Inc.* magazine, author of *Small Giants: Companies That Choose to Be Great Instead of Big*

PREFACE

Thousands of books about leadership and organizational culture exist. Many profess to offer leaders throughout the business world a "silver bullet" that will help them raise performance and solve their deepest organizational problems. Despite what appear as "new" notions, many ideas are simply variations on existing themes. What makes *It's My Company Too!* different? First and foremost, the questions that drove the research behind this book are different from those asked by authors of other books.

How do organizations develop the commitment and loyalty from their employees that propel performance beyond "normal" to "extraordinary" on a daily basis? What makes one organization an award winner versus another that's scrambling to survive? What in the organization leads employees to do the best they can? We sought to answer these questions through firsthand observation, interviews, and archival research that took us to several states and organizations across a range of sizes, industries, markets, and constituents. Whether for profit or not for profit, the top performers shared remarkable similarities. We then matched what we found with evidenced-based research to better understand what we saw and why it worked.

We investigated and ultimately selected eight award-winning organizations to write about. We learned through interviewing more than two hundred people that having the *right leadership* and the *right culture* were important but not necessarily sufficient factors for organizational success. We found organizations that went beyond simply engaging employees and getting their commitment. We found organizations that delighted customers, increased efficiencies and productivity, and gained superior employee satisfaction, but we found more. We found a unique synergy that cultivated *discretionary thinking*, and that thinking motivated employees to give their best efforts every day. In short, we found *entangled organizations* that achieved performance excellence and made them market leaders within the communities they serve. How did they rise to the top?

Discovering Entangled Organizations

When we began this project nearly two years ago, we had no idea we would find what we came to describe as *the entangled organization*; that was not our original purpose. What we were searching for was a better understanding of how truly successful companies distinguish themselves from others. Just as Olympians are different from other athletes, employees within high-performing organizations act differently within their organizational cultures. From our past business experiences and research, we knew that something more than engaged employees and other popular notions stood behind performance excellence.

For more than a year, we traveled across several states to investigate award-winning organizations. Our selection criterion for the organizations was simple but demanding: Each one had to be a recipient of an important award—the Malcolm Baldrige National Quality Award, one of the national "Best Places to Work" awards, the Better Business Bureau's International Torch Award for Excellence in Marketplace Ethics, or some other major industry award for excellence. The criteria we set for ourselves were also simple: We had to be open-minded about the organizations. The final group of selectees would have to represent a diverse set of industries (service, manufacturing, health care, retail) and different types (profit, not for profit) and sizes (several hundred to several thousand employees) to help us determine whether similar behaviors and structural elements such as policies and practices lead to greatness across industries.

Our qualitative research ran the gamut from a two-month ethnographic study in one company to visits in other companies and organizations that ran two or three days. Across the board, we interviewed founders, leaders, employees, customers, clients, and suppliers in each organization to understand what they do, how they do it, and their motivation for working within the organization. In addition, we conducted archival research to examine customer feedback, policies and procedures, communications and reports, and tribal stories that painted verbal pictures of how employees achieved what Bo Burlingham, in his book *Small Giants: Companies That Choose to Be Great Instead of Big* (Penguin, 2005), refers to as "mojo," or company charisma.

From our original list of twenty organizations, we identified eight organizations in eight very different industries that not only had charisma and organizational character but also highly energized personnel and high levels of product quality, profit, and productivity. Although this book is not about companies that profited during an economic slump, each organization was profitable and successful despite the economy, which further captivated our interest. Each company and organization we studied allowed employees to focus on using their discretionary thinking toward solving exciting challenges. And although what each company did was somewhat different, the group of eight shared a common set of values, behaviors, and actions that created cultures that led their employees to achieve more than they thought they could do.

GOING BEYOND ENGAGEMENT TO GET REMARKABLE RESULTS

Saturday mornings during the month of July in the Tasty Catering warehouse are chaotic. Crews are everywhere, waiting to depart for their assigned picnics and special events while the warehouse and kitchen teams are scurrying about moving supplies, loading trucks, and packing orders. Loading crews are mostly seasonal workers—high school and college students whose minds have a tendency to wander to other, more fun summer activities.

This particular day was extremely hot and humid, even in the morning hours. Steven, the supervisor on duty, was a college student and four-year veteran of summer employment at Tasty Catering. He noticed a high school novice loading Indiana-bound equipment on a Wisconsin-bound truck, a critical error in the catering business. To a novice, a truck is a truck and equipment is equipment. This particular fellow had yet to experience the terror and potential disaster of arriving at an event without the proper food or equipment.

Steven caught the mistake, then turned to the offender and yelled, "Hey, stupid, I told you to put that in the Indiana truck. What is the matter with you? How dumb can you be?" An immediate hush fell over the warehouse. Hugo Rios-Tellez, a young full-time culinary worker, overheard the outburst. Silently, he left what he was doing and approached the supervisor. "Hey, Steven, number two!" was all he said as he pointed to a poster on the wall and directed the supervisor's attention to the list of company values. Steven turned and looked at the placards hanging just above the freezers, where he knew he would find "Number two: Treat all with respect."

Staring at Hugo, Steven took a second to regain his composure, realizing he had just violated the company values, something he knew was wrong. In response, he sought out the novice and immediately apologized for his outburst. What those present didn't know was that Tom Walter, Tasty Catering's CEO, was in the rear of the warehouse and had witnessed the entire episode. He silently caught up to Hugo and shook his hand, placing a $20 bill in it as he said, "Thank you, Hugo." Hugo looked down at his hand, then back at Tom. He handed the bill back and said, "Thomas, it's my company too!"

Creating a culture that gives each employee a sense of caring and ownership in the organization is a powerful tool for guiding behaviors. Here was a young employee not only feeling empowered to care about what was happening in another department but also feeling compelled and obligated to speak out when he saw a behavior that did not fit the Tasty Catering culture. Steven, likewise, listened and immediately responded to correct his own behavior. Both young men reinforced the culture and the notion that employees must respect each other, regardless of their assigned jobs. This is what crew leaders are trained to do when they see a violation of company values and when they realize they have made a mistake. But what created this sort of organizational environment? How can you unlock this in your own employees?

Moving from Engaged Employees to Entangled Employees

Recent research has shown how customer satisfaction and the resulting financial gains from repeat, loyal business stem from *emotional engagement* within employee-customer interactions.[1] Yet, organizations that are focused on excellence and high performance go beyond employee engagement to what we have identified as *employee entanglement*.

At first blush, entanglement sounds negative. For most people, entanglement means being caught in a difficult and complicated situation from which it is a challenge to escape. Well, that does not sound like something an employee would want to voluntarily enter, let alone something an ethical leader would want to create. However, let's look at the concept in a slightly different way.

At the core of entanglement is tension, which is the condition of being stretched or strained, a state of mental unrest that seeks resolution and reduction of the psychological and physiological stresses that arise from the tension. Would anyone disagree that the mental challenges one faces in today's rapidly changing environment are tension filled?

We assert that *entanglement can be a positive force* within organizations, driving individuals, teams, and organizations to achieve better results because of the tension between the existing state, the knowledge that things can always be better, and the desire to make things better. At the root of entanglement rests the tension between the present and the desired future, between what is and what could be, coupled with the realization that change occurs in the vacuum between the past and the future along with the collective efforts of dedicated people joined by common values, purposes, or goals. Within our research, we found eight high-performing organizations in which the tension between organizational and personal expectations for excellence and the desire to see their organization excel drove continually better performance, outcomes, and sustainability. For the high performers described in this book, *entanglement is the critical force that separates world-class from common performance, providing an organizational competency that makes leaders among peers.* It's these distinctive competencies that make imitation impossible and competitors irrelevant.

Comparing employee engagement and employee entanglement is analogous to noting the difference between college athletes and Olympians. Carrying over this analogy to for-profit and nonprofit organizations, the "college athlete" is certainly a valued employee; however, the "Olympian" is someone who could change the future of the organization. The average college athlete may be a high performer who is engaged, but chances are he has his sights set on a variety of other things. Of course, part of his focus is on his training and his teammates, but he is also concerned about classes, assignments, his social life, his future—assuming it is not in sport—and so on. The Olympian, on the other hand, has a much narrower focus. She is far more tuned into achieving success at her sport, so her every action is concentrated on attaining her highest level of performance. She wants—no, she needs—to be the best, and all aspects of her life (her diet, her sleep, her training, her family support, her work choices) are entwined in her efforts to be the very best.

Just as the Olympian interlaces all aspects of her life into her quest for gold (perfection in her chosen sport), an entangled employee does so for the success of his or her organization and the perfection of his or her own performance. Each decision, both within the workplace and outside it, becomes organization focused.

Entangled employees are like Olympians. They see each encounter with a customer (client, patient, student) or other key stakeholder (employer, coworker, board member, owner, supplier, the larger community) as possibly their only opportunity to make a positive impression; they don't wait for second chances. They interlace all aspects of life with their quest for personal and organizational gold. Each decision in the workplace and outside it is focused on gaining the best possible result. Where an Olympian asks, "Will this action improve my skills and better position me to win?" the entangled employee asks, "Is this action my best, and will it improve my organization, achieve our goals, and position us for success?"

Hugo Rios-Tellez is the perfect example of an entangled employee. He has a strong personal commitment to the goals and values of the organization. During our research, several entangled employees shared that people outside their organizations had "accused" them of "drinking the Kool-Aid and swallowing the company doctrine." Rather than being insulted when charged with holding an unquestioning belief in their employer's ideology, they embrace the spirit of the culture. The entangled employees are usually the first to admit that others may not fit within their company culture. Why?

OUR LIST OF ENTANGLED ORGANIZATIONS

The following eight organizations had both brilliant leadership and a system to create an exciting workplace. While we recognize that different industries face different challenges, we believe we can all learn from places where leaders create a system with the discretionary thinking that reflects the best of what employees have to offer—in other words, where entangled employees at all levels address problems that others face and achieve outcomes others aspire to achieve.

These are exceptional organizations that do remarkable things. We were energized to see the positive caring and the desire to do the job right that exist within each of these organizations. How they meet their challenges and foster engaged and entangled employees is a fun read, one that has inspired other leaders to improve their organizations. We think you will have the same experience.

Listed below are the entangled organizations from which we continue to learn.

- Advocate Good Samaritan Hospital, Downers Grove, Illinois
- Integrated Project Management Company (IPMC), Burr Ridge, Illinois
- MidwayUSA, Columbia, Missouri
- Mike's Carwash, Indianapolis, Indiana
- North Lawndale Employment Network/Sweet Beginnings, LLC, Chicago, Illinois
- Springfield Remanufacturing Corporation (SRC), Springfield, Missouri
- Tarlton Construction Company, St. Louis, Missouri
- Tasty Catering, Elk Grove Village, Illinois

That is one question, along with several others, that this book answers. We wanted to know why these companies were so special in the eyes of their customers, their employees, the organization's stakeholders, and those who would love to work for them. Let us introduce you to the companies we studied that have an environment that leads to remarkable results.

Moving from Entangled Employees to Entangled Organizations

According to the Institute for Human Health and Human Potential, less than 10 percent of the human brain is involved when processing thoughts related to the task at hand.[2] That leaves a little more than 90 percent of our thoughts—what we've come to label *discretionary thinking*—to wander. While "average" employees use a small fraction of their mental processing capacity for work, entangled employees devote more of their mental energies toward finding solutions to vexing problems, such as improving the quality and quantity of what they do to serve fellow employees, customers, communities, and constituents. In short, *entangled employees allocate and direct more of their discretionary thinking toward organizational challenges*, as Hugo Rios-Tellez and his colleagues at Tasty Catering do.

Within entangled organizations, an overwhelming majority of employees think past the requirements of their position to ways that help the organization achieve maximum performance. This extra effort stems from a strong, developed, and well-maintained employee-focused culture. Leadership recognizes and rewards discretionary thinking so often and in such a way that this behavior becomes commonplace. For example, Dr. Jeffrey Oken of Advocate Good Samaritan Hospital (chapter 8) commented that members of the nursing staff are always asking him, "How can we make things better for you?" The nurses and technicians use their discretionary thinking to devise ways to improve service, which only means more positive action toward making the hospital better in serving others. Within each of the organizations we studied, we found similar instances of behaviors that made the difference in customer experiences and positive outcomes.

Discretionary thinking can be either wasted or channeled, and the high performers we highlight in this book are masters at channeling discretionary thinking toward small as well as large goals. One key question that arose during our research was "How do organizational leaders gain greater access to the discretionary thinking of their team members or associates?"

Creating an entangled organization with entangled employees at every level does not happen overnight. Entangled structures exist because of specific actions leaders take along the way to create unique environments that employees love and protect. Leigh Buchanan, editor-at-large for *Inc.* magazine, has described how emotional commitment has four times the power to affect performance compared with rational commitment.[3] The 11 percent of workers Buchanan described as "true believers" are entangled employees. What would it be like if the majority of your employees were entangled rather than simply engaged or, worse, actively disengaged?

Eight Not-So-Easy Pieces

This book applies to all organizations, in either the public or the private sector, whether for profit or not for profit, whose leaders want to get the most from their people. The organizational challenge both today and in the future is to get more of each employee's attention and discretionary thinking to solve the ever-rising challenges presented by an environment in which the pace of change is accelerating. The entangled organization involves eight critical elements:

- Having leaders who do extraordinary things
- Building an ethical organization
- Focusing all the human capital

- Using processes to guide performance
- Increasing an individual's self-efficacy
- Giving employees freedom and responsibility within a culture of discipline
- Hardwiring discretionary thinking and actions
- Guiding the transformation process to remarkable performance

Throughout this book, these critical factors have been and will continue to be conversation discussion points about organizational survival and success. And we found that the blending of these eight critical elements created a *special synergy and magnetism within entangled organizations* that gave rise to employee loyalty, engagement, and satisfaction—measures of success akin to financial success; customer loyalty, engagement, and satisfaction; and the effective and efficient use of resources. Because employees are key to meeting financial and customer-satisfaction goals, it is crucial to find the best in your staff and to see to it that they are moved from engaged to entangled.

Each chapter of the book tells a story related to one of the eight critical elements, but as with a jigsaw puzzle, one cannot get the full picture of an entangled organization by looking at only one or two pieces. One needs to connect all the pieces to understand the synergy and magnetism between and among the pieces and to align them for maximum organizational effect.

Synergy results from the cumulative power of all eight elements coming together, but *magnetism* results from an entirely different sort of power. Physics reveals that magnetic forces and force fields exist around bodies such as the earth. Magnetic forces help to hold the universe together and to balance opposing forces. In short, magnetic forces sustain relative tension between balanced objects.

We've introduced the topic of magnetism because assembling the parts or recognizing some synergy between them is not enough. The parts cannot be taken singularly; they must be taken as a collective whole.

Although synergy exists in such a way that the whole is much greater than simply a sum of the parts, synergy itself cannot describe the relationships we found among the elements of an entangled organization.

With the entangled organizations we studied, we found that entanglement is positive tension *within an organization*. With high performers, we found that magnetism exists between and among *unique individuals* through shared values, goals, and behaviors—specifically trust and caring—that builds guilds and strengthens relationships. The interviews and archival research helped us identify this quality, and the analysis across the case studies confirmed it.

Each organization we studied had its own quality—Kevin Sheridan[4] called it magnetism—that stemmed from organizational purpose. Similarly, each organization demonstrated the eight elements in different ways and to different degrees, depending on their state of development. To make each element clear, we decided to focus on the story of the company that best exemplified that element. For example, Springfield Remanufacturing Corporation showed us how shared leadership within an industrial, profit-oriented setting generated discretionary thinking that led to performance excellence. And although every organization operated from a strong ethical foundation, we found Integrated Project Management Company exemplified how leaders can build and sustain an ethical company. The other organizations we studied had equally compelling stories to illustrate the other six elements.

Chapter 9 brings the puzzle together and discusses what we refer to as the *entangled organization* as an integrated whole. This integrative chapter describes the essential elements involved in hiring and nurturing a high-performance and engaged workforce that sets out on a path to build this sort of organizational environment.

The chapters within this book serve as the puzzle pieces as well as the road map for achieving performance excellence through entanglement. As you finish each chapter, we hope you pause to think about what you could do, in whatever role you perform, to have a positive impact on the lives of coworkers, employees, customers, suppliers, and others on whom you depend to sustain your organization and make it prosper.

Finally, for the benefit of academics who teach business students about organizational leadership, structure, and related theories, and for those leaders, consultants, and students who want to learn more about the theoretical and empirical foundations of what we saw, we have included support material on our website (www.itsmycompanytoo.com) as well as in the endnotes. Within the realm of business, evidence-based research exists in pockets and silos; in some cases, it is so heavily anchored to a specific discipline that integration of some theories can be either missed or ignored. On the website we frame and integrate the theories behind the practices we observed, from which readers can draw their own conclusions about the strengths and weaknesses of the entangled organization.

Why You Should Read This Book

Other books may address the eight elements discussed within *It's My Company Too!*, but the synthesizing model of the entangled organization makes this book unique. The entangled organization is clearly a performance excellence model for the demands of the twenty-first-century organization. In addition, our concepts are anchored to evidenced-based management research. Our conclusions are based on interpreting research rather than giving our opinions.

Leaders at all levels of a business, as well as those who teach business subjects, should be knowledgeable and conversant on the topics discussed within these chapters.

Senior Leaders and Executives. Getting things done through others is your stock in trade, but this book gives you additional ideas for creating a dynamic environment in which an energized workforce comes to work looking for new ways to delight customers or improve your organization. Changing an organization does not take huge financial investments; what it takes is *a major investment in how you do things, how you structure things, and how you behave.* The entangled organization is an organizational design that can help you accomplish these things.

Middle Managers. Beyond the issues of structural design and leadership behaviors, we found effective leaders were more concerned with guiding the energy of others in the right direction rather than controlling their organizations. The entangled organization can show you the behaviors leaders need to reinforce and support and ways to structure the work environment to keep teams and individuals engaged. You start being a leader by leading yourself—managing your own career and working to enter a leadership position.

Leaders of Not-for-Profit Groups or Government Agencies. Your organization must emphasize to your constituents the societal value you provide. Motivating others toward goals in an ever-shifting and uncertain environment requires more communication and engagement around the vision, shared values, and economic value the organization brings to others. The entangled organization can help you stimulate growth and achieve performance excellence on par with for-profit companies.

Educators, Academicians, and Consultants. While we're confident all readers can benefit from this book's content, the material on the website and in the chapter 9 endnotes were written specifically with you in mind. As business leaders and owners as well as educators, academics, and consultants, the author team saw the need to share the theoretical foundations of our findings with the varied audiences who teach and guide leadership and organizational science, design, or behavior in different venues. Although the literature is wide-ranging, we also wanted most of it to be readily accessible to educators and consultants outside of academia who may not have access to large databases such as EBSCOHost or ABI/INFORM. Thus, sources from *Harvard Business Review* and others are common references. *It's My Company Too!* has resonated with the various audiences with whom we work, from the classroom to the boardroom. The book can help you guide discussions about designing organizations for sustainable success in advanced graduate courses in MBA and doctoral programs, as well as with senior leaders with whom consultants work.

Business Students. The literature related to leadership, organizational science, and culture is overwhelming, so what should you read? How can you best use the limited time you have available to get the most concise picture of critical concepts related to organizational success? Chapter 9 and the material on the website should serve as a foundation for your learning on these topics as well as a springboard for additional research. A critical review of the literature should boost your knowledge and ability to apply the elements that comprise *It's My Company Too!* in real-world settings. We hope that doctoral students will consider additional research into the concepts and model discussed in this book, especially in the domain of positive organizational scholarship and positivity. *It's My Company Too!* can help you see the tapestry of behaviors, thoughts, and actions that lead to the sustainability of winning enterprises.

Noted statistician and quality management guru W. Edwards Deming once said that 85 percent of organizational problems were system-related, while only 15 percent were related to people.[5] Based on our experiences and conversations with leaders at all organizational levels in varied industries, we agree with Deming's assessment that many perceived behavioral problems are really system problems that resulted in such behaviors and attitudes as apathy, complacency, lack of motivation or attention to detail, or indecision. So how do you overcome these deficiencies?

The eight organizations highlighted in these pages have done just that. This book is about real people, real organizations, real challenges, and very real success. The subjects of this book have systems in place that encourage high performance. The leaders within these organizations support the systems and behaviors of their team members or associates who sustain cycles that continually improve their organizations and more deeply entangle coworkers, customers, and suppliers in the process.

Regardless of the industry in which they operated, those we interviewed expressed pride in the values, leadership, and reputation of the organization in which they served. Deep respect was evident in the ways organizational leaders valued employees and honored them through recognition programs, compensation, joint decision making, training, and development. Employees shared this respect and honor through their contributions as discretionary thinkers. While organizational leaders cannot ignore the forces that shape the competitive market, neither can they ignore the deep impact their leadership and the culture they create and nurture has on the internal operations and behaviors of the people who look to them for direction. We hope you enjoy reading this book as much as we enjoyed the experience of learning about these eight remarkable organizations.

Having Leaders Who Do Extraordinary Things

Building an Ethical Organization

Focusing All the Human Capital

Using Processes to Guide Performance

The Synergy and Magnetism of an Entangled Culture

Increasing an Individual's Self-Efficacy

Giving Employees Freedom and Responsibility Within a Culture of Discipline

Hardwiring Discretionary Thinking and Actions

Guiding the Transformation to Remarkable Performance

CHAPTER 1

HAVING LEADERS WHO DO EXTRAORDINARY THINGS:
Springfield Remanufacturing Corporation

When he worked for International Harvester plant in Melrose Park, Illinois, during the 1970s, John P. "Jack" Stack earned a reputation as a kind of "fixer" when it came to dealing with problems on the manufacturing floor. He had a knack for finding creative solutions to long-standing headaches. That kind of reputation cut two ways, though; in 1979 Stack found himself reassigned to Springfield, Missouri, to turn around Springfield ReNew Center (SRC), the division that remanufactured heavy-duty diesel engines for the parent company. Morale was terrible at the plant and so was productivity. Some of it had to do with the uncertain future of the organization—International Harvester itself was suffering mightily at the time—and some had to do with how the workforce was treated. Employees worried about what was going to happen to them next.

Stack spent his first few weeks at SRC wandering the floors and observing the practices and procedures and processes that were in place. The workers, too, were busy observing their new manager. One plant veteran even went so far as to ask Stack in the middle of a staff meeting, "Well, how old are you anyway?" The answer: Stack was a mere thirty years old at the time.

During a recent discussion with us more than thirty years later, Stack said that he knew the workers back then distrusted management mainly because the plant's leadership team kept a tight lid on information. They ran the ship as a hierarchy wherein people were told things on a need-to-know-basis only. That mind-set, in turn, led to doubt and suspicion among the folks on the shop floor. Stack knew firsthand how such a caste system negatively affected the firm all the way to the top; it created an environment consumed by an "Us" versus "Them" struggle.

As someone who began his career in the mail room back in Melrose Park, Stack understood this dilemma all too well. When he eventually accepted a promotion off the shop floor into a leadership position, he was no longer invited out to play pool or to participate in beer and pizza parties with his old friends. He had become one of "them," and his friends began calling him a "suit." "I have never forgotten what they thought about leadership," Stack said, and he didn't want any part of it.

After taking over at SRC, Stack did take risks in trying to break down barriers with his associates on the line. He bucked corporate orders to cut costs by ordering extra fans for the shop floor and fighting for dental coverage. Making incremental moves like that had an impact. Not only did performance at the plant begin to turn around, but employees began to trust Stack a bit more each day.

That trust was soon put to the test, though, when Stack received some devastating news from corporate HQ: The Springfield plant was to be closed. The recession of the early 1980s, combined with the arrival of global competition, struck International Harvester hard. The company was hemorrhaging money everywhere. The only recourse, upper management felt, was to scale back. But with the U.S. economy as a whole struggling, jobs were scarce. Stack knew that closing the plant would strike a terrible blow not just on his SRC associates but also on the town of Springfield itself. No one could afford to see the plant close.

That realization led Stack on an ambitious journey. (The story is told in great detail in his second book, *A Stake in the Outcome*.[1]) He cobbled together about $100,000 from twelve other managers in the Springfield plant to use as a down payment to buy the factory from

International Harvester. At the same time, he somehow convinced a banker to lend the new owners enough money to cover the sale price, which left the new business with a breathtaking 89-to-1 debt-to-equity ratio. "That meant that if we missed one payment, the bank would take everything back," said Stack, who also pointed out that SRC is now a 100 percent employee-owned company.

Stack also came to another realization as he fought to save SRC: He couldn't do it alone. While he had years of experience and training in building engine components and transmissions, no one had ever taken the time to teach him how to build and run a business. Given the sky-high stakes and the razor thin margin of error, Stack knew that if SRC was to become a success, he needed to find a way to engage each and every one of his associates in helping him run the business. Rather than rely on the command-and-control hierarchy of old, where the leaders at the top made decisions, he needed a new kind of system that could turn every single worker into a leader. The answer he came upon, as it turned out, was something that's now called the Great Game of Business.[2]

In this chapter, we'll describe how Stack and his associates at SRC came to implement something new in the world of business: a leadership system that empowers everyone in a company to make good decisions because it's in their best interest to do so. "Look, I believe that people, as a whole, hate to be 'managed' and told what to do," said Stack. "The goal should be to have a system in place where people can manage and lead themselves. Rather than boosting up or tearing down individuals, the system should be about getting to the root causes of problems and enabling anyone—not just charismatic and visionary leaders—to come up with the solutions. And if you doubt that this system works, consider that in its first days, a share of SRC stock was worth 10 cents. Today, three decades later, that same share is worth $237 [split adjusted].

That's a 237,000 percent growth rate if you're counting. The question isn't 'Does SRC's leadership system work?' It is, 'Why isn't everyone playing the Great Game of Business?' "

There Has to Be a Better Way

The inspiration behind the leadership system Stack and his associates created lies within the words "there is a better way and we can do it." Stack knew that most organizations wasted the talents of their workers. But if they could find a way to unlock and unleash that talent, they could create an organization with a supercharged workforce committed to meeting the organizational goals. What if they could change the paradigm from giving workers only enough information to "do their job" to creating a transparent culture in which everyone would be taught to understand how their individual efforts could literally impact the company's bottom line? "If I can connect the employee to the broader picture and create the training and reinforcement structures to encourage that connection," Stack said, "I might get a greater commitment from each employee to do the job well."

Stack recognized that if he and his associates were going to be successful, he needed to knock down all of the barriers that had become so prevalent in modern business. In order to build a leadership system, Stack knew that everyone had to trust the information they were being given. "If you ask associates at most companies how much money their company makes on every dollar of sales, they usually think it's around 60 cents. But the truth is it's usually more like 10 cents—if anything at all. Most employees think owners are lining their basements with gold bricks."

By adopting the practice of what *Inc.* magazine has dubbed "open-book management,"[3] where every shred of information (save salaries) is shared with everyone in the organization, SRC learned to eliminate its Us versus Them culture. It also removed any misconceptions employees had about the financial solidity of SRC, which then enabled them to think of ways they might help their company improve. In other words, the associates at SRC became more deeply entangled in the quality and performance of their duties because they could now see how their efforts paid off. As Mike Lofton, a production supervisor at Heavy Duty, one of SRC's divisions, explained: "This is why my staff enjoys work and stays on the job. They know what they do leads to financial success for the company and for themselves." Rodney Swope put it even more succinctly: "Sharing financial information allows staff to plan their lives."

The Great Game of Business

But simply sharing information isn't enough to turn employees into leaders. To get there the employees have to understand how companies work by mastering the language of business, which is told through the information found on balance sheets and income and cash flow statements. But Stack also knew that most people are scared of numbers, especially if it sounds anything like accounting. Ugh. The answer Stack came up with, interestingly enough, was that most people actually love playing games like Monopoly, where they are almost tricked into handling money and making business decisions. People as a rule also like to win. If he could get people thinking that business was just another game—one they could actually win—it would bring about a major change in how they thought about their job. And, just as with any game, Stack knew players needed three things:

1. They needed to know the rules.
2. They needed to know how to keep score.
3. They needed to have a stake in the outcome.

These three elements are, in fact, the foundation of the Great Game of Business,[4] which, in turn, is the foundation for SRC and its leadership system.

Part One: Teach the Rules

In order to put his leadership system in place, Stack first focused on teaching his associates the rules to the game. Every new hire at SRC attends a training program where he or she first is taught business basics through a case study of a fictitious company that makes yo-yos. The participant learns the basic elements of the financial statements and the principles of costing as they relate to a manufacturing business. Then the training continues with a case study of a more realistic application to SRC. The goal is to show the workforce how the financials fit together at the organization level, which is how you keep score.

The next step is to reveal how each individual unit, down to each individual, contributes to the organization's financial statements. Each line item—for example, an expense item—is then allocated to an individual or a small team, usually in an area they have control over. They then create a realistic budget for that line item for the year. They are responsible for meeting the targets they have created. This sets up an understanding of how an organization operates at a macro level through the financial statements and also how you can drill down to specific line items (the micro level) that an individual can impact on a daily basis.

We talked recently with a chief financial officer of a mid-size organization who went through SRC's training program. He really did not want to go because he thought it would be a waste of time. But after the two-day training ended, he spent two hours on the phone with his wife on the way back home explaining what an important benefit this program would be for his organization.

Part Two: Keep Score

On a weekly or biweekly basis, each of SRC's divisions has a huddle, which is essentially a meeting where the latest performance results are shared with everyone in attendance. (There is also a biweekly huddle where the parent company, SRC Holdings, reviews the performance of each of the separate units.) During the huddles, everyone can see all the expenses and all the revenue and what they mean to the employees if they reach particular critical numbers. By sharing the latest results, each and every associate then knows exactly what the latest "score" for the business is—either relative to their departmental or divisional goals or even to the organization's overall goals, which are called its "critical number." The critical number is chosen at the beginning of each fiscal year as a way for the organization to zero in on and go after its biggest weakness, which could be profit before tax, for example, or debt.

But what makes SRC's huddles really interesting is that they involve matching up actual performance against the projections made by the associates. Rather than obsess about historical information, which would be like driving a car using only the rearview mirror, SRC puts a strong emphasis on looking ahead. Associates are taught how to forecast what the future holds and then, when variances against those forecasts occur, to be able to explain what happened and why. What's truly powerful about this system is that the projected numbers aren't pushed down from upper management; the associates themselves set the targets. "You really have to know your business to be able to forecast," said Stack, "so you tend to study a lot more to get it as accurate as possible."

For the first half of the one-hour huddles, particular line items are called out and actual amounts are compared to budgeted amounts determined by the forecasts. The second half of the meeting involves the whole unit sharing ideas to help those who might be below projected or to suggest what might be done to support meeting the critical numbers of the organization.

The huddles are critical in creating SRC's leadership culture. Not only are individuals involved in managing their own numbers, they are likewise directly involved in helping others reach their numbers. They are working together because they are treated as equal partners in the process. At SRC there are defined trigger points as to what happens if, for example, sales drop to a particular level. Everyone knows that, and they work like crazy to come up with ideas on how to reduce costs or how to obtain more revenue in order to avoid those trigger points. Such engaged teamwork can only happen if workers fully trust that what senior leadership provides in the data is "the real stuff."

As Stack pointed out: "We are making leaders of everyone in the organization and that is important. Each one is now working for the organization—not just on their job but for reaching the quantified targets too. They are thinking of how to do better each day. We can see that by their comments and the discussion in the huddle."

Part Three: Provide a Stake in the Outcome

The third key component of playing the Great Game of Business is to share the rewards that come from winning or, in this case, when the organization reaches its targets. In this approach, there is little to be gained by making a unit or an individual target easy to reach. In the past, as with Management by Objectives, such a practice created an adversarial relationship between management, who wanted higher goals, and employees, who wanted lower targets they could attain more easily and thus gain the bonus tied to those targets. SRC's approach precludes that from happening. By creating a bonus program that is linked directly to the organization's critical number, everyone is given the incentive to work together to earn it. What's so effective about this approach is that when the critical number is chosen well—again, usually around an organization's biggest weakness—everyone on the team is rewarded for actually making the company stronger when they achieve their goals.

For the first quarter, the workforce can receive up to 10 percent of the total bonus if the company is on target to date. Obviously, knowing they can earn some of the bonus immediately (not having to wait a full year) incentivizes the workforce to reach those first-quarter targets. In the second quarter, up to 20 percent of the bonus can be received for reaching the company critical numbers to date. What is also so beautiful about this approach is that if their numbers were low in the first quarter, the workers can make it up in the second quarter if they meet the critical numbers for that period. In the third and fourth quarters, they can receive up to 30 and 40 percent, respectively, of their bonus.

Bonuses are issued as a separate check if the bonus is paid in cash (like with mini-games, which are described below) or as a separate letter with the stock shares indicated. This practice highlights that it is special and further reinforces the outstanding performance it took to attain the company's targeted critical numbers. For organizations that use an Employee Ownership Stock Program, as SRC does, receiving stock acts as another form of incentive for the associate to help drive the performance of the organization further since the better the organization does, the more valuable their stock becomes. In fact, during huddles, a group may question particular planned line-item budgets if they appear to be inconsistent with the overall organizational direction and historical expenses. It is not unusual for employees to express "hoots and hollers," as Stack puts it, when one of the line items is exceeding expectations.

Divisional or departmental bonuses can also be paid out through a system SRC calls "mini-games." Just as with the overarching critical number, each business unit constructs a game to reward associates for tackling a weakness that is, in turn, linked to the organization's goals as a whole. For example, a mini-game could relate to decreasing inventory levels to a specific dollar amount.

On the flip side, if a line item is below expectations, the person or team assigned to that item feels the heat from their associates even if nothing is said. That's because people feel accountable to one another. If anything is said, it's usually just to ask a question about why the variance exists or to make some suggestions about what to do to try to get the line item back on target. In this way, huddles become an environment where everyone truly is a leader.

Tap the Wisdom of the Crowd

When SRC began operating on its own, it faced another massive challenge: All its business came from one major customer—International Harvester. That was a scary place to be, and the company scrambled to land other accounts for its remanufactured truck engines. But it was actually during an early organization-wide huddle that a janitor—yes, a janitor—pointed out that in recessions the demand for truck engines ebbs (because fewer goods are shipped) but the demand for used car engines spikes because people try to save money by keeping their existing cars on the road longer. It was a revelation not just because the janitor was right (SRC soon began remanufacturing automobile engines, which helped diversify its customer base); just as important, it proved that the system of leaders was working. If you teach people the rules and tell them the score, they'll find a way to win.

While structure is important in building an entangled organization, the behavior of the leader is just as important. In creating a company of leaders, Stack has been very careful to make sure that each member of his executive team is supportive, acts as a coach, and acknowledges good ideas and performance. That creates a climate in which every associate can mirror those behaviors and grow as a leader.

A leader who is supportive is less focused on telling a person what to do and more focused on asking the right questions, as a teacher might do. Supportive leaders do not blame; they work toward improving and creating learning moments. Stack wants his senior team to lead the workforce in arriving at an idea. Supporting, coaching, and asking the right questions are skills—skills that a leader must have to build the kind of relationship needed for a culture of engagement and discretionary thinking and action.

Being a coach means being more of a partner than a boss. It means being there to give advice rather than issuing orders. As a coach, you let the employee lead even if it is not done perfectly. As a coach, you are there when called upon to listen, to communicate, to observe, and to interpret meaning and intent in the employees' nonverbal communication. Coaching requires patience, and it involves reinforcing behaviors in the employee to help guide the person in the right direction, which involves knowing the consequences of proposed actions.

SRC reinforces the notion that a group of its associates is smarter than any single individual through a process it calls "High-Involvement Planning," a semiannual process during which departmental heads throughout the company come together to paint a picture of the market and where it's headed over the next five to ten years. That road map is then used to construct the company's sales and marketing strategy for the next year—something that is also presented to the entire company. Every presentation is based on a template SRC has been using for twenty-seven years. Among the key elements that template contains are:

- The overall state of the economy, which might include critical elements like interest rate projections.
- A snapshot of the competitive landscape: Where is SRC weak compared to its competitors?
- The results of the company's most recent customer survey.
- SRC's projected sales-and-marketing budget.
- Twelve-month and four-year sales forecasts.
- A step-by-step plan for how the sales team will make good on those forecasts.
- Contingency plans for what happens if SRC doesn't make its projections.

When these presentations conclude, the associates in the audience get the chance to ask questions and request clarifications. Then, all associates are handed a questionnaire on which they are asked to indicate, on a scale of one to five, how confident they are about both the forecasts and the plan to make good on those forecasts (as well as the contingency plans). The results are then tabulated to determine an overall confidence level. At SRC, rarely do any of the divisions report a confidence score below 80 percent. But if someone has concerns, that individual is encouraged to speak up and make them clear.

Allowing associates to give input into the direction of the organization puts a responsibility on the employees to research and think out the information that is shared with them. Because it's a plan that everyone had a hand in making, when the plan is put into action, no one can look back and point fingers. As Stack said: "We have strength in numbers in contributing toward the direction of the organization. With our different viewpoints, we can come up with the best solutions and course of action." Again, it's a system where everyone is trusted to be a leader.

Keep the Company Growing: SBUs

Driving diversity as a way to reduce risk is a key theme at SRC Holdings, which now owns SRC and thirty-five-plus other businesses, which range from a consulting company to a logistics provider and an electronics manufacturer. When associates think like leaders, they can put their entrepreneurial chops to work by thinking up ideas for new companies, such as the idea to develop a fuel pump plant that will allow SRC Holdings to control price and quality while contributing to the employee stock value. After all, it's their company too! "We want the workforce to understand how to develop a market and use our technical competencies and leadership approach to work to be successful in those new markets," said Stack. "That helps to engage our workforce and reduce our market risks."

Some of the strategic business units (SBUs) created over the years allow SRC employees to be in better control over their particular specialty areas. By using SBUs, you can create autonomous units that are smaller and more decentralized than the whole. That can help the workforce see the results of their actions and more thoroughly comprehend all of the dynamics of the specific business they are in while also creating new opportunities for leaders to emerge and experience different responsibilities. This is particularly important when using the Great Game of Business model because it is predicated on knowing the financials and understanding the business. If any business gets too complex because of the number of customer segments and markets, it may become difficult for the workforce to understand the intricacies for the different markets. Creating SBUs resolves that problem. It also creates within the associates working in those SBUs an entrepreneurial passion to succeed because they can better see the immediate result of their work—something that can potentially be lost in a more centralized organization.

Currently, SRC Holdings includes these key SBUs among its many others:[5]

- **SRC Heavy Duty**—truck remanufacturing, Springfield, Missouri
- **SRC Automotive**—engine manufacturing, Springfield, Missouri
- **SRC Power Systems**—warranty analysis, reverse engineering, new power unit design, wiring harnesses, powder coating, and distribution, Springfield, Missouri
- **SRC Electrical**—remanufacturing of starters, alternators, compressors, Springfield, Missouri
- **SRC of Lexington**—heavy construction equipment remanufacturing, Lexington, Kentucky
- **SRC Logistics**—public warehousing, contract warehousing, fulfillment services, distribution, reverse logistics, and custom software services to manufacturers, distributors, and retailers in a variety of industries, Springfield, Missouri
- **NewStream Enterprises**—packaging, labeling, bar coding, supply chain, Springfield, Missouri
- **NewStream of Canada**—transportation, warehousing, supply chain, Toronto, Ontario

- **Ciona Technologies**—turbo chargers and electronics, Springfield, Missouri
- **Great Game of Business**—seminars, coaching, books, Springfield, Missouri

Each is a separate corporate entity with a majority held, if not wholly owned, by SRC Holdings. The SBU structure facilitates the separate units working together for their own betterment as well as that of the parent corporation. For example, Senior Vice President Jeff DeCarlis talked about the time when one of the divisions lost 45 percent of its business. The unit leader called out for ideas from the workforce and from the other divisions. Help came quickly: The other divisions suggested ways the division could save money to help the overall organization meet its targets and helped the struggling unit through its difficulties. This shows the power of getting a company's associates all pulling in the same direction.

Specific executive vice presidents in SRC Holdings track what is going on in the separate companies, but their supervision takes the form of advising, not controlling. Jeff DeCarlis and Ron Guinn both indicated that their role is mainly to monitor, not to lead. "We are okay with the units making mistakes at times; it's all right to fail—at least to a degree. The leadership of the holding company would intervene, if necessary, but that would be sort of a failure of our role in coaching and supporting throughout the process."

Succession Planning

While SRC will recruit new talent from outside its organization, it also puts a premium on developing existing associates and creating career trajectories for them. That's why a subset of Stack's advocacy of SBUs is his belief in continuing education. "Continuing education is key: Pay or salary buys hands, and the brains come free. SRC Holdings pays for education, no matter the subject, because education stimulates the brain." Stack believes that leadership skills should be taught to all SRC associates so that when an opportunity arises in an external market, they will have leaders ready to seize the opportunity. We saw this happen during the executive meeting when leaders of one of the SBUs would ask for a certain type of mid-level leader, and a leader of another SRC Holdings subsidiary would offer one of his or her staff who was being trained for that type of leadership position.

Promoting—nay, almost *requiring*—discretionary decision making is a policy that supports the maturation of the leaders of the units. And by leaders, Stack means everyone in the unit. In fact, when we interviewed him, he was moving into executive offices away from the plant "as a way to make it harder for employees to check with the boss to see if what they are doing is okay."

Another one of the prudent yet extraordinary things that SRC has implemented in terms of succession planning is the interpersonal plan, or IPP, where each individual has a personal development plan to support his or her own growth. This starts with the employee and then becomes part of the annual evaluation with each individual's immediate supervisor. The plan focuses on how the individual wants to grow in the company. Then a course of action is developed that could include enrolling in college courses, in certification programs (for example, a green belt certification in quality processes), or other experiences relevant to the goals the person outlined. (An employee qualifies for tuition reimbursement as soon as he or she joins the company.) These plans include mileposts to measure progress over time. The employees we interviewed said the IPPs demonstrate in a real and practical way that the organization cares for them professionally and personally. One executive vice president proudly admitted that he had reached that management position as a result of the IPP that was crafted for him several years earlier. In other words, SRC doesn't just talk the talk when it says that it has created a culture where everyone is a leader.

Does SRC's Leadership Approach Work, and Why?

The associates at SRC have worked together to create a very special place. Strong employee engagement is the backbone of this top-notch organization. Through teaching the basics of financial statements and costing items, SRC transformed its workforce from a culture of followers to one filled with leaders. By teaching each and every associate how their efforts impact the company's bottom line, SRC has aligned each person's performance to organizational performance. The use of huddles brings the unit together to look at the overall financial performance and question variances where performance failed to meet projections; then they have a thorough discussion about what to do about getting back on track. Again, rather than merely looking backward at historical information, SRC's extensive use of forecasting among its associates to set targets allows the organization as a whole to look forward as it charts its future direction. Encouraging their associates' discretionary thinking to problem solve and decide the best course of action results in what is best for the company because it is also best for the employees themselves! They set the course of action to rectify problems, which increases the probability that those employees will commit to it. Getting the job done leads to individual employee entanglement, and that is exciting!

The process SRC uses to create a future-looking unit, in which each line-item champion creates a plan for the next year, is a way to get associates to consider what is going on in the environment and how that will affect their numbers. They start looking at what they will need in terms of raw materials and worker capabilities and capacities to get the job done. All this builds a level of maturity in the workforce that is almost unparalleled in most industries. (One of the authors is an academic and would jump for joy to have this become part of the process at his school. A second author is using this at his company with exciting success for it and its employees.) SRC's process frees the corporation to accelerate to maximum potential because individuals can unleash their inherent entrepreneurial ideas to define and meet the needs of the market and to improve the organizational operations because, quite simply, they've been taught how to grow and run a business.

What of the reinforcement or bonus system SRC calls "A Stake in the Outcome"? It seems to do what it is supposed to, namely, create sustained effort. While the individual focus is on specific line items and there are bonuses tied to specific mini-games, the main financial focus is on meeting the organizational critical numbers, which are determined by the company's biggest weaknesses. This is what the huddles focus around and work to meet. The group dynamics and personal pride are such that an employee does not want to come into one of those meetings with bad numbers. But little is said if they do, as the focus is on reaching the goals, not placing blame. They want to find solutions. The result is a cooperative approach within and across every business unit within SRC.

What kind of organizations can benefit from this style of leadership? Our short answer is: every kind. SRC started out with 119 employees; the company now has 1,200, and this approach has been applied at a number of other different organizations with reported success. The approach can be used for sophisticated employees as well as those with little or no educational background in finance. Recall that the Great Game of Business training program begins with a two-day session on basic financial statements, budgeting, and cost accounting analysis. The most difficult challenge in an organization adopting this system seems to come back to these two areas: (1) getting leadership to cease acting in a command-and-control mode and becoming a coach; and (2) getting employees to realize the importance of their role in the process and becoming part of the leadership of the organization.

But, if someone can overcome these hurdles and see the incredible benefits that result from working within a system of leaders, the sky is literally the limit. All you need to do is look at the price of a share of SRC stock today compared to thirty years ago for proof of that.

What We Learned from SRC

How can you build the kind of culture that has led to the success SRC experienced? Here are seven ways.

1. **Listen.** One of the first things Jack Stack did when he became the plant manager was to sit down with the employees to find out their concerns. A hallmark of an effective leader is his or her listening skills. As a leader, you show respect for the workforce by listening, particularly if you move to their location, their workspace, so you can obtain a sense of their environment. By doing this, you are demonstrating you want to learn and you care about employees as people. The key issue that led to alienation of employees was the lack of leadership's responsiveness to the issues they raised. It is simple things like installing fans to cool the work area in summer or adding some refrigerators so staff have a place to put their lunches. However, the end result is the same. If you listen, you learn. If you learn, you can respond more to meet the needs of the workforce. By meeting those needs, you create an environment for more engaged workers because they feel their voice matters.

2. **Communicate.** Stack created the structure to get people talking and as a means through which he could communicate with the workforce and they with him. His goal was to create a transparent organization so the employees learned about the issues senior leadership faced, and senior leadership learned about the concerns and ideas of the workers. Open communications and sharing ideas create a transparent environment, which in turn creates a culture in which people engage in joint problem solving—a perfect way to get the workforce entangled.

3. **Develop Leaders.** "There is a leadership void and a desperate need of leaders," Stack said on multiple occasions. There is a plethora of managers who revel in giving orders, however. It is difficult to teach leadership in the classroom, but it can be taught in high-performing organizations that value the individual worker. SRC Holdings Corporation has many processes in place to make everyone a leader so that opportunities are not missed. Stack encourages his staff to sit on nonprofit boards where they can help these organizations learn how to create revenue streams from unlikely sources. An SRC survivor from the pre-Stack days said that Jack Stack moved the company "from management to leadership."

4. **Address Organizational Weaknesses.** Senior leaders have to be courageous and take action in the face of an apparent weakness. Stack said that real innovation occurs when people are fixing weaknesses. And leaders support innovation even if it may result in failure. Stack's success was due to building the structure and leadership behaviors to generate and sustain a culture of engaged and entangled employees to all do extraordinary things. As Stack would say, "Everyone is a leader here." We think they could likewise say, "It's My Company Too!"

5. **Practice the Four Ps of Success.** Stack was visibly excited as he discussed his idea of the four Ps of success.

   - Position (in the marketplace)—He believes that strategic leaders should be *discovering* markets, not just *following* market trends. This can be more easily accomplished with a highly engaged workforce that lends their own discretionary thinking about new markets and new products. Stack and his team have created some incredible new markets in the past five years and have gained a commanding position in those markets.

   - Positive Cash Flow—Independence is lost when cash flow is lost. Equity loss and increased interest debt are two of the negative outcomes that result from the loss of positive cash flow. Positive cash flow allows an organization to control its destiny.

- Profit—This is a healthy term. Profit is necessary to pay employees, to provide employees a future, and to maintain a sustainable organization. Stack was passionate about capitalism. Creating wealth is important, but he said sharing wealth with those who helped to create it was vital. This is not redistributing, but sharing. The bright side of capitalism for him is the ability to pay taxes to support the economy.

- People—SRC's people are highly engaged in planning, in creating a successful, profitable company, and in reaping the resulting rewards—all of which yield deep entanglement. Stack has proven that transparency leads to competitiveness among the staff. Performance excellence is owned by the person who sees and understands the balance sheet. Scorecards are necessary to keep score, but people also need a clear shot at reward and recognition. His leadership style has led to positive peer pressure. That is, people know what they do and what others do for the organization and they do not want to let anyone else down. When adversity strikes a SRC Holdings unit, Stack says the people rally around the problem and discover the solutions.

6. **Understand.** Stack has never forgotten what it was like to have an entry-level job. He did not segue from college to the office. He had ten jobs "on the floor" in his first ten years with International Harvester. He understands how mental disruptors such as doubt, fear, anxiety, animosity, and contempt can create a dysfunctional organization. He lived it for one period in his life. He does not intend for those disruptors to penetrate SRC Holdings. Sharing information has created a family atmosphere. One employee mentioned that the top three factors in his life are family, church, and SRC. When asked why, he said, "SRC and its leaders understand and fulfill my needs." Stack understood employee engagement

thirty-five years ago, and he has changed the world for the better because of that understanding.

7. **Build Trust.** If you practice the above, you will do much to build trust. Transparency, listening, communicating, and reacting to concerns will help build trust. Walking the talk, living the values, and supporting the vision every day is a major way to build trust. The payoff is a workforce that will work for *you* rather than just for *a salary*. They will have more personal allegiance to the organization than when they do not have trust in the leadership. Stack can teach us all about building the kind of culture and the kind of values that support a sustained effort by the workforce to produce a quality product.

8. **Train the Fundamentals.** The workforce needs to be educated so they understand the fundamentals of how to run a business. In this way, they better understand the dynamics of the organization and the outcomes, and how, most important they fit into making those outcomes happen.

Selected Resources

Here are some additional sources you might find useful as you do extraordinary things in your organization to create an employee-centric culture of engaged and entangled men and women.

1. A more complete coverage of the approach that Jack Stack has used can be found in: Jack Stack and Bo Burlingham, *The Great Game of Business* (New York: Currency-Doubleday, 1992), and Jack Stack and Bo Burlingham, *A Stake in the Outcome* (New York: Currency-Random House, 2003).

2. A super article that addresses the importance of the engaged workforce was done by the Gallup group, which developed the Gallup 12 questions that assess worker engagement. John H. Fleming, Curt Coffman, and James K. Harter, "Manage Your Human Sigma," *Harvard Business Review* 83, no. 7/8 (July–August 2005): 107–114.

3. The *New Yorker* came out with an article recently that addresses the difficulty of finding the right person for a job. It is an interesting read. Malcolm Gladwell, "Most Likely to Succeed: How Do We Hire When We Can't Tell Who's Right for the Job?" *New Yorker* 84, no. 41 (December 15, 2008): 36–43.

4. Being a leader who inspires and empowers others takes introspection and personal growth. This article focuses on steps you must take to become more effective. Bill George, Peter Sims, Andrew N. McLean, and Diana Mayer, "Discovering Your Authentic Leadership," *Harvard Business Review* 85, no. *2* (February 2007): 129–138.

5. A positive work environment can readily support the kind of culture you need to create a cohesive work team. Luthans and others have been a major force in promoting a positive work environment. This article provides a good overview. Fred Luthans, James B. Avey, Bruce J. Avolio, and Suzanne J. Peterson, "The Development and Resulting Performance Impact of Positive Psychological Capital," *Human Resource Development Quarterly* 21, no. 1 (Spring 2010): 41–67. For a more comprehensive review of positive organizational behavior, see D. Nelson and C. Cooper, eds., *Positive Organizational Behavior* (Thousand Oaks, CA: Sage, 2007).

✳ ✳ ✳

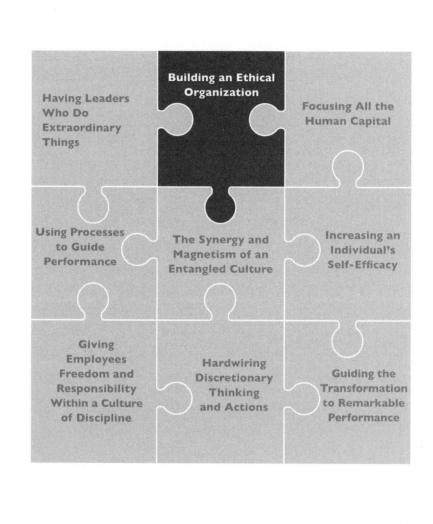

CHAPTER 2

BUILDING AN ETHICAL ORGANIZATION:
Integrated Project Management Company, Inc.

Clients of Integrated Project Management Company, Inc. (IPM) sign an agreement when a project is started that they will not try to hire IPM's staff, as it could distort the working relationship and independence of decision making of the IPM staff involved in the project. A few years ago Rich Panico, CEO, was informed by a client that they had made an offer to one of IPM's project managers who was working for the client and that the IPM project manager had accepted. Panico said, "I know you are familiar with the contract, and it clearly says you cannot offer employment to an IPM consultant." The client indicated he understood and was sorry, but that was what they were going to do, and how could this be resolved? After they negotiated a sizable penalty, Panico said, "Look, I do not want your money at IPM. You write out checks to these five charities, and we will distribute them."

At the next company staff meeting, when employees learned about the decisions, they applauded Panico for how he had followed through on his beliefs. In a similar manner, IPM has refused several million-dollar contracts because the ethics of what the client wanted done were not aligned with IPM's philosophy. As Rich put it:

> We earned the hearts of the employees. We must go beyond engaging the employees' intellect. We have to engage their hearts. Intellect is all the rational reasons for working for an organization, such

as salary. Going beyond the intellect, to connect with their hearts, creates a much more engaged employee. For us to develop a solid relationship with a client involves an employee who is engaged with his or her heart. That is the underpinning of a successful relationship with the client. If we veer only once from our values, we give the employee and the customer a reason not to believe in the values of the organization. You do not want to give your employees any reason not to believe.

This explains, perhaps perfectly, how IPM's beliefs affect employee behaviors, which differentiate them not only from other project management consulting firms but also from other firms in general. This leadership approach of high ethical behavior has led to high-quality outcomes, which in turn has created loyal relationships between IPM and the nearly 300 clients the company has served in more than 3,500 projects. These remarkable results did not happen because of good luck. Rich Panico developed the structure and behavioral expectations that led to them.

A History of Paramount Values

When Rich Panico founded the Integrated Project Management Company in 1988, he drew into the IPM family others who shared his belief that *integrity* and *honesty* are paramount values that can never be compromised. In setting this context, he raised everyone's expectations, especially those of the customers the company serves. For IPM associates, ethical behavior defines the company's character and sustains the relationships that secure organizational success. This chapter shares some of the stories and elements that have set IPM apart as a high-performing company known and appreciated for its high ethical standards.

In a recent monthly newsletter, CEO Panico described the purpose of his company using a rather effective analogy. He compared IPM to the TV show *The Biggest Loser*, noting that IPM project management consultants (PMCs) help clients "accomplish something they have often tried to do themselves but with limited success." IPM's PMCs create the conditions, develop the plans, provide the personal facilitation, and instill the confidence clients need to transform their companies or business units from the "losers"—organizations plagued by waste, inefficiency, and ineffectiveness—into lean, smooth-running operations. Even though the ability to get the project done often lies within client capabilities, they often get bogged down in their own inertia.

Similar to the TV show's coaches and personal trainers, who help weight-loss competitors pursue their target weights, IPM PMCs lead their clients to a desired end point. In doing so, they overcome physical and psychological obstacles and shed years of unconstructive behaviors and often natural tendencies in the process. Panico noted that in the business world these tendencies appear as "lack of accountability and discipline, poor follow-up, ineffective communications, cross-functional barriers, complacency, and lack of motivation and enthusiasm." With IPM PMCs serving as personal organizational trainers, Panico believes, "Clients can be led and reinvigorated to accomplish great objectives when the right conditions are established." He maintains that the incredible talent within IPM has "an honorable and important role in making a real difference in companies and in peoples' lives."

This sentiment is echoed through what one client reported. The client, a pharmaceutical executive who had survived two mergers of his original employer into two progressively larger international companies, fully expected to lose IPM's services because each acquiring company had its own internal project management staff. However, the results achieved with each prior IPM effort were so superior to the new owner's expectations that dismissing IPM was not a viable option.

The client, who had used IPM teams on ten different projects over seven years, noted that IPM's PMCs make the difference because "they invest themselves completely and personally in the outcomes of our projects. IPM managers lead their projects rather than manage them, and they are not afraid to put the elephant in the room, engage everyone in the dialogue, or ask the dumb question." Although the entanglement of IPM's leaders may not have been visible to this client, the underlying entanglement of IPM's PMCs made the difference in the way their clients positively perceived the company.

Perhaps IPM's highest compliment came when this same client said, "If my colleagues were as passionate about driving our projects forward as our IPM PMCs, we would be unbelievably successful."

This belief, which resonates throughout the company and among current and former IPM employees and customers, sets the company apart from its competitors. How did IPM achieve this constancy in belief?

IPM began with four employees in the city of Burr Ridge, Illinois. Today it serves the life sciences, food and beverage, consumer products, industrial products, and health-care industries, as it has for nearly twenty-four years. With success came expansion, and now IPM operates beyond its Chicago-area headquarters in three other major metropolitan areas: Boston, Saint Louis, and San Francisco. Regardless of office location, employees live and promulgate the same beliefs, attitudes, and culture, which are built on core values, ethical principles, and quality practices.

IPM's reputation as a highly ethical company, one in which employees are committed to acting ethically at all costs, resonates positively with clients who want the best value for their investments of time and money. While other companies struggled during the recession and tight economy, IPM leaders reinforced company strengths by encouraging spirited intelligence sharing through which they created the right strategic direction from which "periodic, insightful corrections" could be made to account for the effects of external forces. As a result, IPM has maintained a steady customer base, which has sustained the firm's profitability, financial stability, and continuous innovation. The IPM commitment to uncompromising, ethical leadership at all costs has led to more rather than less business and more public recognition.

Our review of IPM yielded five major lessons for building a strong, ethical organization. The first lesson is that the ethical foundation of the founder, president, and CEO of an enterprise sets the tone and direction for the company. Senior leaders must also reinforce the foundation constantly through personal example and transparency. Second, we found that marketplace differentiation begins with core beliefs that demonstrate a leadership versus a management mentality. Third, a strong ethical culture must be built consciously, constructively, and constantly. The fourth lesson is that designing, nurturing, and reinforcing an ethical culture goes beyond transactional employment agreements to the point of developing entangled relationships. Fifth, leaders of ethical companies transfer their belief in, and inspire others to serve, a higher purpose. Let's take a closer look at each of these lessons as IPM's story evolves.

Ethical Foundations Begin and End at the "Top"

To an outsider looking in, a lucrative contract with an existing client appeared inviting and a "no-brainer," but for Rich Panico, only one option existed: walking away. No contract was worth risking his company's reputation or compromising the ethical principles on which Panico had founded the company, nor was it worth risking the IPM family's security he had worked so hard to safeguard. To Rich and his staff, a client who is not honest or fails to act with integrity cannot be trusted to fulfill commitments. Their reasoning is it's better to walk away from trouble and its associated headaches than to deal with cleaning up messes from project failures.

Leading with Heart and Soul

Rich Panico is the heart and soul of his company simply because he literally leads others *with his heart and soul*. As Panico's assistant, Karen Heiting, puts it: "Rich is never afraid to stand up for what is right, no matter the cost, and he's not afraid to seek wisdom from God to guide his path." IPM employees see Panico as a humble man with a gentle spirit, a giant heart, and the ability to lead effectively. They believe in him because he truly walks the talk, and he walks it every single day. As a result, employees have the same expectations of each other. They share responsibility for sustaining a renowned ethical culture that clients and suppliers appreciate and value because they work for and do business in an environment where integrity, trustworthiness, respect, and fairness make a difference.

Employee turnover is not a significant problem, notes Director of Regional Operations Rob Neufelder. Many IPM employees envision being with the company for a long time, in large part because of the family feelings within the company that stem from Panico's attitude toward his staff. As the CEO himself says: "I'm extraordinarily blessed. I'm surrounded by people who are smarter than me and whom I love dearly. How many leaders can tell you how much they love the people around them? My staff sense and know I love them, even though we disagree at times, and rightfully so because of our different perspectives. Yet they know I trust their intentions as always being noble." We had to ask ourselves, how many organizational leaders feel that way or are comfortable saying that? The answer, we're afraid, is very few.

Being Transparent, Respectful, and Building Trust

Company newsletters and staff meetings report on the financial status of the company, which always operates within its means. Investments are made with cash or short-term debt only, so employees who share in company profits are not penalized with interest on debt or other extended obligations. Despite the tumultuous economy of 2009, employees received bonuses that represented 25 percent of IPM's profits. In addition, and perhaps most important, IPM consistently provides above-average compensation and benefits based on various market standards because IPM's corporate standard for performance is also "above average."

The close family atmosphere stems from the level of trust that permeates the company. The following story of the support that company leaders give staff during tough, ethically challenging situations exemplifies this trust.

While deeply entrenched in a research project, an IPM project manager discovered a potential misappropriation of funds by the client. She immediately notified her supervisor, who forwarded the issue to IPM seniors, who immediately addressed the issue with the client's vice president. An investigation revealed that previously identified problems linked to the apparent misappropriation had been addressed and rectified, and IPM continued the relationship since no ongoing ethical concerns existed. Despite the findings, the project manager felt uncomfortable and asked to be reassigned to another project. IPM's leaders readily complied with her request because they respect the integrity of each person and, as in this case, the conscientiousness with which PMCs approach their work.

When IPM leaders say they treat all employees with the same level of respect, they don't just mean staff at the project management level. Equal respect extends from the top of the organization to the bottom and back up again. During a recent trip to California, for example, while giving the CEO a ride back to his hotel, a PMC asked, "How was your flight out here, Rich?"

"I got a lot done," he replied. "I worked on Jo's Performance Summary and Development Plan." (Jo Jackson is the CFO and has been with Panico since he started the company.)

The PMC was surprised. "What could you possibly tell Jo that's new?"

"I do this out of respect for her, and the process allows me to reflect on all of her contributions over the year. We absolutely learn from each other. I've never missed a performance review, and I'll never miss one because of the deep respect I have for Jo." This is a respect that goes beyond job titles and years of friendship. Respect is deeply entrenched in the organization because the organization is built on it and continues to evolve and grow because of it.

Marketplace Differentiation Begins with Core Beliefs

Most project management companies simply do what their industry requires. They apply the standard management principles of planning, organizing, budgeting, and controlling to a specific project and report progress to clients based on predetermined objectives and a time line. They use various techniques and steps to achieve a completed project—hopefully on time and on budget. Built on the practice of converting work into billable hours, these companies have a "churn and burn" mentality: Get the work done and get out according to the calendar and schedule. In some firms, the pressures and demands of project management lead to employee turnover, which requires continual training and assimilation of new staff into the company's culture and creates quality issues as new folks find their way in a new environment.

Project Leadership, not Management

Not IPM. In stark contrast to its industry, IPM is all about project leadership rather than project management. This leadership mentality permeates all practices, languages, behaviors, and communications throughout the company. From a leadership perspective, IPM's PMCs see their responsibility for guiding and influencing others as equally and sometimes more important than simply keeping a project on schedule.

The impact of taking a project leadership approach to client challenges is best seen within the integrity of achieved outcomes and results. For IPM project leaders, building collaborative relationships with clients is more important than simply accomplishing tasks. Although IPM leaders are very good at getting their jobs done, clients appreciate the critical differences between IPM's project leadership versus other firms' project management approach. The deep respect and loyalty that exist between IPM PMCs and their customers develops beyond what many believe possible in the realm of project management. In short, IPM's marketplace differentiation begins with the company's core beliefs and this leadership mentality.

IPM's one-page mission and beliefs statement (see below) encapsulates what makes IPM different from other companies and serves as the constitution from which all practices and processes evolve. Panico may be the CEO, but every employee accepts a leadership role in modeling and living the expressed beliefs that underpin the business.

EXCERPTS FROM IPM'S "OUR MISSION AND BELIEFS" STATEMENT

Combining a passion for excellence, honest and ethical conduct, and uncompromising integrity, IPM achieves high-quality results and consistently meets its commitment to clients.

IPM derives its competitive advantage from its value-driven, self-motivated, and highly skilled employees—its most important asset. It is the company's intent to maximize job security and to involve all employees in achieving this goal. The company's culture must, in a disciplined yet motivating fashion, forever embrace continuous improvement and teamwork and defy complacency in any form.

IPM must influence the economic and political future of this country to preserve the positive elements of free enterprise. Planning is the key to success; education is an integral part of economic survival.

IPM's mission is honored each time a client's expectations are exceeded, each time an employee achieves his or her dreams, each time IPM earns an employee's loyalty, and each time the company's efforts positively influence our society and the world in which we live.

Structuring a Values-Based Leadership Approach

Larry Meyer, IPM's leader of Knowledge and Process Management, noted that IPM operates from a holistic viewpoint that stems from values-based leadership. Right from the start, a client knows he or she is working with a different company because of the preamble to every master service agreement. The preamble—reproduced below—very simply and succinctly specifies the values that form the foundation of ethical performance.

IPM'S PREAMBLE TO EVERY MASTER SERVICE AGREEMENT

IPM agrees to execute this agreement and conduct business with ethical behavior. Core values of integrity, honesty, respect, excellence, and continuous improvement will guide each decision and interaction. This agreement is entered into with the expectation that any issues arising from it will be dealt with honestly and in fairness to both parties.

Customer satisfaction ultimately indicates the value customers place on a company's character, which is what IPM employees demonstrate through their values-based actions. IPM conducts an extensive, objective post-project evaluation with each client as part of the company's continuous quality-improvement initiative. More than 71 percent of their clients have rated IPM's PMCs as *outstanding* in leading projects with ethical behavior, honesty, and integrity (which are the foundation of IPM's distinctive competitive advantage in the marketplace), and another 21 percent rated these attributes as *above average*.[1] Fully 100 percent reported that IPM's PMCs delivered the project objectives, with 70 percent indicating an above average or outstanding result.[2] These results and others we researched indicate that IPM's cultural foundation in ethical values has a direct impact on performance and outcomes. Nowhere is this more evident than in IPM's reputation, which has led to its sustainability and success despite economic fluctuations, as well as to it being the 2005 recipient and 2010 finalist of the Better Business Bureau's International Torch Award for Marketplace Ethics (see box below).

As with other high-performing companies we studied, IPM's purpose stems from two core components: shared core values and an organizational vision. IPM's recognition as an ethical company with an impeccable reputation rests on four pillars: excellence, ethical conduct, community involvement, and commitment to employees. IPM leaders, PMCs, and associates use these four pillars as the organizational commitments against which they test all their decisions and through which they intend to achieve their vision of being the global leader in strategy development and project leadership.

MAJOR RECOGNITIONS FOR ETHICS & EXCELLENCE	
2011*	**"Best Small Workplace"** (Great Place to Work Institute® and *Entrepreneur* Magazine)
2010*	**"Best Small Workplace"** (Great Place to Work Institute® and *Entrepreneur* Magazine)
	American Business Ethics Award (Financial Services Professional Foundation)
	International Torch Award for Marketplace Ethics Finalist (Better Business Bureau)
2008*	**"Top Small Workplace"** (Winning Workplaces and the *Wall Street Journal*)
	One of 100 fastest growing companies in Chicago (*Inc. 500* Magazine)
2005	**International Torch Award for Marketplace Ethics** (Better Business Bureau)
* *Inc. 500* Magazine cited IPM among the 5,000 fastest growing, privately held companies in the U.S. for five years, beginning in 2007.	

49

Unlike other companies we have studied, IPM established an organizational constitution, of which the vision is only a small part. The documents and guidance that comprise IPM's constitution make company ethics come alive. IPM leaders believe their distinctive competence and impeccable ethics drive clients to select the company as their service provider and motivate candidates to seek IPM as an employer. However, the company's Quest defines the true dream for the company, the destination that IPM associates continually seek but never attain because of its continual evolution and improvement.

The five elements of the Quest (shown in the following box) embody the company's values of integrity, honesty, respect, excellence, and continuous improvement, as well as the ethical behaviors in more specific terms that guide decisions and interactions toward strategic goals. The goals include "peace of mind," which acknowledges that rewards must be acquired through good, honest, hard work rather than ill-gotten means. The goal "professional fulfillment" seeks more than mere employee satisfaction; rather, it speaks of "challenging and rewarding career progression" and personal "engagement" through which each employee sees his or her future fully "intertwined with IPM," to quote Panico. This goal aligns very closely with the concept of employee entanglement we described in the introduction.

Shape an Ethical Culture Consciously, Constructively, and Constantly

IPM leaders have written the company's Quest, but how do they get employees to achieve it? Even families have their differences, but to be truly entangled, employees must see documents such as the Quest as a philosophy to live by. To get this level of acceptance and belief, senior leaders must consciously, constructively, and constantly build the company culture and align attitudes around the core values. How do they do it?

IPM'S QUEST

Global Market Leadership represented by an impeccable reputation, global recognition of our brand, being a leader in our chosen markets and a catalyst for ethical conduct, and providing renowned employee training and development.

Growth and Innovation based on an entrepreneurial spirit and innovative mind-set and ever-increasing influence, size, and customer base.

Prosperity marked by stability, security, strength, financial rewards, pride of association, and peace of mind.

Professional Fulfillment exemplified by an extraordinary culture that embodies Our Mission and Beliefs, challenging and rewarding career progression, and personal satisfaction and engagement.

Philanthropy through which IPM is recognized as a good neighbor and civic leader, an influencer in upgrading the quality of education, and a contributor to the betterment of society and the well-being of children.

Where It Begins: The Management–Employee Agreement

The U.S. armed forces gain immediate commitment from every soldier, sailor, airman, or Marine, regardless of rank or status, by administering an oath of office and subsequently training and reinforcing the culture necessary for each unit to execute on each member's promise to serve faithfully. IPM achieves something similar through its Management Employment Agreement (excerpts are quoted in the following box) and training program. Each new member of the IPM team commits to the agreement as the "rules of engagement" through which values come alive in personal actions. Employees have a clear understanding from the start that working for IPM is not like working for any other company; instead, it is working in a very positive way that aligns everyone, regardless of position, location, or personal attributes.

EXCERPTS FROM IPM'S MANAGEMENT EMPLOYMENT AGREEMENT

I, _____, understand the magnitude of this responsibility and accept it with a complete knowledge of the conduct, behavior, and professional ethics that are nonnegotiable elements of this management privilege.

IPM was founded with a belief and strong desire to provide rewarding and secure futures for above-average performers who possess uncompromising honesty and integrity, to share the profits of the company with those who contribute to its success, and to fortify a culture that exemplifies teamwork.

The company's values and principles cannot be compromised for fame, personal financial benefits, or any other incentive that casts doubt on our mission and beliefs, endangers IPM's long-term viability and reputation, or compromises employees' trust and confidence in its management.

Those who share in responsibility for management of IPM's resources must wholeheartedly understand, accept, and enforce IPM's intrinsic values; these are referenced in our mission and beliefs and are most clearly defined as IPM's character elements.

PROVISIONS: "As it relates to the company's mission . . . our mission and beliefs will not be modified or interpreted in any manner that compromises the company's integrity, its values, or the security and well-being of its employees.

"As it relates to IPM's culture: I realize it is my responsibility to promulgate open and honest communications within all levels and among all individuals within the company; to do what is in my power to discourage selfishness; to encourage teamwork and synergy; to promote continuous improvement; to foster caring and concern for each other; and generally provide a motivating positive environment that is founded on trust. To this end, I promise to address parochialism, selfishness, and other negative influences immediately upon observation or awareness."

If you're thinking, "This is too good to be true. What employee will buy this?" you're not alone. Panico says that outsiders and even new hires are skeptical when they first read the mission and beliefs and find it hard to accept because of past experiences to the contrary. In fact, he says, "People do not accept the philosophy as real and are waiting for us to trip, but I guarantee them it's the stone-cold truth."

The most prominent issue when it comes to winning hearts, or turning skeptics into believers, is finding top performers who share IPM's values and passions. As the CEO noted, "After that, the only thing we have to do is ensure they have challenging and rewarding work and a supportive environment. When we fulfill these desires and behave according to our values, employees trust us all the time."

Setting the Structure for Today and for the Next One Hundred Years

He went on to tell us he believes "we should be running companies for the next generation of employees because that will force us to do a good job." This future-oriented mind-set reflects how IPM develops leaders to build a legacy that perpetuates the principles and practices evident within the company.

Panico started the company before project management was "cool," but from the beginning he wanted two things: an impeccable reputation and longevity. "For it to be around for a hundred years, I figured I needed to build our company on values since these help us stay the course." He also believed he needed to design an environment in which those around him "felt comfortable because they were being treated fairly and consistently." He wanted to attract to the firm others whom he could trust and who would work in a high-performing fashion, where he didn't have to second-guess anyone's intentions because doing so "sucks energy from whatever we are trying to achieve."

IPM leaders believe the ability to celebrate the company's hundredth birthday does not depend on the CEO, the CFO, or any other senior leader waking up tomorrow but rather on the right decisions in hiring the right people. According to IPM employees, individual talent is important, but never compromising IPM's character, standards, or values is more important. If leaders tolerate bad behavior—say, for example, a person is making money for the firm by doing a job well but violating core values and principles—the company will falter eventually. That type of behavior is analogous to cancer cells within the company; all it takes is one employee to compromise the company's integrity for the entire organization's reputation to be damaged, which can cause the culture to collapse.

For these reasons, IPM is very selective in hiring only top performers who will contribute positively to the company's culture and results. In 2011 alone, the company received 5,470 résumés. From those, IPM staff selected 443 candidates (8.1 percent) for a phone interview, followed by 191 (3.5 percent) for first-round face-to-face interviews, which led to 71 (1.3 percent) second-round interviews. Eventually 20 candidates were hired, which is merely four-tenths of one percent of the total field.

As selective as IPM is, you can imagine that hiring the people with the right skills is only part of the formula for longevity and sustainable success. Manager of Human Resources Jill Cochrane emphasized that cultural fit is just as important as skill fit when it comes to selecting an employee. Each candidate who passes the initial experience and skills screening undergoes several interviews during which team members have a say in who will be brought into the IPM family. As part of the collaborative effort to bring on the best talent with the best fit, the CEO conducts interviews with candidates that focus on character elements and leadership rather than anything technical. This personal interest of senior management extends to the orientation process, during which everyone is accessible and approachable. Panico goes to lunch with each new employee, who is also assigned a mentor to help that newest member of the family acclimate to the culture.

SKILL SET	DESCRIPTION	EXAMPLES
Tactical	Allows an individual to analyze a fairly well-defined need and originate tasks or activities to satisfy the need.	• Adaptability • Cost Awareness and Control • Decision making • Follow-up • Planning • Problem Solving • Technical Competence
Strategic	Allows an individual to apply insight and foresight to the development of a plan in order to accommodate environmental influences, anticipated reaction, and the evaluation of risk influence/anticipated obstacles.	• Flexibility • Foresight • Insight • Negotiating • Strategy Development
Management	Tools which ensure proper integration and deployment of personnel, dollars, and other resources to accomplish specific objectives.	• Conflict Management • Continuous Improvement • Delegation • Interviewing • Managing Change • Meeting Protocols • Presentation Skills • Subordinate Development • Time Management
Personal	Attributes born out of experience, environment, sense of self, and vision which shape an individual's approach.	• Initiative • Leadership • Leading by Example • Active Listening • Motivation • Organization • Professional Maturity • Relationship Building • Verbal Skills • Writing Skills
Professional	Factors that influence the perception an individual creates.	• Appearance • Assertiveness • Courtesy • Diplomacy • Poise • Teamwork

Cochrane strives to ensure that good psychological chemistry exists between the mentor and mentee when making matches because developing strong relationships early in one's IPM tenure has a direct impact on job performance. As every new employee progresses deeper into the two-week orientation period, he or she gains a fuller understanding and appreciation of the value and depth of performance excellence, IPM style. To be successful, each employee develops performance skills in five areas—tactical, strategic, management, personal, and professional—that allow the employee freedom within a culture of discipline (see previous page).[3]

Again, IPM builds its ethical culture through conscious, constructive, and constant reinforcement. Performance reviews are a major component of that. The way in which IPM conducts these evaluations garnered the company a lot of attention and praise from the *Wall Street Journal* and Winning Workplaces, which recognized IPM as a "Top Small Workplace" in 2008. IPM's Performance Summary and Development Plan (PSDP) is designed not simply to evaluate performance but also to review character traits, such as dependability, fairness, and common sense, as well as an individual's ability to elicit trust (see the following box).

Despite what appear to be very strict guidelines, only two absolutes exist within IPM: honesty and integrity. Someone who lies will be discharged immediately; it's as simple as that. However, IPM leaders know that people make mistakes and errors happen, and when they do, an individual receives immediate feedback, and corrective action is taken.

According to Panico, real-time feedback creates a culture of highly motivated staffers because the best development occurs when people know how well or how poorly they have done on a project or task. IPM leaders told us they do not allow any criticism to appear on a PSDP or other review document if the immediate supervisor did not address the problem with the individual well before the review session. Leaders at all levels explained that numerous opportunities exist for offering feedback, from weekly one-on-one performance meetings, in which staff members review specific events or aspects about existing projects, to formal reviews at the end of every project. In response to criticism that IPM's leaders devote too much time annually to developing employees rather than increasing profits, Panico's response is very simple: "How can we treat our clients well if we don't treat our own employees as well?"

IPM'S PERFORMANCE SUMMARY AND DEVELOPMENT PLAN OVERVIEW

The primary objective of the Performance Summary and Development Plan© is to motivate and develop employees to reach their full potential; this serves the employees' and IPM's quest for excellence. The objective is accomplished through recognizing past achievements, highlighting future opportunities, and developing a strategy for employees to attain their potential while addressing performance shortfalls.

Relying on mutual respect and trust, both the employee and the supervisor share responsibility for professional development—a never-ending process that ensures that aspirations are discussed, understood, and integrated into an evolving career plan. The Performance Summary and Development Plan provides a structure for the process and addresses how well the two parties are serving this critical responsibility.

IPM's highest priority is developing employees to their fullest capability. The company requires loyal employees who are well-trained and driven to excellence if it is to achieve its objectives to provide employment security, ensure company growth, and satisfy its mission. The Performance Summary and Development Plan is a key element of IPM's strategy to produce these high-caliber individuals and serves as a testimony to the company's commitment to individual growth.

Go Beyond Transactional Agreements to Transform Others into Entangled Employees

In today's environment, company leaders are concerned with the legal limits and boundaries of employment contracts or agreements, which usually include a job description, a hierarchical relationship with a boss, and a set of performance expectations. These elements constitute the transactional nature of any employment but address nothing of the relational side. Another challenge with contractual relationships is that staff members have little incentive to do more than simply what the contract or work agreement specifies. Other than a possible monetary reward for early delivery, what motivation exists for doing something exceptionally well? Unfortunately, our society has become so accustomed to the transactional nature of contractual arrangements that performance expectations have deteriorated to the point of accepting mediocrity rather than excellence.

Building Trust

Unlike the immediacy of a transaction, relationships take longer to develop and evolve because the two parties must build trust by satisfying each other's needs in a timely fashion. Here's how Panico explains it: "All relationships begin as transactional contracts. As we build trust, the relationships transcend contracts and become transformational. Transformational relationships are influenced by the mind and heart. These often evolve to trusted friendships and in its highest state, love relationships." Numerous articles and books directed toward corporate America target the development of "trusting relationships" between management and both vendors/suppliers and employees as a key to long-term success.

Within IPM, we found the unconditional trust that exists within organizations where entangled employees operate. Trust and caring are the foundation blocks underlying sincere relationships through which employees openly share new ideas for improvements and innovations that lead to breakthrough thinking and performance.[4] Entangled employees drive these breakthroughs because they constantly search for ways to do things better. A major human resource challenge exists with this mentality because few employees have been exposed to environments like IPM's, and some are honestly intimidated by the concept of unconditional trust and caring because it does not reflect what the majority of American workers face every day.[5] "It's like someone trying to get close to you when you've never considered this possibility within the work environment. Yet once you can move employees slowly forward, this practice becomes tremendously addictive because they will search forever to find it again," observed Panico. Members of the IPM family have found a way to make this a reality.

According to Larry Meyer, the shared beliefs, along with the consistency with which the company culture is reinforced, help all employees believe in themselves and believe that one should always strive for a better outcome. Having served in the U.S. Army as an officer as well as having worked for General Electric, he believes IPM represents "a well-balanced existence where employees draw comfort knowing their leaders 'have their backs' and will do the right things ethically regardless of what's going on outside." This sense that we are "all in it together working for the best organizational, client, and personal outcomes" builds a culture that supports discretionary thinking and the entangled workplace. It creates "an attitude that supports your best, and you will do the things that are right for the company, right for the client, and right for each employee." That sort of attitude and behavior is what truly makes IPM a family—even when someone leaves the nest.

M.W. is a former IPM employee who spent twelve years doing engineering and project management work before moving up the ladder in a different company. He expressed his appreciation for the skills and lessons learned through his IPM experience in a letter addressed to the entire company after his departure: "The IPM family really helped me learn about people, organization, and management in general. The lessons learned went well beyond work and business and apply to everyday life, family, and relationships. I owe much of my professional success to the things I learned from my coworkers at IPM." What IPM does for its employees only reinforces the entangled relationship between employee and organization and builds the family environment at IPM.

The Organization as a Servant to Others

The unity evident in professional matters spills over to philanthropy and social responsibility, which strengthen team member entanglement around shared purpose. For example, newborns of employees are welcomed as the newest members of the IPM family. Babies receive a car seat and a savings bond, and the mother receives flowers from the entire staff. Similarly, those who experience a death in the family receive either flowers or a donation to a charity selected by the mourning family.

Some might say these actions are not remarkable because other organizations do similar things; however, what we found remarkable at IPM is the consistency in caring for others, especially the ways in which team members rallied around significant family events and serious illness. When a team member's son was diagnosed with leukemia in 2009, for instance, IPM staff formed Team Sammy to walk and raise funds for leukemia research. This event has developed into an annual company commitment that joins team members from all over the company, regardless of their physical location.

Such impulses resonate throughout other top-performing companies. When employees align and identify their personal values so closely with the organization's values, when leaders create the right culture where employees feel nourished and nurtured, when employees have total trust and know they are valued by the senior leadership team, the foundations for entangled relationships and breakthrough performance exist.

Serve a Higher Purpose

In chapter 1, we discussed the power of discretionary thinking and how significant changes and efforts can occur when a group of people shares a high level of entanglement and commitment to a cause. In IPM's case, company leaders have done a great job in building the right culture, one in which employee entanglement continues to drive ethical and moral behaviors and leadership. IPM employees have taken it upon themselves to serve the greater good outside the company walls.

Within IPM, Karen Heiting glows as the perfect example of a discretionary thinker. For the last nine years, she has served as assistant to the CEO. Seven years ago, she was diagnosed with cancer and spent five months recuperating. During the entire time she was out of work, coworkers called, e-mailed, and visited her, bringing food, support, and love to encourage and motivate her to fight and get back in the saddle.

Out of such a dark personal situation came light, as Karen saw an opportunity to unite her coworkers' generosity with the company's efforts to "step out into the community" with a larger corporate commitment to social responsibility. She presented a proposal to the executive team five years ago that served as the seed for Integrated Project Mercy, which continues to grow each year.

Integrated Project Mercy supports IPM's mission and beliefs by focusing efforts on the needs of children, education, veterans, and the homeless—both globally and within the communities where IPM employees work and live—as well as educational programs that serve community needs. The charities the company supports rotate on a quarterly basis; the decision as to which charity the company supports also rotates quarterly among the regional offices, where employees choose a cause near and dear to their hearts. National as well as regional programs have benefited from IPM's generosity and charity, as is seen in the following table. In addition to Integrated Project Mercy, coworkers help others through donating their time and money to other local, national, and international causes.

SOCIAL RESPONSIBILITY BENEFICIARIES	
Nationally	Regionally
• Action Against Hunger • Feeding America (formerly named America's Second Harvest) • Compassion International • Habitat for Humanity • Intrepid Heroes Fund/VA Hospitals • Ronald McDonald House • World Vision Program-School Tools • YMCA • Mercy Home for Boys and Girls	• Restoration Ministries Collection (coats, hats, gloves, scarves, and mittens) • Special Operations Warrior Foundation • CPT Joe F. Lusk II Foundation • Heartland Blood Centers: IPM Blood Drive for Sam McLeod • St. Louis (MO) Area Food Bank • Alameda County (CA) Community Food Bank • Walk for Leukemia (Sammy's Team)—Chicago and San Francisco (6/18/09)

All it took was one entangled employee to make a proposal to a room full of other entangled employees. Just as Panico's *The Biggest Loser* analogy exemplifies how IPM's project leaders make a difference in the lives of clients' employees and the performance of the client, Karen's idea planted a seed in the heads and hearts of her coworkers that in turn has changed and will continue to change the lives of people across the country.

What We Learned from Integrated Project Management

Corporate scandals over the past fifteen years have caused many company leaders and governing boards to address ethical behavior and individual characteristics such as honesty and integrity as organizational practices.[6] Such leaders have found that corporate standards of behavior must integrate the values and behaviors of their employees because values originate within the people individually, are expressed in the ways in which they interact with others, and comprise a major part of organizational culture.[7] Within organizational settings, leaders set the context and expectations; they also provide examples of ethical behavior and ideals, and what employees see at the top permeates the thinking and behavioral patterns of those who follow and becomes the definition of acceptable behavior.[8]

During our quest to find and report on high-performing companies, IPM stood out as the logical example for explaining how company leaders should build an ethical organization. Based on the lessons we learned from IPM, here are four ways you can adapt in your business.

1. **Differentiate your company** within your industry and markets by defining core values, building a well-defined philosophy and belief system around those values, and demonstrating a leadership rather than management mentality. Refusing to follow others and adopting a market leader mentality requires dedication, energy, and moral consciousness, as we saw within IPM. Its leaders exemplified the three value disciplines that characterize market leaders: *customer intimacy*, through the relationships PMCs establish and nurture with clients; *project leadership*, through the ways PMCs deliver project results; and *operational excellence*, through maximizing efficiency at the lowest relative cost.[9] To be a market leader, follow IPM's example. Positive results do not happen by chance but rather through effective leadership and management that stem from core beliefs.

2. **Consciously, constructively, and constantly build a strong ethical culture** by refusing to compromise on core values and beliefs. IPM's culture evolved from a basic set of principles to a well-defined constitution and set of best practices that

establish the discipline for achieving excellence. Great companies allow employees significant freedom to operate within a culture of discipline, and IPM's culture exemplifies this practice.[10] Holding everyone within a company to a higher standard requires constant vigilance, especially by leaders whom everyone is watching and from whom everyone else takes their lead. Future employees must understand they will be held to a higher standard at every stage, from the interview to full immersion in the culture. A strong ethical culture also brings with it the responsibility for constantly protecting that high standard through one's personal discipline and strength of character.

3. **Nurture and reinforce an ethical culture** by going beyond transactional employment agreements to build trustful relationships in all directions. Several core values exist within ethical cultures, but trustworthiness, respect, caring, and fairness are commonly found in codes of ethics around the globe.[11] Build on these core values to create open environments where employees will eventually express deep respect and caring for others. However, this begins with the leaders at the top. To create the right culture, leaders must set the right example. By living the Golden Rule as part of one's work culture, leaders can develop mutually trustful relationships that no employment contract could begin to describe. Mutual trust can lead to constant innovations and new ideas that stem from the discretionary thinking of fully entangled employees.

4. **Seek to serve a higher purpose** through which you can create high, positive ambition. Strong economic returns stem from entangled employees who give their all because they want to do so, not because anyone or anything is forcing them in any way. Financial capital stems from the social and community capital that rests with the productivity, commitment, and energy of the employee base. Creating strong economic value for customers and clients produces benefits for a broader community. Moral leadership does

not require heroics but rather people who work quietly behind the scenes to "prevent moral wrongs in the workplace."[12] When leaders show their personal strength of character by committing themselves and their companies to a transcendent purpose over the long term and do not allow anyone to fall prey to the temptation of compromising core values by even the smallest margin, they gain wider commitment and eventual entanglement from the people nurtured within the culture.

Selected Resources

Here are some additional sources you might find useful as you build an ethical culture of engaged and entangled men and women within your organization.

1. Kenneth R. Andrews, "Ethics in Practice," *Harvard Business Review* 67, no.5, (September–October 1989): 99–104, addressed the three-part challenge of developing moral managers, building an ethical culture, and instituting polices that support and safeguard ethical performance. Andrews noted how ethical cultures make standards and values central to a company's strategy and also make an explicit estimate of a candidate's character part of the hiring and selection process.

2. Ben Heineman, "Avoiding Integrity Land Mines," *Harvard Business Review* 85, no.4 (April 2007): 100–108, presented tools companies can adopt in creating a culture of high ethical standards. Heineman provided real-life examples from GE, particularly the company's response to scandals such as Enron and WorldCom, from which we can all learn. Rosabeth Moss Kanter addressed the concept of creating an institutional logic that looks beyond company goals and plans for advancing societal goals in "How Great Companies Think Differently," *Harvard Business Review* 89, no.11 (November 2011): 66–78. IPM's Quest and philosophy represent

examples of institutional logic that guides behaviors.

3.   To create an ethical foundation, leaders must acknowledge that negative behaviors occur for any number of reasons. In "Why 'Good' Managers Make Bad Ethical Choices," *Harvard Business Review* 64, no.4 (July–August 1986): 85–90, Saul Gellerman discussed the rationalization behind unethical behaviors and addressed the need for establishing clear ethical guidelines for all employees to avoid potential situations that could jeopardize a company's reputation.

4.   Finally, leaders must not only set the example within ethical cultures; they also need to think differently. Douglas Ready and Emily Truelove, in "The Power of Collective Ambition," *Harvard Business Review* 89, no.12 (December 2011): 94–102, discussed the centrality of organizational purpose in creating an ethical foundation. In a similar vein, Ikujiro Nonaka and Hirotaka Takeuchi defined the practical wisdom, or *phronesis,* that represents the experiential knowledge through which people learn to make ethically sound judgments; see "The Wise Leader," *Harvard Business Review* 89 no.5 (May 2011): 58–67.

�✦ ✦ ✦

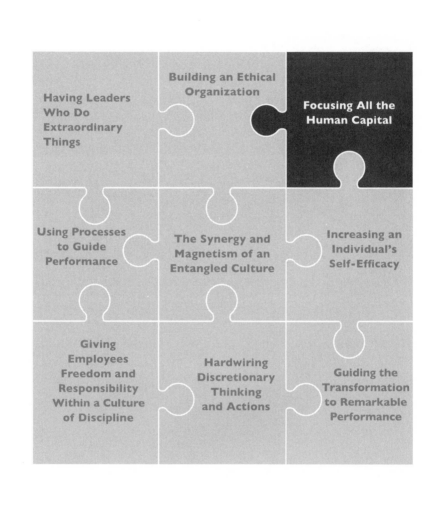

CHAPTER 3

FOCUSING ALL THE HUMAN CAPITAL:
MidwayUSA

"If you take all the theories and concepts in business research and codify them into one practical guide, it would be the Malcolm Baldrige Criteria for Performance Excellence. If you just read it and understand how the parts fit together, you can see how it becomes a fantastic road map to help an organization," Larry Potterfield said as we were leaving a Baldrige Quest Conference in Washington, DC. MidwayUSA was a 2009 recipient of the Malcolm Baldrige National Quality Award. The company's founder and CEO and his team were in the nation's capital to talk to others about the company's journey to quality. Here was a person so committed to the approach that he was creating a Baldrige Performance Excellence Group in Columbia, Missouri (his hometown and the company's headquarters), and encouraging others to form groups around the country. This was definitely someone we wanted to know more about.

MidwayUSA is a family-owned catalog and Internet retailer that offers "Just About Everything^{SM}" for shooters, reloaders, gunsmiths, and hunters. Ninety percent of the company's total business is with U.S. retail customers; dealers and international customers make up the remaining 10 percent. MidwayUSA has 243 full-time and 100 part-time employees. Many in the company's workforce have a deep passion for shooting, hunting, and outdoor sports, and they draw on that personal knowledge and insight to better serve their customers.

Even though MidwayUSA had a history of good results prior to adopting Baldrige, Larry realized the company needed more. Larry had always been a very strong, entrepreneurial leader who was a major contributor to the company's success. As MidwayUSA grew, he realized the company needed a management structure that would provide sustainability and continued growth. He turned to the Baldrige Criteria for Performance Excellence to obtain that framework.

"I wanted this business to be the best it could be. I wanted to serve our customers so they will keep coming. It is [the] simple dynamics of survival in a competitive market," he explained. So search for a survival technique he did. And he found something to latch onto—or so he thought.

"I discovered the Baldrige award through some of my reading, and as I read the material, it spoke to me as more than a gimmick. [The basis for the award] was a way of leading, of conducting a business." Larry thought the Baldrige method might be the answer to leveraging the company's reputation of quality. "I got pretty excited about it, told my team to apply, and it was a failure. I was so discouraged that I backed off of the approach and let it go."

Clearly he didn't keep that attitude, so we wondered what led Larry to get the organization involved in the process and try the Baldrige approach for a second time.

This chapter looks at how applying for and, eventually receiving, the Baldrige award helped Larry create a focused approach toward setting organizational goals and translating those goals into action plans, process performance measures, and individual performance expectations.

Out of Africa

Several years went by. Larry was still convinced there was value in the Baldrige approach but could not figure out why MidwayUSA had failed

THE MALCOLM BALDRIGE NATIONAL QUALITY AWARD

In 1987 the U.S. Congress passed into law the Malcolm Baldrige National Quality Award, named for the Secretary of Commerce at the time. The Baldrige Program is a national public-private partnership dedicated to performance excellence. The Malcolm Baldrige National Quality Award is designed to help businesses follow the lead of world-class competitors by:

- Raising awareness about the importance of performance excellence in driving the U.S. and global economy
- Providing organizational assessment tools and criteria
- Educating leaders in businesses, schools, health-care organizations, and government and nonprofit agencies about the practices of best-in-class organizations
- Recognizing national role models and honoring them with the only Presidential award for performance excellence

An appointed Board of Overseers is charged with developing the criteria based on what they determine to be the best practices of organizations. The board tracks the performance of benchmark organizations and learns what these organizations do that make them so competitive. What the board learns is then translated into a set of "Criteria of Performance Excellence." The board has created criteria for several organization types: profit, not-for-profit, and government; health-care; and educational organizations.

Six process categories exist in the current Baldrige criteria: leadership; strategic planning; customer focus; measurement, analysis, and knowledge management; workforce focus; and operational focus. The seventh category focuses on results. The grand design of the Baldrige approach is a set of systematic processes that are aligned to bring an integrated approach to leading and managing an organization.

—Adapted from the 2011–2012 Criteria for Performance Excellence (Gaithersburg, MD: National Institute of Science and Technology, 2011).

the first time. It wasn't until reading Malcolm Gladwell's *The Tipping Point*[1] while he was on safari in Africa that the lightbulb went off in Larry's head.

"I realized the approach I had taken with the Baldrige was all wrong," he explained. "The foundation of Gladwell's book was that little things can make a big difference. The first time I tried to adopt the Baldrige approach, I just delegated it to a team of people who did not understand the approach and did not understand what I wanted done. It's like I threw it on the table and told them to do it. Because I wanted them to embrace it instead of it being my baby, I gave it to them and was not personally involved. I needed to be involved. I realized that you need to get a few people to buy in, and then a few more, until you reach a point where you have a critical mass of people who know the approach and support it."

So began MidwayUSA's second Baldrige quality effort. Realizing that no one really understood the approach or how it could help the organization, Larry sent several senior leaders to a Baldrige informational conference. Among them was Linda Bounds, vice president of financial services. When she and her colleagues saw what Baldrige had to offer, the "aha" moment arrived. "It was clear why Larry believed that Baldrige is a great common way to communicate. I have been in organizations where senior leadership jumps from one latest management trend to the next and employees just get confused." Together, the senior leaders quickly came to the conclusion, "Why not adopt the Baldrige terminology and approach?" Enter the beginnings of employee engagement, commitment, and entanglement.

"I came back from participating as an examiner and told Larry that if he really wanted all senior leaders to embrace Baldrige as a management approach, he should send the rest of the senior leadership team," Linda continued. She and others knew that the entire company wouldn't commit to concepts that management, especially senior leaders, did not immerse themselves in fully.

At MidwayUSA, the balance began to tip in the direction of the Baldrige criteria, and as that balance was tipping, so were employee devotion, belief, and perhaps most important, discretionary thinking.

Now, nearly one-third of MidwayUSA's employees are state or national Baldrige examiners[2], a solid core of people who know the program and *want* to apply it to their organization. That makes a huge difference.

Larry himself learned that he needed to be a part of the program; it wasn't something he could just delegate. If he wanted employees to devote hours of discretionary thinking toward MidwayUSA and the Baldrige award, he needed to show that he was doing the same.

Identifying Values, Vision, and Mission

After building the critical mass of supporters and believers, MidwayUSA needed to discuss how the different elements of the Baldrige approach could be applied. They started by having a team of leaders and a cross-functional set of employees develop a statement of values that outlined how they were going to do business. They then translated the core values into a specific code of conduct. These values underpinned the mission and vision, which set the framework for the rest of the goals of the organization and provided a set of statements that could inspire employees and other stakeholders who also shared these values. Research has shown that value statements play a significant role in creating a positive culture within an organization.[3]

MIDWAYUSA'S CORE VALUES

The family principles that guide us:
- Honesty
- Integrity
- Positive Attitude
- Respect
- Stewardship
- Accountability
- Teamwork
- Loyalty

MIDWAYUSA CODE OF CONDUCT

All members of the MidwayUSA Board of Directors and all employees, from entry level to the CEO, are committed to the following—both on and off the job:
1. A high level of integrity and honesty at all times
2. Respect for all stakeholders (customers, employees, vendors, shareholders)
3. Strict adherence to all laws, regulations, and company policies
4. Fairness in all dealings
5. Loyalty to the company and coworkers
6. Candor with respect
7. Teamwork through participation
8. Conduct worthy of your trust and confidence
9. Friendly, helpful, and courteous behavior
10. The promotion of safety through actions and instructions

Next, the team worked on defining the vision and mission of the organization. While the values and code of conduct stated how they wanted to run the business, the vision and mission set the direction for the type of organization they were striving to become.

MIDWAYUSA'S VISION & MISSION

Vision: To be the best-run business in America for the benefit of our customers by systematically applying the modern leadership and management principles from the Baldrige Criteria for Performance Excellence.

Mission: We are a catalog and an Internet retailer of shooting, hunting, and outdoor products relying on high-performing employees, cutting-edge technologies, and the modern leadership and management principles from the Baldrige Criteria for Performance Excellence.

MidwayUSA's values, code of conduct, vision, and mission provide a clear sense of the direction and how the organization wants to do business each day. Larry and Matt Fleming (the current president) and the rest of the leadership team worked to build the culture to support these sets of statements. As Larry said: "We have progressed since we began on this journey, but the journey is not over; we think it is just beginning. My goal, as CEO, is to continue to work to institutionalize our values and vision and use the Baldrige criteria as a road map to be the best-run business in America."

Indeed, having the statements was not enough. It was important to live the statements so that "nonbelievers" would understand that MidwayUSA leaders meant what was said. Watching the example set by the leadership team and seeing how leaders embraced and lived the mission, vision, and values led to more employees becoming entangled in the quality effort and wanting to go to the examiner training program to learn about the Baldrige approach.

The next phase involved defining the key measures—aligned with values, vision, and mission—that would be used to determine how well

Rank	Company Key Measure
COMPANY KEY MEASURES	
#1	**Customer Satisfaction – Overall** CG: Customer Satisfaction
#2	**Company Goals Performance** CG: Customer, Employee, Vendor, and Shareholder Satisfaction
#3	**Gross Sales – Overall** CG: Shareholder Satisfaction
#4	**Net Income Percent of Net Sales** CG: Shareholder Satisfaction
#5	**Earnings Distribution** CG: Shareholder Satisfaction
#6	**Inventory Turns** CG: Shareholder Satisfaction
#7	**Employee Satisfaction and Engagement** CG: Employee Satisfaction
#8	**Vendor Satisfaction** CG: Vendor Satisfaction
#9	**Baldrige Self Score** CG: Modern Management Practices
#10	**Strategic Plan Execution** CG: Customer, Employee, Vendor, and Shareholder Satisfaction
#11	**Donations by Key Community** CG: Shareholder Satisfaction
#12	**Percent of Customer Orders with NRA Round-Up** CG: Shareholder Satisfaction

the organization was doing. These key measures would drive the strategic plan and the measures throughout all of MidwayUSA. Many organizations embed measures in the strategic plan to drive the company, but that leads to changes in emphasis each time a new initiative is started in a new strategic plan. MidwayUSA keeps the focus on those key areas that are central to the success of the organization. These metrics do not change with a new strategic plan; they are intended to guide and influence all actions over time throughout the company. The exhibit titled "Company Key Measures" lists these key company measures and then shows which strategic company goal (CG) relates to each measure.

The strategic planning process involves multiple meetings, one for each of the six Baldrige approach/deployment criteria areas: Leadership; Strategic Planning; Customer Focus; Measurement, Analysis, and Knowledge Management; Workforce Focus; and Operations Focus.[4] From the strategic plan come action plans that may be related to the department or to the primary building block of the Baldrige approach, which are processes.

Action Plans and Individual Performance Evaluation

Action plans are developed based on the strategic plan, which is aligned to the organization key measures. Each action plan specifies a time dimension, a deliverable, and an owner—either an individual or a team. The action plans are aligned to outcome measures in the strategic plan. How well the team meets the various metrics in the action plan becomes an important part of individual annual appraisals, along with the members' other responsibilities. For example, in the first action plan listed in the table following, the 3-Year Hunting Category Expansion Plan, the merchandising team as the owner would be responsible for (1) creating the plan along with sales growth projections and (2) enacting the plan and striving to meet the growth projections developed in the plan.

SAMPLE ACTION PLANS FOR MIDWAYUSA

Priority	Action Plan	Owner(s)	Plan Description
1	3-Year Hunting Category Expansion Plan	Merchandising	Create a plan to expand the hunting category to continue growth to plan
n/a	Server Virtualization (2008 AP)	IS-Network	Continue to virtualize servers
1	Improve Web App: Account Management	Marketing	Rewrite account management application/page
n/a	Product Families/Attributes (2008 AP)	Merchandising	Develop a new product numbering system to group similar products together with a common number
1	Future Sales Multiplier (FSM) Modification	Administration	Improve In-Stock Rate by changing FSM to reflect variation in product groups/types
2	Delivery Restrictions	Merchandising	Improve Delivery Restriction Management process to allow for agility. Example: Cannot add NJ FPID card as a license to allow shipments to NJ
3	Quantity Limits	Administration	Create the ability to systematically limit quantities on products
n/a	Batch/Wave Picking Handheld Technology (2008 AP)	Logistics	Ability to use handheld for tote induction, batch/wave picking (reduce totes on the conveyor)
1	Contact Center Move	Contact Center	Plan and implement new CC facility

However, action plans are only part of understanding how MidwayUSA guides its employees' performance. In addition, defining processes and setting forth process performance goals are an essential part of aligning goals and strategic plans to the core of what MidwayUSA does.

The Primacy of Processes

Processes are the foundation of the Baldrige approach, for they are the primary building blocks upon which we measure performance improvements. Processes are the drivers of performance in any organization because these key activities help the organization reach its overall goals. Part of MidwayUSA's commitment as a Baldrige training advocate involved mapping out the company's 1,500 processes to better understand what the company does and how it does it. The company did this to better match the process performance measures with customer needs.

Because many of these processes are tied to meeting customer needs, MidwayUSA would have to have a better way of knowing what the customer wanted. For example, the process for the area of shipping (see following table) would consist of all the steps involved in shipping an order, drawn out on a process map. Such a map helps everyone in the organization understand what is done and what steps might be wasteful or could be done better. In addition, setting performance measures is part of setting performance goals for any process; in this case, the company used the percentage of orders that were shipped on the same day, the numbers of orders that were shipped accurately (complete orders and shipped to the correct location), the package quality (the number of packages that may have been damaged or the contents may have been damaged), and the average total cost of shipping per invoice. In the table, the measures are linked to stakeholder requirements—in this case, customer requirements.

Each of the other 1,500 processes that MidwayUSA has identified is similarly mapped out by each department to reflect work being done by the department, the position responsible for doing the work, and the measures used to determine the effectiveness of the process. At every step along the way, processes are designed to meet the key requirements of the stakeholders affected by the process. This provides performance goals for those executing the strategy and starts the process of discretionary thinking; such thinking leads to remarkable results as these teams become engaged in making the process better through lower costs, greater reliability (fewer errors), faster execution, higher stakeholder satisfaction (if there is direct interaction with the stakeholder), or greater capacity in the process to handle the changing level of demands for the process.

Larry Potterfield states, simply, "An organization gets things done through processes. If you do not have processes well defined with measures of performance that link to meeting the requirements of stakeholders, you are not managing your company very well."

A SAMPLE OF KEY PROCESSES AND RELATED STAKEHOLDER VALUE				
Key Process	Area Process	Measure	Key Requirements of Stakeholder	Stakeholder
Logistics	Shipping	Same-day shipping	Fast delivery	Customer
		Shipping accuracy	Accurate, intact shipments	Customer
		Packaging quality	Accurate, intact shipments	Customer
		Total cost per invoice	Profitability	Shareholder

A SAMPLE OF KEY PROCESSES AND RELATED STAKEHOLDER VALUE

Key Process	Area Process	Measure	Key Requirements of Stakeholder	Stakeholder
Marketing	Publications	Response rate-flyer	Timely, relevant information	Customer
		Response rate-catalog	Timely, relevant information	Customer
Merchandising	Product Selection	Number of new products	Product selection	Customer
	Inventory Mgt	In-stock rate	Product availability	Customer
	Pricing Mgt	Competitive pricing	Competitive pricing	Customer
	Product Selection	Gross sales growth	Financial performance	Shareholder
	Inventory Mgt	Profit margin	Financial performance	Shareholder
	Pricing Mgt	Inventory turnover	Easy to do business	Shareholder
Order Taking	Floor Operations	Time/service factor	Easy to do business	Customer
		Abandoned calls	Easy to do business	Customer
	Results Mgt	Total cost per call	Easy to do business	Shareholder

But how do you determine customer and other stakeholder requirements? This question was a real challenge since no customers were wandering around store locations ready and willing to provide answers; in fact, determining customer needs was and is an ongoing process. The company went out to its customers around the country and the world and asked, measured, and tracked customer satisfaction data. "We use all kinds of data when setting processes that drive customer satisfaction," Larry explained.

He continued, "A major part of the Baldrige approach is focusing on the things you do or your processes. If we can manage the processes, we can better keep a focus on customers. For example, if customers tell us they expect to have the product they ordered from us in five days, then we have to set our processes to meet that time frame. We set time goals for order processing, order fulfillment, and how long it takes the order to reach the customer. We track and measure each of those metrics so that we can meet or exceed customer expectations." And, we might add, this is something many companies neglect to do.

Larry pointed out: "Each of the processes has measures of performance that can be tracked and benchmarked with other organizations to help us meet the organization's vision to be the best-run business in America, for the benefit of our customers, by systematically applying the modern leadership and management principles from the Baldrige Criteria for Performance Excellence. In addition, the process performance measures are aligned to key requirements of stakeholders, which align with the organizational key goals."

By combining process performance measures, action plan performance measures, and resulting individual performance expectations, everybody in the company knows what they should be doing and how they should be doing it.

As Sara Potterfield, vice president of the contact center in 2009 and current vice president of public relations, explained:

We want to make it clear to supervisors and employees the full gamut of what is important in [each] employee's job. Then we want to make sure that we reinforce each of those elements to demonstrate that these are the things that matter in a person's performance.

How can I get an employee to be customer focused or show respect for others unless I also reinforce what I want done and acknowledge it when it is complete? You can't say customer focus is critical and then focus rewards only on the number of calls that call center representatives handle per hour. You can't encourage making the calls shorter and expect customer satisfaction will improve. You have to reinforce in their reviews what you value as an organization. We focus first on what will satisfy the customer and then look at those things that will make our processes more effective and efficient while creating a great environment for the employees.

Those in the call center shared with us that their supervisors were more like coaches and partners,[5] who helped them do their work well and asked them about how to improve different aspects of the work or work environment. "It is great to be asked for your input," said Christina Carver. "It shows they care about you as a person, and it shows that they care about your ideas. As I work on my own improvement plans, my supervisor focuses more on what I think and how I can best improve, instead of telling me what needs to be done. The way they do things is just as important as getting things done. At Midway, the way things are done builds commitment and trust rather than creating bad feelings." Those are good ways to build engagement and entanglement, we would say.

Moving Beyond Performance Reviews to the Culture

Larry Potterfield was drawn to the Baldrige criteria because of the alignment of items and the importance of measures as well as the focus on more than pay-for-performance as the key to reinforce work behaviors. The Baldrige core values recognize the importance of valuing workforce members and partners beyond just worker satisfaction.[6] That supports the focused effort Larry and his leadership team make to sustain a culture that encourages employee engagement.

"How do I do that? Well, I must do that through two different approaches. I can create the system or the process [keeping with the Baldrige vocabulary], and I do it through my personal behaviors and those of all the leadership team to encourage, acknowledge, and demonstrate the importance of what the employees are doing."

This, according to Larry, is one of the problems with some of the textbook approaches to empowerment. The view they champion is that the senior leader empowers the employees and then lets them work on the project with minimal contact. In MidwayUSA's view, if the project is important to the organization, the senior leader should be involved—not to direct, but to support, to encourage, and to help. "The second time we got involved, I made sure we all got involved. I was there as a cheerleader supporting the development of this fantastic approach to leading a business," Larry revealed.

At MidwayUSA, they start building culture the minute they consider a new hire. As Larry noted:

> We want employees who embrace the shooting sports[7] that we support. We want an employee who has an attitude that supports a caring focus toward customers, other employees, and doing the job better than good. We want an employee to have a commitment to MidwayUSA. We seek that out in our hires. We then train them in their technical skill but also in our values, which are central to building the culture that we want. To have employees believe in these values, every leader must live them every day—in every action taken by me or Matt Fleming or any of the other leaders of this organization.

How important is the culture to new employees of MidwayUSA? It would seem that most of them are outdoor enthusiasts, and that interest appears to be an important factor in their engagement. Administrative Assistant Bridget Whetstine came looking for a job at the company through a pretty unusual route. A friend of hers, a fellow outdoor enthusiast, was a longtime customer of MidwayUSA. When Whetstine was looking for a job, her friend suggested she apply there. Essentially, the customer became the spokesperson for the company because he had seen Larry on TV, bought merchandise from the company, and ultimately had several positive experiences with MidwayUSA.

Nic Klein, an industrial engineer, shared with us how he ended up with the company. "I was working as a manager at a Dairy Queen. I had been dating the same girl for quite some time, and I wanted to propose to her. So I went looking for a higher-paying job so I could buy her a ring. I took the job to afford an engagement ring for my girlfriend, but I stayed at this job because of the quality of the people I work with, the quality of the leadership, and the quality of the company I work for."

An employee in logistics who was going to the University of Missouri commented: "The organization helps me do well at my university by being flexible with my work schedule. I love this place and have changed my major to business in the hopes that I can stay with Midway when I graduate. The place cares about me and my development. I have never experienced that from another employer."

To help build a performance-focused culture, the value statements and various Baldrige terms are posted throughout the organization. The posts change weekly to reach different employees and to combat staleness and overexposure. Larry wants to live the values and support employees who embrace them as well. He wants the values to be the way every single person acts at MidwayUSA. "These are not words or just a public relations statement. These are how we want all employees to live. It starts with us, our behavior, and the behavior we will or will not tolerate with others."

We asked a former supervisor in the call center if the signs about quality and customer focus on the wall become routine after a while. He replied:

> You would think so, but it doesn't. The signs change every week and have a new message that is designed to make us think about different aspects of quality or keep us focused on the customers. It is just another example how the senior leadership from Matt Fleming and the Potterfields [Larry, Brenda, and Sara] demonstrate the values of the senior leadership and the values they want each employee to share. It also demonstrates, to me at least, that the organization cares about the employees and how what each person does is important to the success of the organization.

MidwayUSA also trains employees in ways to enact those values in the jobs they have. Larry works hard to develop an environment where people know each other. For example, whenever employees drive to Kansas City or St. Louis for a trade show, Larry creates a seating chart for each car to encourage people to become acquainted with other people in the organization. Halfway through the trip, they change locations, so another set of people can meet.

Many organizations tend to have functional silos or departments whose employees want to stay together because they know each other. When it comes to improving the total organization, however, the silo approach can lead to dysfunction. To combat that silo feeling, MidwayUSA uses the "farm" to build a culture that brings people together. Larry explained the significance of the farm that MidwayUSA owns and operates. "We have a farm several miles from Columbia. We use it for some meetings but more for social gatherings. I want people to become friends and to know each other. If you know who you are working with and working for as a friend, it will help create a climate of respect and help to get people working together."

Nearly every person we interviewed at Midway had something to say about the farm, which is about an hour away from headquarters. The company holds its quarterly State of the Business meeting there, and on other occasions staff members conduct team-building experiences on the grounds. The farm is a place where memories are made. For example, Christina Carver said she shot and cleaned her first pheasant out there. She and Stephanie Buckner chuckled as they recalled MidwayUSA's head of financial services calling her a "tiny little thing" as she toted around a huge 12-gauge shotgun; she is apparently a really good shot. The two women couldn't wait to tell us about George, the designated cook whenever he goes to the farm, who makes a "mean pork steak." MidwayUSA employees often use the farm to shoot clay pigeons, and a former employee even held her wedding there. It is a place of business but also of recreation. The farm functions to help promote teamwork and a family environment. The farm symbolizes so much more than an outsider might think.

"Even the inclusive nature of meetings," according to Fleming, "is central to developing the culture we want to create. For example, our strategic planning meeting includes multiple levels of organization representatives. By having greater participation, we get more diverse ideas that can help us understand what is going on in the market and how MidwayUSA can best fit in that environment."

Some of the employees that we interviewed said it was the open communication that made them feel that organizational leaders really cared. "Our leaders want input from us and are very open as they communicate to the company through such formalities as the State of the Business quarterly briefings and State of the Department meetings, which they call 'Department Knowledge Sharing.' The ability to talk to our leaders, including senior leaders, creates a culture of caring and a family environment; we are part of the decision making at Midway."

"It is a joint effort," confirmed Larry. "Matt Fleming or I cannot do it alone."

How Aligned Measures Have Worked for MidwayUSA

Senior leaders at MidwayUSA, using the Baldrige criteria, create a focused direction for the organization through a range of activities: from setting values and writing both vision and mission statements, to clarifying key organizational goals and strategic plans, to identifying process performance measures and action plans, to customizing individual performance metrics. In addition, they use Baldrige principles to go beyond acknowledging performance to get each employee involved in decision making, which builds a culture of discretionary thinking, engagement, and entanglement. Has it really helped? Larry would answer that with an emphatic yes.

The financial numbers given earlier validate the CEO's response, but what is also important are the people numbers—that is, the customer satisfaction numbers and employee engagement and employee satisfaction measures. MidwayUSA's 2009 overall customer satisfaction rating was 93 percent, demonstrating improvement over the 2007 and 2008 scores of 91 percent. Overall customer retention is at an all-time high: 98 percent for the current year-to-date (2011). Overall customer loyalty, measured as "likelihood to shop again," is 94 percent.[8]

Results for indicators of workforce engagement and satisfaction in MidwayUSA's contact center, as well as employee satisfaction in its merchandising, marketing, and logistics departments, show levels comparable to national benchmark-performance ratings of 77 percent and 80 percent, respectively. The annual aggregated employee satisfaction survey score has improved from about 60 percent favorable in 2002 to 82 percent in 2008. These are some of the best improvement scores we have seen across organizations.

Even more affirming, however, were the employees' stories, which demonstrate their level of engagement and their focused efforts to see the organization succeed. For example, a customer once drove from

Kansas City to pick up an order, which is a bit of a drive. He expected to find his package ready, but that wasn't the case. The warehouse employee took it upon himself to get to the heart of the problem instead of passing off the responsibility to someone else in another department. He discovered the order was on hold, addressed the issue, and got the gentleman his package. Had he himself not felt empowered and responsible for taking care of the problem, a very unhappy customer could have left the warehouse that day—and the company for good. Instead, the customer went home with his package, satisfied with his experience and with a positive attitude toward the company.

Dave Loucks and Jim Swofford, two line employees, both recalled a time when the order processing center in logistics failed, which created a major backup of packages that needed to get out. Instead of leaving the mess to the packaging department, Larry Potterfield's wife, Brenda, vice president of community and industry relations, and several managers put their job titles and work aside and started sorting packages to ensure that customers would get their orders on time.

What We Learned from MidwayUSA

"MidwayUSA," Larry Potterfield declares, "is a Baldrige platform, using the Baldrige criteria as the road map to help guide the organization to its vision to be the best-run business in America for the benefit of our customers, by systematically applying the modern leadership and management principles from the Baldrige Criteria for Performance Excellence." MidwayUSA is a Baldrige award recipient, but that fact is less of a central issue than how Larry Potterfield has set the direction for the leadership and for employees by focusing on measurable and aligned objectives to guide the organization. The work is structured, the processes are identified, and employees are engaged and recognized for their contribution to the organization. Larry's personal leadership behaviors demonstrate the values and vision that he wants the organization to strive toward, and he shows that he believes in the mission and values through the way he runs the organization, the way he values people, and his belief in the Baldrige criteria as a means to improve any organization. This latter point is demonstrated by the Baldrige Performance Excellence Group Larry founded and supports in Columbia, Missouri, and through his advocating that chapters be formed throughout areas where performance excellence is desired.

Here are nine steps you can take to become more focused on aligned and integrated goal setting. These nine steps reflect the ideas that Larry believes in, as he develops his workforce to be able to communicate in similar ways through the Baldrige process. Through the Baldrige processes, the entangled culture is created that builds discretionary thinking and acting through the empowered workforce.

1. **Articulate your goals and how you want to run the business.** Developing a purpose statement with values, vision, and mission is an excellent tool to help set the direction for the organization and how it will conduct itself in its relationships with customers, the community, and its staff members. This gives the employees goals they can believe in and commit themselves to make happen. Posting and reinforcing the values, the vision, and the mission on a daily basis is an important step in building a customer-focused environment and an environment that values each employee.

2. **Align and integrate goals at all levels.** Separately from strategic planning and after you have a cohesive set of values, mission, and vision, set the key organizational goals as a stable measure to guide the organization. Strategic plans focus on current initiatives that would support these overall key goals, but those plans will most likely change as initiatives change. Action plans and process performance goals should be measurable and have a direct correlation with influencing key organizational goals. Defining action and process performance objectives as part of individual performance goals helps to align each employee's behaviors with their contributions to organizational goals.

3. **Link incentives and recognition to performance.** This step demonstrates the importance you are placing on performance goals. Each employee's contribution to the goals should be defined with performance metrics to support what is expected of the employee. However, incentives take organizational performance only so far. Research reinforces building a culture that has values, a vision, and a mission that employees support and internalize, which leads to superior efforts and more focused performance that exceeds mere monetary incentives.[9]

4. **Value employees.** One of the core dimensions of the Baldrige award is valuing workforce members. Research studies released by the Gallup organization found that engaged employees are more focused on doing things well and on having quality interactions with customers. This, in turn, leads to engaged customers—a significant step beyond satisfied customers. You will have an engaged workforce when you include workers in decision making, recognize good performance through compensation, and acknowledge them, plain and simple.

5. **Behave in ways that are consistent with the values you profess.** Continually we find organizational leaders must be actively involved in supporting the direction and culture they want to create. Leaders can do much to support focused performance and the culture that is best for the organization through day-to-day personal behaviors that encourage, support, and praise employees, build relationships, and connect the values, vision, and mission to daily work life. This means that the toughest job for leaders may be managing their own behaviors to conform to the message they want to see reflected daily throughout the desired organizational culture.

6. **Construct a positive work environment.** At MidwayUSA, Larry Potterfield crafted the organization to support customers and the workforce through cross-functional improvement groups; rewarding good work and innovative ideas; developing employees

through training; hiring the best people—not only those with the best technical skills but also those with good attitudes; and being there to demonstrate daily that his company works as a team. It is a strategic way of thinking that goes beyond day-to-day operational interactions; it reflects and focuses on how to build a world-class organization.

7. **Support leaders and employees to become national or state award examiners.** Becoming an award examiner can be life transforming. While it does require an annual time commitment by the organization and the employee (8–12 hours of training preparation, 3–4 days of training, 40 hours to evaluate an application, 1 day for a consensus meeting, 3–4 days for site visits), the value it can bring to the organization can readily pay for itself, as MidwayUSA has experienced. Add one or two more leaders and employees each year to the state or national Baldrige examiner training programs until you have reached a critical "tipping point" where enough people are trained in the Baldrige approach to start making improvements based on the criteria.

8. **Become more Baldrige focused.** The Baldrige website (www. nist.gov/baldrige/) provides many resources to support a better understanding of the Baldrige approach. In addition, you can download or order copies of the criteria in three categories: business, not-for-profit, and government; health care; and education. These eighty-plus-page publications give a concise look at the Baldrige approach, its criteria, and its core values. The criteria book is rather technical, so we would encourage looking at some of the other sources first. There is a pen-and-paper survey you can do on your own, or you can pay for the online Baldrige Express, which allows you to take a survey of employee and leadership perceptions of how well the organization meets the criteria in the seven categories. With the Baldrige Express, you can specify how you want the data to be presented (for example, by departments, by

employee type, by location) so the results are shown in these categories. Results are tabulated by Baldrige and presented for each question with a Pareto chart that demonstrates the areas and questions, if addressed, that will have the greatest effect on results. We find it interesting to look at the variances in responses between leadership and employees.

9. **Form cross-functional quality teams.** To help keep a focus on the desired direction of the organization, develop quality teams that include leaders and employees from different departments. This broadens communication and encourages different perspectives from the workforce. It also helps focus performance toward systematically meeting customer needs rather than just improving departments. A good start is to have each team chart some of the key work and support processes, and address these questions: "How do we measure how well this process is doing?" and "Do these measures support improving customer or stakeholder requirements?" Find out what customers or other stakeholders really value, measure that, and then align process performance measures so they match with customers' wants and needs.

Selected Resources

Here are some additional sources you might find useful as you develop an employee-focused environment in your organization to create a culture of engaged and entangled men and women.

1. For setting values and creating a culture, good sources include Mark Baetz and Christopher Bart, "Developing Mission Statements Which Work," *Long Range Planning* 29, no. 4 (August 1996): 526–533 [it has some good examples], and Patricia Jones and Larry Kahaner, *Say It and Live It: The 50 Corporate Mission Statements That Hit the Mark* (New York: Doubleday, 1995).

2. Setting performance measures is important. The work of David Norton and Robert Kaplan in developing the Balanced Scorecard provides a good framework; see, for example, the first article on the scorecard in *Harvard Business Review* 70, no.1 (January–February 1992): 71–79; or the article that ordered the elements of the scorecard, in *Harvard Business Review* 78, no. 5 (September–October 2000): 167–176. In "The Aligned Balanced Scorecard: An Improved Tool for Building High Performance Organizations," *Organizational Dynamics* 37, no. 4 (2008): 378–393, Kenneth Thompson and Nicholas Mathys demonstrated the needed alignment between outcome measures (finance and customer satisfaction) and internal process elements of the scorecard.

3. For insight into creating involved personal leadership, we recommend two articles by Clark Aldrich in the journal published by the American Society for Training and Development: "The New Core of Leadership," *T+D* 57, no. 3 (March 2003): 32–37, and "Using Leadership to Implement Leadership," *T+D* 57, no. 5 (May 2003): 94–100.

4. Much understanding of the Baldrige process can be gained from Mark L. Blazey, *Insights to Performance Excellence 2011–2012: Understanding the Integrated Management System and Baldrige* (Milwaukee: ASQ Quality Press, 2011), and the Baldrige website: www.nist.gov /baldrige.

✳ ✳ ✳

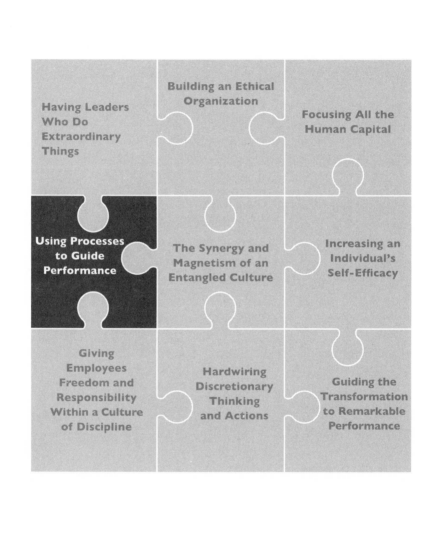

CHAPTER 4

USING PROCESSES TO GUIDE PERFORMANCE:
Tarlton Corporation

Imagine your organization's biggest competitor. On paper, you actually seem quite similar: You're both centrally located in the same area; you offer similar services; you have workforces of relatively similar size. Now think about the competition between the two of you. You fight hard for customers, using price, service, and other differentiators to your advantage. One day, in walks a really big client you both really, really want to serve. The client is so big, in fact, that when you land the contract, you can't do all the work yourself. Who do you have to approach for help in serving the client? Your number one competitor, of course.

Although such a situation is relatively unusual in other industries, it isn't that uncommon in the construction industry, where the need to deal with partners and subcontractors on a regular basis can be challenging. Part of the challenge is in dealing with complex customer requirements and articulating very specifically what the customer desires to all parties involved. Add to that the need for much of the work in construction to be done by multiple subcontractors and, on many larger jobs, by partners because of the various expertise levels required, and you have a recipe for possible disaster.

How does an organization unify the work within this complexity to reduce the probability of errors? How does an organization create an environment in which employees successfully work together as well as with outside organizations? We found this challenge across the board in the construction industry and at Tarlton Corporation in particular.

Tarlton has provided general contracting and construction management services in the Midwest since 1946. More recently, when Tracy Hart, her brother Dirk Elsperman, and sister Wendy Guhr took over the business from their father in 1999, it became certified by the Women's Business Enterprise National Council, which allows the organization to participate in projects that specify diverse contractors.

You might think that a woman-owned business would face a struggle in such a stereotypically and heavily male-dominated industry as construction; however, it seems the exact opposite is true. Whether or not the company is woman-owned is virtually irrelevant when it comes down to the facts: Tarlton is a $150 million company capable of managing $100 million projects for corporate, power and energy, government, and institutional clients. And Tarlton has a quality reputation, developed over sixty-five years, that comes from its work, its people, and its processes, an entangled culture that supports discretionary thinking and action and a customer focus.

The company's philosophy is simple: Take care of the client first and treat others as they would like to be treated. Tarlton's experience and business maturity have built on that philosophy to provide client services for successful construction of new and renovated facilities. No project is too large or too small. The company has worked as a general contractor and construction manager to successfully complete large complex buildings for specific purposes; to upgrade existing spaces, including offices, laboratories, manufacturing/industrial floors, and power plants; and to provide ongoing maintenance through annual and long-term contracts. Tarlton leaders and staff love the challenge of complex builds even more than the standard "big box" project.

The workforce is skilled in fulfilling clients' needs through lean construction and integrated project delivery, design-build, construction management, and general contracting. A particular niche is concrete restoration of all types, and in 2004, the organization established a competency in sustainable construction, having since completed projects that include LEED (Leadership in Energy and Environmental Design) certification at the Certified, Silver, and Gold levels. In 2010 Tarlton joined *Engineering News–Record*'s (ENR) Top 400 Contractors list at number 382 and became one of *Inc.* magazine's Top Small Company Workplaces. In 2012, Tarlton moved up to number 351 on the *ENR* Top 400.

Although they have on average two hundred tradespersons, including laborers, ironworkers, carpenters, operating engineers, and cement masons, Tarlton itself performs only about 40 percent of its volume on an annual basis. When less than half of an organization's work is done by its own employees, certain skills and processes must be established and perfected in order to complete a project that's up to customer standards.

Internally, the organization has three major challenges in keeping true to its customer-focused strategy. The first is translating customer wants into an understanding so the customer can visualize what the end product will be. A portion of clients approach Tarlton as the first step in their own process even before they have formalized their plans through an architect, and Tarlton helps them consider their options. At this stage, the company gives the client an overall estimate of what the cost might be, given the different options that it and the client formulate. This process takes a lot of give and take with the customer, as Tarlton often bids on unique, complex projects for which the designs conceptualized by the customer are one-of-a-kind, aesthetically unique, and/or LEED registered.[1] Such projects can involve some surprises (such as underground issues), permit and approval issues, and volatile raw material costs. Tarlton excels at this part of the process because of its experience with unique designs, its innovative construction approach, and its expertise in the use of prefabricated and other basic materials.

The second challenge is effectively managing collaborative partnerships. Because of the nature and scope of the technical requirements of a contract, Tarlton is at times called upon to work with direct competitors. In these cases, the corporation has to have project managers who know the technical side of the work and have the communication and negotiation skills to get the job done on time, on budget, and up to standard. The same is true in managing subcontractors and union workers. If Tarlton wants to earn bids and please customers, it needs to attract the best "subs" while simultaneously demanding effective cost-and-quality controls. Time management is critical too, because in many cases, particular subs need to complete their work before the next subs can do theirs.

The third challenge Tarlton faces is keeping employees aligned with the values of the organization even though they may be widely dispersed on different projects at different locations. In addition, keeping a loyal and dedicated workforce in a very cyclical work environment is challenging. When there are significant variations in the amount of work available, organizations must reduce their workforce. How does Tarlton nurture employee loyalty and dedication when it seems the organization or the industry itself is not dedicated to them?

Later we will see how Tarlton aligns its culture to meet the needs of the customer. But first, we will review how Tarlton takes customers' visions of what they want done and creates a plan of action to translate vision to reality.

Translating Customer Wants into a Plan of Action

As with the customers of most other service industries, Tarlton's customers have three major requirements: Projects must be completed on time, on budget, and at the promised level of quality. To manage these activities, Tarlton has developed step-by-step processes that all of its project managers are trained to follow. These processes ensure continuity in the building and management process if there is a change of project managers or a hand-off during any part of the process. Tarlton consistently documents the stage the project is in at any given moment,

USING PROCESS MAPS TO DEFINE THE WORK

Tarlton uses process maps to help guide its employees on completing all aspects of the work. Many integrative systems approaches to management, such as the Baldrige approach, consider processes to be the major building block of the organization. A process map is a step-by-step diagram—a road map, if you will—of what is done during the defined process, whether that process is as complex as assembling a car or as simple as taking an order at a fast-food restaurant. The example below represents a contract-specific Communication Flow Process map Tarlton uses to facilitate communications on a $21.5 million hospital expansion project. Mapping the process helps team members understand what should be done during each step in the defined process. In addition, there is a review of the process, which can occur at the end of a project or during periodic reviews.

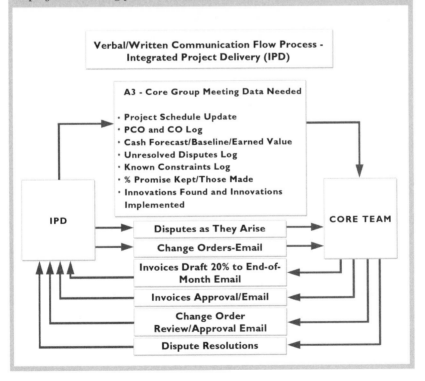

> The process map is a beginning point for analyzing what the process does, and it helps to answer questions about what can be done to improve the process. Tarlton uses process maps, starting with the initial stage of determining customer wants and continuing through planning, bidding out segments of the project, and the actual construction and completion stages.

as well as the stage that comes next. The company's leadership believes that using this process is a major tool in making sure customer needs are monitored and met. They have seen firsthand that following clearly defined steps reduces overall project time because less time is wasted correcting errors and backtracking to perform a missed critical step.

Tarlton uses a standard and consistent set of processes to help translate the customer's goals into a reality. For example, see the process map below. The illustration provides an overview of each set of areas in which multiple processes are defined. Which processes are used depends on the nature of the project. In most cases, the client brings architectural and engineering drawings to Tarlton staff who then review the drawings and conduct an extensive interview to better understand the expectations of the client. Based on the information compiled from the drawings and the interview, a detailed cost estimate is prepared. These initial steps ensure that all aspects of the client's wants are discussed, documented, and properly articulated in the project description Tarlton's crew will use.

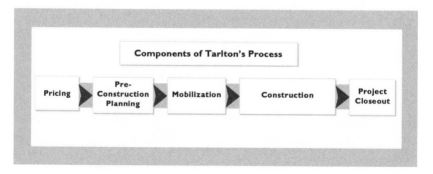

Bidding proceeds after the detailed cost estimate is prepared. Tarlton needs to translate client desires into descriptions the various subcontractors can understand and bid on accurately. Tarlton's preconstruction team outlines, in clear and efficient language common to all parties, a detailed list of what needs to be done. This step of the process is critical because Tarlton and the client can't sit down with each person bidding on a portion of the job. The accuracy of the drawings and the client's list of specific expectations are exceptionally important because these become the detailed plans for the organization and subs to follow in developing an accurate price. Once the budget is approved, the detailed plans become the project specifications. In most contracts, a contingency budget line would be added to cover any surprises that might emerge during the process, for example, finding dangerous pollutants in an old dump site uncovered during excavation.

Before any project begins, the final wants of the client and the final cost of the project must be determined. Doing this successfully depends on the costs of the various options available, including such details as flooring material, lighting, and window shading. If Tarlton is not specific in this part of the process, it runs the risk of dissatisfying the client as the client is expecting "A" but winds up with "C." This happens because all details were not clarified in the initial project development and budget processes.

Once agreement exists between Tarlton and the client as to the specific nature of the project, the cost, and the expected completion date, the project moves from the pricing and preconstruction planning processes to the mobilization and construction stages. By this time, subcontractors will have been confirmed, based primarily on price. The mobilization stage involves ordering and gathering the materials and equipment at the site. After the pricing process is completed, construction begins.

To help its employees manage the process during construction, Tarlton invested in a software package called Building Information Modeling (BIM), which has been found to be a remarkable process.

BIM allows Tarlton's people, subcontractors, and clients to better visualize the project by bringing together various elements—architectural, structural, mechanical, electrical, and plumbing—and plots each separate component onto a single, integrated model. This federated model helps detect project clashes and gives the various parties a better representation of what the finished project might look like, at least spatially.

Through this technology, construction problems surface and can be corrected at much lower costs than if they are caught in the midst of construction. Steve Moore, one of Tarlton's superintendents, showed us the savings that were realized by using BIM in one hospital construction project. BIM showed that part of an air-conditioning duct protruded into a hallway used by the hospital staff. The duct had to dip down to avoid a drainpipe, which had to meet particular gradient specifications because it was a gravity drain. Discovering the problem during construction would have caused a delay and added cost since it would involve retrofitting the area so the hallway would meet clearance requirements. It also would have cost significant money to make the correction. Using BIM, Tarlton's project team and the related designers and subcontractors could see the problem early in the process and rectify it.

Scott Green, PE, LEED AP, manager of construction technology, said BIM is a major tool used on the construction site and in the home office. "BIM is used during the construction process to monitor what is done, who is on schedule, and what work may need to be held until another subcontractor has completed their assigned work. BIM is a time saver, cost saver, and a way to solve problems before they get serious."

Tarlton's commitment to using very precise processes to direct the behavior of their project teams is evident in every aspect of their projects. Project managers must deal with the complexity of the project schedules. Processes clarify what each and every person involved in the project must do. When there are upward of two hundred people working on a specific project, a site that lacks processes is a dangerous one. Building Information Modeling is one tool in the process, a tool that not only helps find problems early but also helps people work together in problem solving on the job.

In one final process, the project closeout process, all the construction costs are reconciled with the cost of the project and customer satisfaction is determined. In addition, Tarlton assesses the satisfaction of the subcontractors with Tarlton. The company also assesses its satisfaction with the subcontractors and suppliers and provides feedback on their performance.

Managing Collaborative Partnerships

Let's go back to our opening scenario. Imagine that you are in the construction business. Your team has put a lot of time into submitting a bid for a job and has won the contract. Now, because of project requirements, you have to contract out part of the work to a direct competitor, perhaps a company that bid for the same job. Your competitor will be working under your name. How do you control the atmosphere at the job site? How do you keep the competitor's staff on schedule? Or consider the reverse. You've lost a bid to a competitor, but they've come to you to contract out part of the work. How would you feel going to work on a project for a competitor? And even when partnerships aren't with direct competitors, a sense of disconnect between contractors and subcontractors can occur.

The construction industry serves as a role model for other industries regarding the many different relationships that require delicate care and the special kind of organization that can capitalize on those relationships. While other companies are just starting to delve into outsourcing and partnering in order to meet the scope of products and services needed for both B-to-B (business-to-business) or B-to-C (business-to-consumer) relationships, construction companies are thinking, *Been there, done that.*

Each organization, competitor or not, has a different culture, different skill level, and different ways of doing things. These sorts of relationships require that everyone involved, from senior leadership all the way to on-site construction foremen and administrative employees, work with these differences smoothly, effectively, and efficiently. Tarlton faces this challenge through both the processes they create to help guide actions and through the training they provide for their project managers and staff to help them navigate the behavioral dimensions associated with dealing with partners and subcontractors.

Tarlton's structure facilitates communication, anticipates problems, and builds in a system of checks and balances to support coordination of each task so that it can maintain the planned schedule and cost estimates. While discretionary thinking is valued at Tarlton, coordination between different specialists helps to develop a way to anticipate problems, use a system of checks and balances, and solve problems before they get more expensive.

Especially when project sites could be miles, if not states, away from the home office, coordination is crucial. As a spider weaves a web, Tarlton's senior leadership weaves a web that connects person to person, leader to leader, and on-site personnel to off-site personnel throughout the company. The more strings in the web and the stronger those strings, the stronger the coordination and the better the anticipation of problems. The stronger the coordination, the stronger the culture. And the stronger the culture, the stronger the company. What does the company do to strengthen its strings?

Senior leaders are expected to visit their project sites once a week and to remain in contact with the project management team as needed during the week. In addition, a project team works together and uses specialists on call from the home office and other sites to work on problems they might encounter. Project Manager Sondra Rotty, LEED AP, worked as a senior project engineer on a major government project and spoke to us about her experiences with Tarlton's web of communication. "I feel comfortable knowing I have people I can rely on to help me do my job well. The focus is on serving the customer and doing a quality job. If I need help, I have people on the job site, and I have people at the home office just a mobile phone call away. They are there for me if I need it, and we work out the problems. That is simply part of the culture."

The tools used to aid the decision-making process, both on-site and off, include decision trees for mapping out the consequences of particular decisions. Gantt charts and process maps help staff members keep the whole project on schedule.

Tarlton uses these sorts of structural approaches (teams, communication responsiveness, BIM, decision trees, processes) to support the coordination between groups in the organization, with its partners, and with subcontractors. However, some behavior training is necessary to ensure that staff will be equipped to maintain good relations among these diverse players.

For example, Rotty told us of a problem her team faced. Partway through a job, someone discovered that the fire alarm wires were not channeled in metal pipes as required in the project specifications. The client's inspectors did not catch it nor did the designers or the subcontractor doing the job. While this would not have been a big deal if it had been caught before the walls were put up, it became an expensive proposition when the error was discovered after the concrete and wallboards had been installed—in fact about a $100,000 error! How does the project manager handle this issue? Who pays for the error? In this case, through negotiation, the costs were settled among the sub, Tarlton, and the client, with each party feeling a little of the pain.

It's usually necessary to work with subcontractors to solve problems and negotiate solutions on a daily basis. Mistakes do happen, and when they do, being sensitive to both clients and partners/subcontractors is a must for Tarlton to stay in business. The company must keep quality people on board who have those skills, in addition to developing them internally. Tarlton provides classes for their staff that help support good relations with customers, partners, and subcontractors. Leaders can directly assess the quality of an employee's behavior in responding to different situations. A project manager might challenge a trainee by asking, "What would you do in this situation and how would you do it?"

Formal and informal training focuses on doing what is right for all the stakeholders. The company provides training in effective listening, feedback, conflict management, negotiation skills, teamwork, and providing diagnostic comments. Having effective communication and strong stakeholder relationships are two reasons Tarlton has an impressive company culture. As CEO Hart told us, "Building positive relationships is an important job for each employee of this company."

Aligning the Culture of Tarlton to the Requirements of the Customer

Each customer is unique, not only in its project but also in its need for interaction. Tarlton had to find a way to develop a culture that met particular customer demands. If the corporation could not find a way to align its workforce culture, they could not have met the challenges of a competitive market.

What sort of culture did that need to be? Given the differences between work-site locations and the home office, the workforce needed to be rather autonomous. It would be impossible to have an effective organization if each major decision had to be made by the senior leadership team. Given the complexity of each project, the problems that might occur, and the cost of delaying a project, the workforce would have to have a high degree of discretionary judgment. Likewise, the workforce would have to feel confident that the senior leadership team supported these discretionary decisions, some of which represented thousands of dollars of costs to the organization. It became very clear that Tarlton needed to have a culture that supports rational decision making by an intelligent workforce that understands the issues and, perhaps more important, the consequences of their decisions. Let's look at the processes Tarlton implemented in order to achieve this culture.

The Structural Dimensions

Tarlton has consciously developed several different structural elements to support a culture that develops the employee and encourages discretionary judgment. These structural elements begin with hiring and include training, keeping a stable workforce, having an open-door approach among the leadership, using job-assignment strategies, and having key resource people for the employee to call upon.

Tarlton seeks potential hires who have both the correct technical qualifications and the temperaments to handle the numerous and varied personal interactions required when dealing with clients, subcontractors, and partners. Hence, for many of the jobs, a second battery of interviews looks for the ability of the candidate to work with people, find solutions to problems, and negotiate when necessary to resolve issues. As CEO Hart indicated, hiring quality people is essential for Tarlton's success and long-term sustainability: "If we do not have the best people in knowing the business and in knowing how to work with people, we will not succeed in the market segment that we have defined."

Once Tarlton hires the right candidate, the main focus turns to developing that employee for the current job. What is unique about Tarlton's development process is that they also factor in the longer term and develop the employee for the next few levels of promotion. It all sounds pretty great, right? Well, it's great, but not all that easy.

The nature of the industry is such that there are wide fluctuations in demand for the product. The corresponding result is significant shifting in the number of employees needed to handle projects. Because Tarlton's services require certain technical skills, it has its own staff of skilled tradespersons. Maintaining that workforce, with its specialized knowledge, becomes a top priority, for those employees also know the company culture inside and out. In addition, a broad range of technical and behavioral training makes the employee more adaptable for different jobs and increases his or her ability to handle the next level of promotion at Tarlton.

Herein lies a significant challenge for any company in the construction industry: maintaining a workforce in a fluctuating work environment while providing career development for employees. Tarlton uses a training approach that supports both of these goals.

According to COO Dirk Elsperman, Tarlton tackles the issue by providing much of the training during the slower periods to keep the employees engaged while building their skill sets. The training covers the gamut of specialized skills needed for the key areas that Tarlton provides for its clients. For example, Tarlton specializes in the following preconstruction services:

- Detailed scheduling/phasing plans
- Strategic procurement goals
- Accurate budgeting tied to a sound cost estimate
- Value engineering
- Comprehensive constructability review

They also specialize in the following construction services and processes:

- Safety planning and implementation through a Site-Specific Safety Plan
- Quality planning and execution through a Quality Assurance/Quality Control program
- Schedule adherence using pull planning based on lean practices
- Cost control and variance reporting
- Subcontractor coordination

Particularly concerning the elements of sustainable building approaches, essential technical training opportunities abound for the workforce to be current in their understanding of new construction practices.

Many soft skills are likewise in demand in this industry. Tarlton supports training in negotiation skills, teamwork, time management, project management, and feedback skills. Both Hart and Elsperman believe this training is essential to keep workers current in their fields and to provide them with the skills essential for effectively making discretionary decisions to support the goals and values of the organization. In addition, both leaders agree that the training Tarlton provides demonstrates a commitment to the workforce—that the company cares. "Our training helps to create the culture we want to build to have a customer-focused, high-performance work environment," said the COO.

Another structural element that supports the culture Hart and Elsperman have developed is an open-door policy. While that is just words in many organizations, the corporate headquarters (which is LEED Silver certified) was built by Tarlton with an open floor plan that facilitates the interaction of senior leadership with the workforce and with special events held in the building, both scheduled and impromptu. However, the open-door policy is much more than just having an open design concept. There is a strong family mentality at the organization. To reinforce this interaction, senior leaders are assigned to every project as support, employees have other support specialists in the organization, and there are periodic team meetings at the corporate offices just to discuss overall problems and what can be done to improve cooperation and collaboration between Tarlton's people, the subcontractors, and the client. In addition, many senior leaders have people they can call upon outside the company for help in working through problems. These senior leadership resource people are paid for their services and come from universities or are otherwise experts in the field.

Selection for job assignments is not a random event. If there is a history of good relationships between a customer and project manager, every effort will made to again link the two. In addition, as the executive group creates the team for the job, they will pick from among the Tarlton employees who will best meet the requirements of the job and who have the temperament that will work best with the subcontractors and other stakeholders in the project. Some of the Tarlton staff members have served Tarlton so long that repeat customers will ask to have a particular person on the job site.

Leader Behavior Dimensions

While Tarlton uses structural elements to support a customer-focused and performance-centered culture, it is equally essential that senior leaders exhibit behaviors that support the desired culture and communicate in a way that says they expect the rest of the workforce to mirror those behaviors. The leadership, by its own behaviors and by how it sets up the work environment (the structural elements), creates a positive organizational culture, not unlike that advocated by Fred Luthans (see sidebar below). A positive culture creates an engaged workforce whose members are willing to exhibit discretionary thinking and actions and come up with innovative ways to make the organization better (that is, an entangled workforce). This sort of leadership style fits well with the needs of Tarlton and its workforce as it unleashes employees' energy and ability to work independently while knowing the senior leadership will support their good-faith efforts.

POSITIVE ORGANIZATIONAL BEHAVIOR (POB)

What Tarlton does is similar to the positive organizational behavior (POB) work environment that Dr. Fred Luthans at the University of Nebraska has demonstrated as an effective approach in his research. POB builds on the notion of building a positive work environment by developing and supporting hope, optimism, self-efficacy, and resilience in the workforce. Research by Luthans and others has demonstrated that there is a direct relationship between these four dimensions in improving performance, job satisfaction, work happiness, and organizational commitment. Underlying improving employee satisfaction and work engagement is the correlation that the Gallup organization has found between employee engagement and customer engagement. Customer engagement is a stronger relationship than just customer satisfaction, according to Gallup. An engaged customer is one who is much more committed to the organization, will tell others about the organization, has a higher rate of return sales, and will stick longer to the organization. In Tarlton's case, the engaged employee is critical to engage the client and the subcontractors out in the field. One might think a subcontractor is a subcontractor, that there is not much difference between them. However, the more intricate work that Tarlton does and Tarlton's passion to have a positive relationship with its clients can be translated into the need for a solid core of capable subcontractors in the same focus and passion for being customer focused. That approach may limit the number of subcontractors that Tarlton wants to use, but it creates an aligned set of values between Tarlton and those it works with.

The CEO and COO demonstrate, by their actions, a very open leadership style that is supportive of employees and focused more on solving problems, when needed, than on placing blame. In addition, they proactively engage with others to learn of the progress on a project, what the roadblocks might be, and how they can help in resolving any issues. For example, Michelle Spires, in marketing, talked about how people work together to help each other meet deadlines. She said that the notion of functional silos does not exist at Tarlton. While people have different skills and levels of expertise, they are available to help out in other areas if needed; she herself has helped in estimating and has had help from Tarlton's resident expert in BIM in developing marketing copy that differentiates Tarlton from its competitors.

The leadership approach extends beyond the workforce to Tarlton's clients. In one instance, the company hosted a meeting for clients to demonstrate the use of "post tensioning" on concrete procedures. Tarlton hosted the event in their corporate offices and, at this event, partnered with the Post-Tensioning Institute, which offered Level I Inspection and Installations Training for those attending the session. The event gave Tarlton a chance to show the attendees its latest procedures in concrete restoration and gave it a chance to network with its own potential and existing clients to demonstrate what it could do. This sort of open approach to keeping in contact with clients and the work-force creates a climate that says loud and clear that Tarlton cares for its customers and its workforce.

Quality performance is an important aspect of Tarlton's culture, so we wondered about the evaluation system. Steve Moore indicated that it is very easy to assess most performances. "You look [to see whether] the subs did the job correctly, on time, and on budget." His whole job relates to comparing performance with specifications. If he is not happy with a subcontractor or a subordinate, he will try to work with the individual(s) to get them up to the quality that is required and expected at Tarlton. If that does not work, Moore just makes a note not to use the individual in the future or he reports the problems to the particular subcontractor, which leads to a discussion with senior leadership at that subcontracting company. The general approach is to make the review process a developmental process. As Rotty said, "You have to realize we may work with these people again. So you want to work with the client and with the subcontractor. You want to develop a solution that is best for everyone to serve the client and do well for the project and the organizations involved."

Our interviews at Tarlton revealed that the company does not employ a punitive evaluation system. Employees do not fear a poor evaluation; rather, they are engaged in a stimulating work environment, and they are motivated daily through the nature of the projects and the trust the executives have in them. It is Tarlton's culture and pride in what the organization does that motivates the workforce to do well. This was echoed across the board by Steve Moore, Sondra Rotty, Scott Green, Daniel Fahey, and Michelle Spires.

For example, Green is working on developing new technology and learning what is going on in the industry that Tarlton can apply to its processes. Fahey, LEED AP, Tarlton's manager of field operations and quality control, worked at three other construction companies previously and noted how Tarlton has a great culture.

If we make mistakes, let's learn from them. We have project engineers meeting every other Friday to share what we have learned on different projects, or we might learn of new techniques. We have project managers, project directors/estimators, and others who come to Thursday meetings to share experiences and new ideas the organization has come across. It reinforces learning and that we are a family. It gives each of us an opportunity to influence the rest of the company and to learn about different experiences—or that labor may have issues with using employees from another state or a jurisdiction issue and what craft does what. These meetings help us learn how to deal with these issues.

Recognition and creating a family atmosphere are important to the kind of culture Tarlton wants, and the workforce seems to respond to these behaviors. For example, Spires indicated that the holiday celebrations the organization sponsors are a great way to renew friendships and just enjoy each other's company. In the same way, the weekly meetings seem to be used not just to share information but also as an opportunity to say thanks to someone who shares an improved process or best practice that they might have learned during the prior week.

Staff members appreciate simple daily recognition from senior leaders. They also appreciate watching how senior leaders approach problems every day: They focus on the questions "How can we get it fixed?" and "What have we learned so it will be less likely to happen in the future?" As one person said, "You know you made a mistake and you already feel bad about it. Instead of getting hollered at to make you feel worse, leadership takes the high road. Does that mean it is okay to make errors? Absolutely not. Will I make the same mistake again? Absolutely not. They treat me as an adult; we work to resolve it. The end result is I feel they respect me; they work for us and the client. I love it here."

Another employee simply said, "In my last job, they treated compliments like they cost $1,000 each. Here, they look for ways to thank you. It makes you want to do your best each day. The job is interesting; the challenges are exciting. I love this job." These are the signs of an engaged workforce. The environment requires discretionary thinking, creating an entangled worker looking for better solutions and ways to solve problems.

What We Learned from Tarlton Corporation

For Tarlton, processes are a major part of guiding employee behavior. They are an effective way to maintain quality control in complex projects where one mistake may cost thousands of dollars. Tarlton has challenges like many other businesses. Their employees are sometimes scattered across the countryside, out of reach of close performance monitoring. In addition, through the process, employees interact with clients and partners as well. The ability of the employees to make a positive impression and to work with these parties is critical to the success of the organization. Process maps chart what needs to be done and strengthen employees' confidence that they can make competent decisions and use discretionary thinking.

Tarlton's leadership uses structure (such as processes, training programs, and connected leadership teams) and behaviors (such as creating a positive organizational behavior culture) to create a dynamic work environment that gets the best out of the team through engagement and discretionary thinking; all of this leads to entangled employees.

To bring this home to your setting, you need to focus on how you organize the work and what behavior your leadership will model and support. Here are a few steps that can help.

1. **Define and reinforce processes to guide performance.** If the process is complex, create a process map to guide behaviors. If the process is less complex, try using a checklist. These tools help employees succeed in their jobs and avoid errors. This is an

excellent way to focus the efforts of employees and build their confidence in themselves as discretionary thinkers. Get them engaged and entangled in defining the process or checklist and have them make it even better.

2. **Have lifelines.** Although the project manager is out in the field, technical and leadership sources are there as needed to support that person. Subcontractors must have confidence that the on-site project manager knows what she or he is doing; this is especially critical for good communication in complex projects.

3. **Train, train, train.** If the workforce has confidence in what they are doing, they will have more optimism, resilience, and hope that the job can be done. They build their confidence through training. Training also builds commitment among the workforce. Laura Lusson, communications manager at Tarlton, reported that training and mentoring have paid off, a lesson they have learned as a result of using tracked surveys with clients and project managers after a project closes. Ted Guhr, director of business development, interviews each client after the project closes, asking questions about each individual on the project team so detailed developmental data is created and the data supports the effectiveness of Tarlton's individual development approach.

4. **Solve problems; don't lay blame.** People make mistakes. Dwelling on them does not correct them. Working on solutions builds a team mentality. Developing the employee builds engagement. Does that mean all employees can make many mistakes without consequences? No, not at all. If the employee does not learn or become a better employee through the experience and keeps on making the same mistakes, even after training, maybe that employee does not have the attitude or aptitude to do an exceptional job for the organization. A leader's actions reflect on the culture of the whole organization. You cannot allow consistent substandard performance to be the norm or you will drag

down the whole organization. Encouragement and recognition for high achievement and customer-focused performance is essential in building the desired culture. Reacting to poor performance is essential too.

5. **Create a positive organizational environment through your behavior**. Focus on building the sort of culture that supports hope, optimism, and resilience. Do this through your actions as leader, and through training, policies, and the development of self-efficacy within the workforce. Self-efficacy comes from training and from having clear goals and direction, moving from defined processes to reachable goals.

Selected Resources

Here are some additional sources you might find useful as you use processes to guide performance in your organization to create a culture of engaged and entangled men and women.

1. Mark L. Blazey, *Insights to Performance Excellence 2011-2012: Understanding the Integrated Management System and Baldrige* (Milwaukee: ASQ Quality Press, 2011). This book provides a good review of Baldrige and the use of processes throughout an organization.

2. Carolyn Youssef and Fred Luthans, "Positive Organizational Behavior in the Workplace," *Journal of Management* 33, no. 5 (October 2007): 774–800, did a splendid job discussing the research that supports the notion of the importance of building a positive work environment through the use of the principles of positive organizational behavior. Luthans is internationally known for his work in the area and has published multiple applied and research articles on the topic.

3. Rodd Wagner and James Harter, *The Elements of Great Managing* (New York: Gallup Press, 2006). This book provides good direction

for leading behaviors and structures that can support an engaged workforce.

4. Fred Luthans, Carolyn Youssef, and Bruce Avolio, *Psychological Capital: Developing the Human Competitive Edge* (Oxford: Oxford University Press, 2007). This book provides a comprehensive treatment of positive organizational behavior and applies the concept to leading and motivating the workforce.

5. Fred Luthans and Carolyn Youssef, "Human, Social, and Now Positive Psychological Capital Management: Investing in People for Competitive Advantage," *Organizational Dynamics* 33, no. 2 (2004): 143–160. This article provides a concise yet pithy view of the positive psychological capital concept, the process of focusing on the development of people and creating a culture to support an engaged workforce.

6. James Harter, Frank Schmidt, James Asplund, Emily Killham, and Sangeeta Agrawal, "Causal Impact of Employee Work Perceptions on the Bottom Line of Organizations," *Perspectives on Psychological Sciences* 5, no. 4 (2010): 378–389. This article provides a foundation for understanding the relationship between an engaged employee and how that has a positive effect on the organization's overall performance.

Having Leaders Who Do Extraordinary Things

Building an Ethical Organization

Focusing All the Human Capital

Using Processes to Guide Performance

The Synergy and Magnetism of an Entangled Culture

Increasing an Individual's Self-Efficacy

Giving Employees Freedom and Responsibility Within a Culture of Discipline

Hardwiring Discretionary Thinking and Actions

Guiding the Transformation to Remarkable Performance

CHAPTER 5

INCREASING AN INDIVIDUAL'S SELF-EFFICACY:
North Lawndale Employment Network and Sweet Beginnings

Paul Suggs Sr. is a graduate of the Sweet Beginnings program. He now works for a baking company doing maintenance work, and his job there has sparked in him a desire to become a baker. After experiencing some time at an IDOC (Illinois Department of Corrections) facility, Paul said that he had a lot of time to think about his life and where it was going. He knew he had to find a better way but didn't know how. Once he got out, life was discouraging. He really felt that people were, and are, just watching him and waiting for him to fail and go back to jail.

"It is hard to change your life," he told us. "It's difficult to find a job. Without a job you do not have money to support yourself. It is so easy to go back to the ways that got you into trouble in the first place." His parents and church taught him about respect, honor, and caring about others. However, when he was out on the streets, it was different. "In the streets, people watched out only for themselves. There was little caring, little sense of honor. You always had to watch your back."

Paul learned about North Lawndale Employment Network/Sweet Beginnings through neighbors. He lived in the Rockwell Gardens housing project in Chicago. People told him, "Go to the bee place." Because Paul wanted to change, he decided to try the bee place. So one day he went to NLEN/Sweet Beginnings to see what it was all about, not expecting much, because life had not ever given him much. As he entered the house on West Flournoy, people asked him how they could help. He was welcomed, and that hadn't happened to him before.

Paul met with Coretta Rivers, one of the workforce developmental coaches, and she encouraged him to go to the church where NLEN held orientations and selected people for the U-Turn Permitted program. She told him that the training would not be easy and that orientation starts at 8:30 in morning, at which time the doors would close; if he was late he lost his chance to go through the program for that month.

Though Paul made it to NLEN's orientation, he didn't have something from his parole agent that he needed. Paul had no phone to contact his agent, and so he thought that his turn was over. He would have to wait until the following month to try and get a spot.

Another employee, however, lent Paul his personal phone to contact his agent, and Paul was flabbergasted. "It was like they were stalling for me," Paul revealed. "They gave me some time to get the things I needed. I asked why, and they said they really thought I needed this program." This kind of treatment was almost the exact opposite of what Paul had come to expect.

"When you get out of a situation of long-term incarceration, you need someone to really listen to you. Sometimes, when you get out, you have friends and family that sit back and are like, 'I'm going to see how long this transition takes from the streets to being 'corrected,' I'm going to see how long it will be before he starts getting high again.'"

Paul's orientation group numbered about 130 people. "After I heard the orientation," Paul told us, "I said, 'This is the place I need to be.'" And he was lucky to be one of twenty accepted in the U-Turn Permitted program. Paul's first leg of training began.

"The anger management program was really tough but very helpful. I think now before just reacting," said Paul. "After the program was over, the coach asked if I would want to be considered for the bee program (Sweet Beginnings), working with the bee hives and marketing. I said yes and landed in the marketing part of the program. It was a great experience." Paul learned a lot through both programs; most important, he learned how to be confident. "I did well and felt better about myself. Afterward, they helped me to find a job, and I still come in to talk with my coach and others. If I look back, I probably succeeded because I did not want to fail myself, and I would feel awful to have failed my coach and all those who gave their time to help me."

Paul now has a job as a baker and is rebuilding his life. He owes much of the credit to those at NLEN and Sweet Beginnings who helped prepare him for the work environment and helped him find a job. As Paul said, "NLEN/Sweet Beginnings is giving people hope and the confidence that they can make it in today's economy."

Research has identified self-efficacy[1] and esteem as two critical elements that are present in employees who are more assured of their ability to succeed and more persistent in sustaining their efforts when success is more elusive.[2] Organizations can hire people with those traits, but can they develop them within their employees?

To help us answer this question, we called upon the organization on the west side of Chicago, North Lawndale Employment Network (NLEN), that is the home of Sweet Beginnings. Though they are deemed an employment network, NLEN is more in the business of changing their clients' perceptions of themselves, much as an employer would. The overall goal of these two programs is to help people prepare themselves for stable employment. This is done through developing the person and providing them the resources and training to find the right job and have the attitudes that will give them the persistence to succeed even when the going gets tough. The NLEN and Sweet Beginnings programs are unique in that they offer a comprehensive range of services to help individuals coming off the street or getting out of jail to transition into jobs that provide them with independence, dignity, and hope.

You might be thinking that this program's practices are unrelated to those of your own organization. But, in reality, maximized success can only truly happen at an organization in which all elements are working at full potential. How can you get employees working at full potential? They must be satisfied with themselves. And if NLEN can generate self-efficacy and esteem to the degree that they do, any organization can. Want to know how? First you must understand who their clients are and what they face each day of their lives.

A Comprehensive Approach

North Lawndale is a poor, mostly black neighborhood with a high unemployment rate and a high dependence upon welfare.[3] The vicious unemployment cycle that many residents face spans across generations. This kind of unemployment is dangerous because it creates a pall of hopelessness, despair, and lack of resiliency to climb out of the environment. It might seem superfluous to compare this community to an organization; yet leaders at organizations across the country struggle with the issue of their own employees' hopelessness, despair, and lack of resilience to climb up from the lower rungs of the so-called corporate ladder. When even one person in an organization feels as though he or she is working at a "dead-end" job, motivation and performance diminish. That behavior is visible to others and spreads through an organization's veins like poison.

In 1997 several people got together to fight the poison—particularly in the form of unemployment as the root cause for much of the high crime rate spreading through North Lawndale. The Steans Family Foundation and the Sinai Community Institute commenced planning the NLEN concept in 1997 with an eighteen-month planning period. At the end of the period in Feburary of 1999, Brenda Palms Barber led the program in a transformation that, by 2003, had evolved into a new mission statement. One of the top priorities of Barber, CEO, was to commission a 2001 study which indicated that more than 57 percent, or 22,137 adult individuals in Lawndale, were "involved in" the criminal justice system.[4]

The study revealed that before and after arrest and incarceration, this particular population of ex-offenders struggled with drug addiction, poverty, low levels of education, unemployment, unstable housing, and homelessness. If NLEN was going to be successful, it had to find a way to remove the negative stigma attached to such residents, which obviously affected their self-efficacy and self-esteem. It had to break the cycle. That was the whole mission of NLEN (see boxed material below).

THE MISSION OF NORTH LAWNDALE EMPLOYMENT NETWORK

The mission of NLEN is to improve the earnings potential of North Lawndale residents through innovative employment initiatives that lead to economic advancement and an improved quality of life.

NLEN has four strategic goals:
- To better meet the increasing and urgent need for employment of North Lawndale residents;
- To provide solutions to unemployment for people with significant barriers to employment;
- To incorporate green employment and workplace strategies into NLEN's work force development model; and
- To serve as a catalyst for economic development in North Lawndale through its social enterprise.

The journey to break that cycle begins with the organization's headquarters where they moved in 2003. The NLEN "office" is a converted two-flat in the North Lawndale neighborhood. From the outside, it looks like a house. Once inside, we saw several comfortable sofas and chairs; it looked like a home rather than an office setting. We were warmly greeted and asked how we could be helped. Purposefully missing from this setting was any feeling of being in a government office;

this was not an impersonal place where visitors were met with the hurdle of tons of paperwork to fill out before they could be helped.

Ron Tonn is NLEN's acting COO. According to him, the agency's goals are to make all people feel welcome, to view each person as an individual, and to treat everyone with dignity. As Tonn put it, "This is the first step in efforts to create a feeling that each person is valuable and should be treated with respect." The golden rule is often overlooked in many internal organizational interactions, but never within the companies studied in this book. NLEN is no exception. As soon as someone walks in the door, that individual's level of optimism and hope starts to improve. The organization underscores for visitors the notion that they can succeed and that this is the organization with which they can find success. Then NLEN provides training in the various skills to help them reach that goal.

NLEN offers three different and distinct programs, all designed to help the community of North Lawndale and its citizens: U-Turn Permitted, the NLEN Resource Center, and Sweet Beginnings, LLC. Each of these is predicated on creating an environment where the participant will feel comfortable enough in the surroundings to ask for help and receive the support needed to rebuild their confidence that they are, as Tonn said, "someone who can succeed if they put their mind to it."

For most visitors, however, a warm atmosphere isn't enough. They are coming from a hostile environment in which trust isn't something you get; it's something you earn. Consequently, not all are really open to accepting help.

Felicia Griffin is a social worker with NLEN. She shared with us that the main thing clients think when they first walk in is that they are misunderstood. "Clients might look at me and think, 'Oh, she doesn't know why I'm here or what I go through.' If I see someone that seems to be resisting, I have to sit them down and tell them why I do the type of work I do and how I understand what they might be going through." Part of the reason she's doing the work she's doing is because of her family, and that helps her relate to clients. "I'm doing time too because my son has been in [prison] for fifteen years." She earns trust by being open and honest and relating to her clients, a common denominator throughout NLEN and Sweet Beginnings. After all, that's how you build trust.

WHAT PROFESSIONALS SAY ABOUT NLEN AND SWEET BEGINNINGS

Before we delve into the heart of both programs, we wanted to share what other professionals are saying about the organization as they look at it from three critical levels of success. The first is program success—that is, the client outcomes; the second is building a culture of helping in the organization; and the third is the success in obtaining the grants needed to fund the program. Dr. Richard Kordesh is the Principal Investigator for Housing as a Productive Family Asset, funded by the Annie E. Casey Foundation, for 2005–2008. He is Director of the GAPS Initiative, a statewide capacity-building project for nonprofits and small municipalities in Illinois. Other recent projects include an examination of comprehensive community development initiatives in five U.S. cities. Kordesh is outgoing president of NLEN's board; he is also the author of several books, including *Restoring Power to Parents and Places.*[5] We asked him to share his insights on the effectiveness of NLEN and Sweet Beginnings. He replied that NLEN works at several different levels of intervention—the policy level, the community level, and the individual level—and that its people-building effects depend on all three.

"At the policy level, Brenda [Palms Barber] is well-known and respected as an innovator and as someone who knows how to combine state and federal resources effectively with private donations, foundation grants, and, more recently, sales revenues from Sweet Beginnings, LLC. She and her staff know how to work within the opportunities and limits posed by the government grants and contracts to design and effectively carry out the programs that further NLEN's mission." Just as with any organization, NLEN's and Sweet Beginnings's success starts with leadership.

"Her ability to mobilize an amazingly diverse array of public and private resources around the core operations . . . creates a positively charged and hopeful atmosphere for the staff," Kordesh continued. "Then she hires sharp people to fine-tune and run these programs. The clients who come in the door and experience the personal service and programs pick up on the reality that this is a highly motivated agency that knows inside and out what constitutes quality with respect to its programs."

Indeed, we aren't the only ones who believe NLEN, Sweet Beginnings, and their fearless leader, Brenda, are on to something here. "Some of these strengths are an extension of Brenda's unique package of charisma and skill sets," Kordesh continued. "Those are not easy to find in just one leader. But the program elements and the multilayered strategies could be transferred elsewhere with awareness that they would have to emerge from varying types of leaders or leadership teams."

U-Turn Permitted is a program for men and women with records of criminal conviction; Sweet Beginnings, LLC, provides work experience for graduates of U-Turn Permitted; the NLEN Resource Center consists of the various support resources available to the whole community to help them find jobs and be better prepared for job interviews. Its staff are there when problems occur on the job.

U-Turn Permitted

NLEN's U-Turn Permitted program is designed to train men and women with criminal records in the skills, habits, attitudes, and values that support success on the job and in daily life. In addition, the approach addresses the habits and thoughts that often set the course for self-destructive and antisocial behavior.

Candidates undergo an extensive interviewing process to determine the suitability of each applicant for U-Turn Permitted. The program directors look for people with a strong desire to change their behavioral patterns rather than a casual desire to give the program a try. They select applicants for attitude, not necessarily for skill. Those admitted to this program must first and foremost sincerely want to change.

As Brenda Palms Barber told us: "A lot of these folks are sick and tired of being sick and tired. People come predisposed to wanting to change their life, and that is really key in our approach and methodology. We're not interested in converting you. We think that the greatest investment of state and taxpayers' dollars is to invest in individuals who don't need to be convinced that they need to turn their lives around, but that they're already in a state where they want to turn their lives around, and that's the difference."

For selected applicants, job behavior training begins on day one in the U-Turn Permitted program. The first day of orientation begins promptly at 8:30 a.m., at which time the doors close and no further admittance is allowed. As the COO explained:

> We start the training immediately. We want the applicant to understand that we are serious about their training and their introduction to the work environment and, if they are not serious, they will not be permitted for this cycle. If they come late and are denied access to the orientation, they can apply for the next orientation program in about a month. We have thrity to one hundred thrity people who want to get into our program in a given month, and we can handle only about twenty participants at a time. We always have more who want to get in than we can accommodate.

As we found out, numerous roadblocks make changing for the better difficult for ex-offenders. As Tonn tells his clients: "In prison, you are kept from society. Now, all of a sudden, you are out and the real challenge begins. You will find since 9/11 that fewer jobs are open to those who have criminal records. The challenge will be to keep focused on finding that hard-to-find job."

Without the means to support themselves and their families, it is easy for many in this neighborhood to slide back into a life of crime. They have had little training in prison to develop new skills, while some have never had a job and don't even know work expectations. U-Turn Permitted helps by stabilizing the client's initial needs. As Tonn explained:

> We can help them find assistance through different agencies and even cover some temporary essential needs for resources. We try to address the whole person, including their family's situation. If they need medical or dental help, we make it happen. We need to do that so the person can focus on improving job skills and improving self-concept. This also builds trust in us. We realize many of our clients have been in a world on the street where taking advantage of each other is the norm. We want to build a sense that they can count on us for help.

This leadership behavior is an extreme example of what it takes to build trust in the workplace. At the same time, it addresses a serious issue program graduates will experience in the workplace. As Tonn said, if people don't have the right kind of investments in their personal well-being (health needs, dental needs, etc.), they aren't going to perform to their potential while going through the program. The same goes for the workplace. When people are worried about so many other things (putting food on the table, personal health, etc.), how can they also devote full attention to the organization?

In the U-Turn Permitted program, participants spend four weeks learning to recognize and redirect destructive thinking patterns and employing conflict resolution tactics to circumvent angry confrontations and resolve disputes amicably. Deer (Re) Habilitation, Inc. administers this anger management course and family counseling training program.

Dennis Deer grew up in the North Lawndale area and had family members who had frequent run-ins with the law. As Deer went through college, he always had the desire to return to the area and give back to the community. In fact, he helped start the U-Turn Permitted program.

The anger management program begins with Deer earning participants' trust. When working with clients, he has them focus on the mind, the body, and the spirit, and getting those aligned so anything can be accomplished. "We want to create right thinking versus 'stinking thinking,' or start thinking about the thinking that will lead to more successful outcomes," Deer explained. In other words, when Deer presents the right kind of ideas to the participant, that person starts thinking about and considering different alternatives to what they have been doing in the past.

Deer's approach relates to intervention and prevention. "We want the clients to use judgment to think ahead of time to avoid an anger situation," he explained. "We use street terminology to help translate the curriculum to more understandable language. For some people, we do not make a difference. However, we do help those who are ready to accept change."

Deer continued with his description of proactive thinking:

> We say you have three choices in life—death, department of corrections, or change—which would move your life in a whole different direction. We want our program participants to consider the consequences of their actions before they happen. We want to prevent problems, but it has to be the choice of the person in the program. We want the program participants to think they can change their destiny, maybe go to college and be able to create a more successful life. We want to build confidence in them so they know they can improve. You start by little successes that you reinforce, then more challenges that they can reach and [therefore] feel better about what they can do. A pattern of successful outcomes in these

training sessions helps them start believing that they have abilities and they can overcome. This is what we are all about.

There is a clear focus on improving communication skills and on presenting an affirmative, confident, positive demeanor in all contacts. "Again," said Tonn, "the focus is on building the confidence of the program participant. We want them to believe in their own ability to make things happen and at the same time give them the strength to persist when they suffer setbacks in their lives. It is all about building a belief in their ability, to have confidence in their choices."

U-Turn Permitted offers direct job placement assistance and opportunities for self-directed job acquisitions in addition to continued workforce coaching to help the program participant work through issues that may arise at work. As long as the client would like to keep in touch with NLEN, assistance will be provided to help that individual build greater confidence in his or her ability and to work through setbacks.

NLEN clients are constantly working with a motivator—"You can do it, you can do it"—and Felicia Griffin looks for something that's important in their lives to use as motivator. For instance, male clients, in particular, want to connect with their children. So she motivates them by saying, "You're one step closer to getting that job, and now you're three steps closer to buying the bike for Christmas for your daughter." That kind of responsibility keeps clients going even when the going gets tough. "You're not going out to get that job for you, no," Griffin explained in an example. "You're going to get that job to do something for your family."

We asked a couple of graduates of the U-Turn Permitted program to share their thoughts about their experiences. Sterling G. said the most difficult part of the program was changing his thought process. He came to the program with a negative and closed mind but left with broader horizons, opportunities, and a positive perspective of life and on his own abilities. "My goal is to come back here and help others. Our thoughts lead to actions, which reflect our character, which shape our destiny. If we can keep the focus on the positive and on what we want to be in life, we can and will succeed. That is what NLEN and Sweet Beginning are all about, and I am so grateful for what they have done for me." Elesha W. felt the change in attitude helped her to have a better life both at home and in a job situation.

The U-Turn Permitted program helped Sterling and Elesha learn how to help others, how to help themselves, and how to accept help from others—all part of having a sense that they can succeed and that they have the ability to persevere. The organization that devotes resources to building those feelings within its employees is the one with the highest entanglement. After all this organization did for these two graduates, how often do you think they and others like them think of (and thank) the U-Turn Permitted program and those affiliated with it? Constantly, for in so many cases, it has saved their lives.

Sweet Beginnings, LLC

Graduates of the one-month U-Turn Permitted program can then apply to get into the Sweet Beginnings program. However, because of the size of the Sweet Beginnings program, only 10 percent of graduates are chosen. Sweet Beginnings is an urban social enterprise business program designed to provide transitional employment for formerly incarcerated individuals and other low-income North Lawndale residents. It is a for-profit program to promote community economic development.

Sweet Beginnings sells honey, honey-infused skin-care products, and a honey-based lip balm, all under the Beeline® label. Individuals employed at this business are trained on the job as landscapers, beekeepers, food processors, and marketers of the products to buyers for retail operations.

Individuals are employed for twelve weeks at Sweet Beginnings to provide them with work experience and the beginnings of an employment history. In addition, the graduates will have a better sense of themselves through the responsibilities and positive experiences they have. "It is all about the client, how we can build their sense of the ability to succeed, personal efficacy, and confidence or self-esteem," says Brenda Palms Barber. "About 80 percent of the employees of the Sweet Beginnings program have jobs within three months after 'graduation.' "

Eighty percent might seem like a high statistic, especially considering the challenge of many graduates' pasts. However, Sweet Beginnings graduates have more than just job experience for their résumés. They've added on to the foundation of self-efficacy and esteem that U-Turn Permitted helped them build. Once they've achieved certain levels of self-confidence and responsibility for not only themselves but also for their families, succeeding in the workplace is much more important and realistic.

Sweet Beginnings has four different departments in which employees can work. Each department teaches something useful and aims to encourage certain behavior post-employment that ranges from furthering education to joining the business realm.

Beekeeping

John Hansen has been the bee-farming instructor and head beekeeper at Sweet Beginnings since 2006. He teaches his student-workers to monitor the health of the hive and bees and to maintain the hives and the colony.

The beekeeping course provides participants with "continuing education" college credit, and they are encouraged to continue their college experience. "It helps them to develop a record that will help them get into a college. This is appreciated by many of the students because it gives them more confidence in their abilities and gives a measure of success in their life," said Hansen.

The overall point of the training is not beekeeping, of course. After all, how large could the city of Chicago's demand for beekeeping really be? The beekeeping training teaches participants how to handle a different work environment and to build their confidence in relating to people and being responsible for their work expectations. This is the next phase of managing emotions and giving them the "right thinking" that they can succeed in their work and in their life.

Production

After the honey is harvested, the production phase is the next area of training for the students. While the production facilities are very small and capacity is very limited, there are still training opportunities. "The development we focus on is building an attitude of caring about the work and about the quality of what you do," said Holly Blackwell, Sweet Beginnings's general manager. "The whole notion of Sweet Beginnings is to develop a profitable business in Lawndale. The profits of this business can contribute to developing the community. In addition, the attitudes we build in those participating in the process create a more positive experience for them and increase their probability to be successful in their life and job. If you feel better about yourself, you are going to feel better about life knowing you are contributing to the betterment of the community."

The production process itself consists of mixing material and filling jars and containers. The person working on the line needs to keep the area clean, mix the right material in the correct bottle, and store the inventory in the right boxes. Entering production numbers on the status chart teaches attention to detail and that everything a person does affects others in the organization. "It builds confidence and responsibility. We have weekly meetings with the team in order to get input into improving what we are doing. Everyone pitches in, and that helps give them greater ownership and confidence that people care about their opinions," Blackwell said.

Marketing

According to the general manager, marketing is one of the more difficult parts of the program for participants. Those with more outgoing personalities are often put into marketing. "These are the people who go out to buyers in a grocery store, department store, or other outlet to sell the product. In addition, participants will staff booths at conventions to introduce the product to the buyers at trade shows," Blackwell explained. She went on:

> This is not easy. You have to be able to be confident, know the uses of the product, and be able to communicate on the level of the store buyer to understand what they are looking for in a product, product prices, and delivery terms. When the product was "sold" to Whole Foods recently, there was an opportunity to celebrate the success. This meant a lot to Sweet Beginnings but probably more to the program participants who made the sale. What a morale boost to them and to those who learned that day that, yes, it can be done. We can be successful in what we do.

That is an important lesson in their life training. Sweet Beginnings employees gain much during their sales experience because they are not only learning how to promote a product but, more important, they are also developing the sales skills they need to sell themselves in an interview and other life experiences.

Train-the-Trainer

Another fascinating part of the program is Train-the-Trainer. Exceptional performers in the program are invited to learn how to train other participants in the program. The level of responsibility associated with these roles really helps to build the confidence and attitudes of the trainers. As General Manager Blackwell put it:

> The participants are thinking: "The organization trusts me to teach others. What a rush, what a responsibility they have given me, and I will not let them down." This aspect of the program is an important part of participants' development. We want them to make

decisions. We want a participant to decide how the training should work. We are their resources, but they are the ones who make the choices. We want the choices to be positive ones, ones that will lead to successful outcomes.

The NLEN Resource Center

Members from the local community, as well as graduates from U-Turn Permitted and Sweet Beginnings, LLC, can use the resource center at NLEN. Users of the NLEN resource center receive the support they need in the job search. As COO Tonn explained: "We can track our success rate through our processes for U-Turn Permitted, Sweet Beginnings, and just the neighbors who use our center. As Brenda said, 80 percent of graduates of Sweet Beginnings find a job within three months. We are proud of that."

The results testify to the effectiveness of their program. While the national recidivism rate among ex-offenders is 52 to 60 percent, the rate among NLEN/Sweet Beginnings graduates is *less than 4 percent*. This is a remarkable performance outcome that rivals even the most impressive of organizational employment statistics, especially considering that many of those whom the graduates interact with on a daily basis have not participated in the programs and are part of the street life that many of the graduates are trying to leave behind. That is truly where some of the greatest challenges lie.

For example, Sweet Beginnings graduate Darryl would have to walk past people selling drugs on his way from the safe house/adult transition center where he lived to the resource center. He himself used to be a drug dealer, and that's what landed him in trouble. As he said: "It was so hard at one point, but every day I felt myself getting stronger and stronger because I knew I was doing something different to improve my life. But it was still hard to face that temptation every day. But because I felt I had a family and people counting on me, it gave me strength to walk past those folks." Darryl now works for the Chicago Transit Authority and is proud of and happy with his change.

Kim used the Resource Center, and it has made a difference in her life. In 2007 the North Lawndale resident began to watch her life spiral out of control. Her mother was diagnosed with cancer, and soon thereafter she passed away, leaving Kim all but broken—with no job, no money, and no food.

Though Kim had no electricity and no gas in her home, she had her dignity, and she had her child. Each and every morning, Kim would get up early and leave the house. She felt it was important to teach her daughter that you need to get up each morning and go somewhere— anywhere—to be a part of society.

Where did Kim go every morning? She was reaching out to resources in her area west of Chicago, seeking any help they could offer. But none of them empowered her to improve her situation. She had no job prospects, she had no clothes to wear to an interview, and she had no transportation. These obstacles seemed insurmountable. Yet every day, Kim got up and searched for help.

Eventually she learned about the NLEN Resource Center, and that became her daily destination. There she would be welcomed and given a cup of coffee when she walked in, and that coffee was often her sole form of sustenance for the day.

Soon after Kim began visiting their offices, NLEN provided her with the resources to put her living arrangements in order and to feed her family and herself. They coached her in financial management, on interviewing skills, and on how to prepare a résumé—all of which helped boost her self-image and build confidence in herself. In addition, she focused more on improving her own image and started jogging. As a result, she lost 120 pounds.

NLEN helped Kim to buy clothes and to secure rides to inter- views. Pretty soon, she got a job. Palms Barber, who shared Kim's story with us, said, "Kim is providing for herself and her family, and she still comes in periodically to talk with her coaches. She also talks to others about what a gift NLEN has been in her life. Kim is now one of our best salespersons to encourage other people to use NLEN to help build their lives."

Kim is so enthusiastic, in fact, that she still comes into the resource center on the days she is off work. She is there to greet folks who face the same obstacles she once did and to encourage them that NLEN will bring out the best in them, just as they helped her climb out of a very dark place in her life.

What We Learned from NLEN and Sweet Beginnings, LLC

Empowered workers always begin as employees who have confidence in their own abilities, as well as confidence that their employers will listen to them. A critical stage in having a workforce that uses discretionary thinking is nurturing each worker's self-efficacy and esteem. The clientele NLEN and Sweet Beginnings serves have experienced only a cycle of failure. Consequently, the organization and its programs focus on four different activities to develop each of their graduate-employee's self-efficacy and esteem: building trust, setting expectations, building self-efficacy, and providing continual support throughout the experience to help guide the transformation process. Let's look at each of these in greater detail.

1. **Building trust** is critical with the clients at NLEN. It would seem that those using the service did not have to be convinced of the need; they already had a desire to change their lives and wanted to find a way to make that change. However, some of those who had sought help had previously tried to do so at other organizations, with different levels of success. For example, Kim desperately tried to get help from a variety of organizations and did not find what she needed. As a result, with some applicants, NLEN

had to overcome a factor of mistrust before they would become more engaged in the process.

The same is true for your organization. It takes actions to turn company slogans into more than just words, into something the employee can believe in and trust. At NLEN and Sweet Beginnings, clients are treated as guests as soon they come in the door. In essence, they sense that they are someone the organization cares about. Do you treat your employees as someone you care about? We encourage leaders to go on "rounds," to use the hospital term, or to practice management by walking around as a means to demonstrate that you do care about your employees. Talk with them; ask them what ideas they have for improving things. Demonstrate you do care and that "respect for each other" is more than a set of words.

2. **Setting expectations** is an important concept at NLEN. To experience success in the workplace, NLEN and Sweet Beginnings's participants need to clearly understand and cultivate the behaviors and skills that will be expected of them. The organization prepares its participants by setting clear, reachable goals that are the critical foundation upon which to build confidence. These expectations and goals play over and over in the minds of the participants as they develop self-efficacy and esteem.

Throughout the training at NLEN and Sweet Beginnings, the real focus is on learning and accepting responsibility. From the first day in orientation, to taking care of bees, to making a sales presentation to retailers, and to stocking the Beeline products— all of these activities underscore that the men and women must take responsibility for their actions. Their actions affect others as well as the success of the organization. Knowing what is needed in the workplace in terms of behaviors, attitudes, and the ability to think through issues is very important for any organization. These are critical skills to strengthen in your own employees so they have more positive self-images and become more valuable assets to your organization through their increased engagement.

3. **Building self-efficacy** is a key part of what NLEN strives to do with its participants. A person with a high degree of self-efficacy is confident he or she can do a certain job and has something to contribute. Self-efficacy can come from reaching goals and being able to perform a task, but it also can come from believing that the goals can be reached. Training, individual coaching, a supportive climate, and setting reachable goals can all help improve a person's feeling of self-efficacy. With high self-efficacy comes higher self-confidence and an improved ability to apply persistent effort to reach a goal.

Every time a participant succeeds, it helps others to believe in the process and in their own ability to succeed. What we find in this organization—or any other, for that matter—is that the leader needs to focus on the individuals and instill within them the confidence that they have the skills, that they can succeed, and that others believe in them. These are some of the principles that Fred Luthans[6] and others use as they advance the notion of building the organization's culture by using positive organizational behavior and using the positive psychological capital approach to leading an organization.

Change comes from within the individual. Organizations need to create the climate to unlock changes by helping individuals believe in themselves. When things go wrong, as they sometimes do, employees will have the persistence to correct the situation and carry on. When employees believe and have confidence in their own abilities, their self-esteem increases; they feel better about themselves. An ex-offender keeps working to better his or her life even though many doors may be closed. A single mother works for better days when she has food, heat, and water in her home. Your employees keep working diligently at a problem until it is solved.

4. Supporting others to do their best is essential as self-efficacy is developed within participants and employees. The developmental process is somewhat fragile in that a setback may lead to a lower sense of confidence. NLEN monitors and provides counseling to participants and tracks each graduate for at least a year after graduation to support, encourage, and reinforce the participant's success.

If NLEN and Sweet Beginnings can successfully change lives against the backdrop of poverty and crime in their community, you can be successful in changing the attitudes and decision-making quality among your workforce. It takes building trust, setting clear expectations, building self-efficacy, and providing continued support. A culture of empowerment and engagement comes from an employee-focused work environment. As you build this environment, you develop a charged workforce that will be in a position to better serve your customers and provide creative solutions to improve your organization. It is within your power as leader to unlock these skills in your workforce. It all starts with building a workforce that exudes self-efficacy and personal esteem. The process completes with a team of men and women who have the ability to contribute to the organization and have the confidence to articulate their views.

Selected Resources

Here are some additional sources you might find useful as you increase each individual's self-efficacy within your organization to create a culture of engaged and entangled men and women.

1. Fred Luthans, "Positive Organizational Behavior: Developing and Managing Psychological Strengths," *Academy of Management Executive* 16, no.1 (2002): 57–72, gives a good concise overview of positive organizational behavior; it looks at it from the perspective of a

leader developing employees or, in NLEN and Sweet Beginnings's approach, developing the client.

2. The original foundations of the POB movement was the notion of positive psychology, a well-researched concept. Two early articles on this concept are M.E.P. Seligman, "Positive Social Science," *APA Monitor* 28, no. 6 (April 1998): 17–22, and M.E.P. Seligman and M. Csikszentmihalyi, "Positive Psychology: An Introduction," *American Psychologist* 55, no.1 (2000): 5–14. As Luthans stated, having model development based on research separates positive organizational behavior from atheoretical, popular, self-help literature.

3. For a comprehensive summary of the body of work on self-efficacy, see Albert Bandura, *Self-Efficacy: The Exercise of Control* (New York: Freeman, 1997). Also see J. E. Maddux, *Self-Efficacy, Adaptation, and Adjustment: Theory, Research, and Application* (New York: Plenum Press, 1995).

4. Alexander Stajkovic and Fred Luthans provided a summary of various applications of self-efficacy in "Self-Efficacy and Work-Related Performance: A Meta-Analysis," *Psychological Bulletin* 124, no. 2 (1998): 240–261.

5. To understand self-efficacy within an individual, see C. Lee and P. Bobko, "Self-Efficacy Beliefs: Comparisons of Five Measures," *Journal of Applied Psychology* 79, no.3 (1994): 364–369.

6. For an example of the impact of a positive leader on culture, see Suzanne J. Peterson and Fred Luthans, "The Positive Impact and Development of Hopeful Leaders," *Leadership and Organizational Development* 24, no. 1 (2003): 26–31.

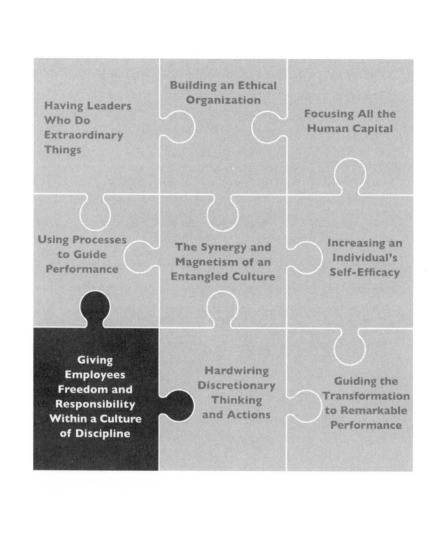

CHAPTER 6

GIVING EMPLOYEES FREEDOM AND RESPONSIBILITY WITHIN A CULTURE OF DISCIPLINE:
Tasty Catering

Tasty Catering springs to life in the wee hours of the morning each day. At its plant nestled within the largest industrial park in North America, staff members prepare scrumptious meals, appetizers, and desserts to deliver to corporate clients that range from Fortune 500s to small, privately held companies throughout the Greater Chicago area.

Tasty Catering's first employees of the day arrive about 2:00 a.m. and immediately check the orders for the day. They set about pulling various food items from the refrigerators, freezers, and dry goods inventories, and getting to work. They need little supervision because they live two values of the company: an enduring culture of individual discipline, and freedom and responsibility within the culture of discipline.

The company's culture of individual discipline evolved from two sources: Jim Collins's book *Good to Great*, and the work of Immanuel Kant, an eighteenth-century philosopher who believed a human being was most free in a circle of clearly established discipline.[1] The circle would allow an individual to decide when and what to do without being "managed," and would, therefore, be "free."

Tom Walter, Tasty Catering's CEO, explained:

Our Good to Great (GTG) team first established the notion that everyone must accept and operate within a culture of discipline so leaders could allow them the "freedom" to do what they needed to do within that culture without micromanagement. By being responsible for their actions within this culture of discipline and their own circle of influence, the employees themselves serve as checks and balances for each other, which encapsulates our seventh core company value—freedom and responsibility within a culture of discipline. Each team member is responsible to the rest of the team, and then the company, for achieving the vision which is "to achieve success through teamwork, innovation, and community involvement."

This culture has had a direct impact on company performance. Recognized nationally as one of *Inc.* magazine's and Winning Workplaces' Top 20 Small Workplaces, and *Catering Magazine*'s National Caterer of the Year, it was also among the top five Best Places to Work in Illinois for five straight years, winning first place twice. Tasty Catering's leaders and employees have built a culture known for customer intimacy and operational excellence. Loyalty among customers runs deep.

Tasty Catering's identity is clearly grounded in the way people think and behave inside the company as well as in the field. These behaviors and thoughts stem from the values, beliefs, assumptions, and practices employees share as well as the responsibility each assumes for doing the right thing. Leaders and employees throughout Tasty Catering embrace the company culture as their distinctive competence. Employees at all levels feel empowered to innovate, change, and improve processes, procedures, and practices that drive exceptional results and outcomes.

It All Started with a Hot Dog

In 1984 the Walter brothers—Tom, Larry, and Kevin—opened a hot dog stand called Tasty Dawg in Elk Grove Village, a municipality located due west of Chicago's O'Hare Airport. Tom brought twenty-three years of experience as a serial entrepreneur and owner-operator of many businesses, including fast-food and full-service restaurants, real estate ventures, nightclubs, college bars, and retail service businesses. Larry, a natural leader quick to find solutions, brought his incredible passion and knowledge of operations and logistics. Kevin, a deep analytical thinker, brought expertise in cost controls, purchasing, and human resources. Their first stand, called Tasty Dawg, eventually expanded to three other suburban locations, including a shopping center they developed. The stands were highly successful, in large part because of the three values the Walters used in building their business: quality, quantity, and service. Twenty-seven years after the brothers sold their first hot dog for $1.00, the spin-off business, Tasty Catering, grossed $6.25 million in sales.

No one among the three brothers has a college degree, but they are all lifelong learners with superior intellects and passion for their work. As three of eleven siblings the brothers learned at a very young age the importance of hard work, ethics, core values, and taking care of each other. The Walter family learned about quality, a core value of Tasty Dawg, from their father, Gordon, who was a fan of Frank and Lillian Gilbreth's biography, *Cheaper by the Dozen*. The Gilbreths' work on time and motion studies placed them at the forefront of the scientific management movement during the early-twentieth-century industrialization of the United States. Gordon Walter made his children read this book and follow the principles it contained. He was the vice president of quality assurance at Zenith Radio Company for more than twenty years, well before the quality movement hit American businesses in the 1980s. Quality and service were two values he instilled in all his children from an early age.

Tasty Dawg's clients had asked for meals to be delivered and company outdoor events to be catered. In 1989 the brothers started Tasty Catering to focus on building a catering business from the client base of the fast-food restaurants. Kevin, Larry, and Tom watched their opportunities in the catering market increase. Over time, they sold two of the fast-food units in order to grow the catering company. Each decision to expand required some tweaks to the basic business model of quality, quantity, and service, but it wasn't until the three brothers decided to sell their last Tasty Dawg restaurant and move solely into the catering business that the company went beyond organic growth and the need for simple adjustments. What model was going to yield the best outcomes for Tasty Catering? How could they retain customer loyalty, which they had built on their quality product and services in face-to-face transactions with Tasty Dawg, now that they were undergoing a business model change that relied on telephone, fax, and e-mail orders?

Changing the Focus to the Employees

The change in service style was critical. No longer could staff engage a client and generate loyalty by in-person contact. The approach to service had to be re-tooled. The Walter brothers realized that if they focused on the needs of their employees and on building employee loyalty, the service model would become contagious. The internal customer, the employee, became the focus of the owners. This was a radical mind shift.

As opposed to straddling several responsibilities when the catering and restaurant divisions had coexisted, employees now had to focus more on a specific area of business and operations. This shift was problematic. Company growth revealed the existence of knowledge and competency gaps that needed to be filled to sustain customer loyalty and success. To attack the knowledge gaps, Tom created a board of outside advisers so employees could benefit from expertise not readily available within the company. As he saw it, targeting and combating knowledge gaps presented a double opportunity. In engaging advisers as cohorts in shaping the company's direction and future, Tom saw the opportunity to obtain fresh ideas and bring "best practices" from other industries into discussions. In engaging those same advisers as paid consultants in identifying, and at times filling, knowledge gaps with the staff,

Tom identified opportunities for self-improvement, including his own skills as CEO.

Expanding the catering business required constant introduction of new menu items, which added to preexisting knowledge gaps. Adding Chef Joe D'Alessandro as the culinary expert on the advisory board was a critical and integral piece in taking the company forward. The menu and service expansions required more chefs and kitchen staff with more technical knowledge. Yet more important than technical knowledge was the need for critical thinking about ways in which employees would execute the processes for delivering quality products on time, every time. Chef Joe presented Tom with a copy of Jim Collins's *Good to Great*, which resonated with Tom.[2] It was time to take his focus on employees a step further.

Defining a Disciplined Culture

Tom intuitively knew that the motivation for achieving higher goals and expectations depended on how well employees understood and extended their foundational values of quality, quantity, and service in a more sophisticated business model and a more exacting culture. Rather than dictating direction from the top, however, Tom ordered several copies of *Good to Great* in English and Spanish for all of Tasty Catering's leaders and employees to read. To this day, each new employee is given a copy of the book to read along with a set of notes on how the ideas apply within Tasty Catering.

Defining Core Values

Providing copies of the book to employees at all levels stimulated a company-wide dialogue on the knowledge, abilities, skills, and habits (sometimes referred to as KASH) required to go from good to great.[3] Step one in transforming the company had to do with core values. Although the company already operated with family-style values, they were not well defined or specific enough and were not employee generated. Tom believed employees needed to be part of the creation process if they were really going to embrace the values. After all, how would Tom and the other leaders know what's important to employees without asking them? How could they help satisfy needs of which they weren't aware? Larry affirmed this position. "The character and the values have come forward as a clear-cut path for the direction and character that the organization would take. We recognized that it was the cumulative character of everybody who works here that makes up our organizational character."

Ellen Harte is director of key accounts and was the very first Tasty Catering employee hired. When the Good to Great process started in early 2006, the employee roster had grown to forty-five employees. Ellen was a respected leader and was a part of the process to establish a clear set of core values. Teams were created within the business; every employee was part of a team. The teams met independently and determined what members felt were important core values. One representative from each team met in the Good to Great Council to establish the core values as well as the rest of the culture statement. They discussed morals, ethics, and values such as respect and responsibility. Ultimately this employee collaboration paid off (see the table below). These values serve as beacons for directing the individual and collective behaviors and actions of everyone involved with the company. Tom stated that having core values formulated by employees from the bottom to the top of the company made the values easier to follow and live by as well as easier to enforce. In short, the values were everyone's possession, which they would protect.

To embed the values firmly within company culture, leaders had them duplicated on oversized placards and posted prominently in high-traffic areas, including the conference room, where all major company meetings are held. The values play a large role not just in company-wide decisions but in everyday transactions as well. "In the heat of an argument, even among partners," said Tom, "you can look to the wall—we all look to the wall—to find an answer to solidify your point. The values have been the foundation for the company. While every major decision revolves around what's good for the company, it's now clearly stated in our culture, and the role of values in our company is what has made us almost a utopia." Very simply, these core values are the decision-making guide for the company. This was an important first step in Tasty Catering's process of developing freedom and responsibility within a culture of discipline because the core values were part of the discipline of the company.

TASTY CATERING'S CORE VALUES

1. Always moral, ethical, and legal.
2. Treat others with respect.
3. Quality in everything we do.
4. High customer service standards.
5. Competitiveness: A strong determination to be the best.
6. An enduring culture of individual discipline.
7. Freedom and responsibility within the culture of discipline.

In addition, before every meeting of three or more people, the culture statements, including the core values, are stated out loud by the meeting participants; each participant reads one value or one culture statement until all are vocalized.

Living and Working with the Core Values: It's My Company Too!

We opened this book with the story of Hugo Rios-Tellez, at the time a culinary worker at Tasty Catering, who intervened with members of the logistics team to ensure that company values were being followed. That story is typical of cultures in which living shared values are not only a conscious action for all employees, regardless of role, longevity, or position within a company, but a moral imperative as well. Hugo's comment "It's my company too!" reflects an attitude we found expressed within entangled organizations in similar yet distinctive ways.

Like many companies throughout the United States, Tasty Catering employs a large number of workers for whom English is a second language. Many came to the company through personal referrals from other employees. About 40 percent of full-time employees are related to at least one other employee by blood or by marriage. Family ties are important to Tasty Catering's value and culture. However, having a heavy population of workers who may not speak English well can present a communication problem.

Although Hugo's English skills were virtually nonexistent when he began working for Tasty Catering, he learned English over the course of several years so he could perform effectively in the diverse roles in which he is called to serve. True to the company value of treating all with respect, communication in native languages is important. The company's operating philosophy hangs on the wall in both English and Spanish to ensure all employees clearly understand the company's guiding tenets. At the same time, however, in an effort to improve communication both in and out of the facility, Tasty Catering leaders established an internal university, called TC University, that offers two levels of English as well as four other main competencies: business, sales, food service, and professional development.

Not many companies provide such a seemingly small yet drastically important benefit to their staff. Recognizing and helping staff work through a language barrier is a classic example of the employee-first attitude that drives the Tasty Catering culture. And just think how an employee is going to perform, knowing that her company is so committed to her personally that they would create an English-language learning program specifically tailored to her needs. It's a two-way commitment. Both sides are invested, and both sides are working hard for each other.

A central part of giving employees freedom and responsibility within a culture of discipline is senior leaders demonstrating that they care and can be trusted. This creates a collateral feeling that the employees will care for the organization and want to do all they can to support *their* company. Tasty Catering's leaders could have ignored the communication challenges of a portion of their staff, but they didn't. They demonstrated the company's responsibility and their commitment to help the workforce. But there is more involved than just supporting the core values; certain structural elements are necessary to complement those employee-generated and -enforced values.

Building the Structure to Sustain the Culture of Discipline

Here is how CEO Tom Walter explained the structure Tasty Catering uses to sustain the culture of discipline.

The culture of discipline is created by the employees and their team. Each person decides what they as an individual want to do within a team. This happens about ninety days after they begin full-time employment. For example, in the Corporate Sales Team, which sells drop-off catering—as opposed to designing special events with servers, liquor, and so forth, which is the responsibility of the Special Events (sales) Team—each person is trained as a salesperson, which is their primary responsibility. In addition, the team assigns additional responsibilities based on allocating the work and the varied interest of each team member. For example:

- Karen is responsible for the team's spreadsheets that track customer loyalty, clients that have dropped off, and potential territories/clients.
- Jodi is responsible for the delivery schedule, making sure that the promised time for food service delivery matches available trucks with drivers and a specific company name.

- Peggy is responsible for bringing in new hotel clients and maintaining customer loyalty with existing hotel clients.
- Kristen is responsible for the team; she is team captain.
- Patrick is Kristen's assistant, responsible for the team in her absence, and he is responsible for most of their largest clients.

Each member focuses on his/her areas of responsibility, and the whole team has performance goals. For example, in sales the team is responsible to the company to hit its sales and profit goals. Profit, in the sales area, is defined by dollar per guest at an event. The team has the freedom to do whatever is necessary to satisfy individual and team responsibilities, but it has to be done within the guidelines of our culture in terms of ethics and a value to serve the customer. For an example of how the circle of discipline works, the corporate sales team cannot sell a wedding to hit its sales target because that is a special event, not a corporate event. That would be a violation of core value #1—Always moral, ethical, and legal—and core value #2—Treat all with respect. So the wedding client is transferred from Corporate Sales to the Special Events Team. The sales team cannot overcharge a client to hit a dollar-per-person goal because that would violate core value #1.

The application of these two values provides the self-control or discipline to guide the team's behaviors rather than constant management oversight. Everyone knows their circle of discipline. They know what they are responsible for and know that they can do anything within our core values to accomplish their responsibility, be it a repetitive task or achieving a goal. And they know the guidelines of how they must act—follow our core values. Therefore, no one is telling them what to do, when to do it, and how to do it. They agree with their direct reports on expectations, deliverables, and timelines—and then just do it.

GIVING EMPLOYEES FREEDOM AND RESPONSIBILITY

Entwined with values and clarifying job roles are other structural elements, such as training, involving the workforce in decision making, having clear metrics of performance, and having a leadership team that corrects issues when the core values are not followed.

Training at Tasty Catering takes the form of formal training through specific classes on-site, online, or off-site on technical and behavioral topics, as well as informal training by members of the team about norms, customs, and how to do things. If the team structure is strong, it can be an important force in training members.

Senior leadership at Tasty Catering has involved individuals in the decision-making process to support the culture of discipline and the notion that "it is my company too." One great consequence of having discipline and responsibility coupled with the ingrained value system occurred on January 31, 2009. The Good to Great Council, comprised of a member from each team, meets the third Monday of every month. This council had formulated a "disaster" plan that would help the company survive if the economic downturn continued. The first decision was that the owners should take an immediate 30 percent reduction in pay. They did. One of the other steps was agreeing that if sales fell to a certain dollar figure for each month, everyone would take a 10 percent reduction in pay, and five hourly workers would be released. These results were published in the weekly in-house newsletter.

The critical drop point occurred in January 2009. On January 31, Tom and the leadership team called all the hourly team captains together to discuss the pay reduction and layoffs. Tom mentioned that the decision about which five to lay off must be based on low productivity and not seniority. He said he would return after informing the salaried teams that the time had come.

He returned to the operations room and asked the team captains to identify who the five would be. One culinary team leader said she had two questions. "Will we survive this problem?" Tom responded that if the country survived so would Tasty Catering. Then she asked, "Are we a family?" Tom said yes, we are a family that contains many families.

The team leader then responded: "We lay off no one. We have all looked for jobs, and there are no jobs. We all have families and need to take care of them."

Silence followed. Tom was hot. Afterward he said that he was shocked because that answer was in contrast to everything they had worked toward. He asked, "What should we do?"

She responded: "We talked about what we could do. We decided that if we all went down to twenty-five hours a week from forty and some overtime, we could still feed our families and the company would save the same as seven people being laid off."

This was a defining moment in the company's history.

The CFO, a member of the leadership team, immediately mentioned to Tom and his brothers that they were losing 18 percent in their rainy-day investments. They could cash in their investments and place that money in the employee assistance fund, Touhy Capital.

Tom then said, "This is a wonderful idea, thank you. Let's keep our productivity high to keep our debt low. And everyone must not worry about family money issues. My brothers and I will place enough funds in Touhy Capital so all of our families can borrow money to satisfy financial needs."

The interest rate was low, and employees were told they could pay back as much as they could afford or suspend payments until the summer, when overtime was plentiful. However, these funds should only be used for family needs. Kevin Walter, Tom's brother/partner and chief purchasing officer, then mentioned that Tasty Catering would sell employees food at cost plus 5 percent for handling and sales tax. This was a net savings to the families of about 20 percent from their grocery purchases.

The end result was a more committed workforce that stood together to support the company and the "family." Tom later said that he wanted to remove all the disruptors from his staff's minds, allowing them to focus instead on how to keep the company profitable and generate more market share, rather than worry about meeting family responsibilities.

Having Tom support the team's decision was a demonstration of encouraging and supporting discretionary decision making, and innovative ideas to sustain the organization and demonstrate that the culture works. This episode allowed the employees to realize that it is their company, and what they say matters. We saw this at all levels in the company, even when the team leader disagreed with the group's decision. Team leaders should honor their team's decision if that decision fits within the value system, or culture, of the company.

The availability of metrics and the transparency of those metrics further supported developing freedom and responsibility within a culture of discipline. The workforce and team could see the data and know how they were doing. The amount of data sharing helped teams to better understand what worked well and what did not. In addition, they learned how they could trust the process and the leadership. Having the data cultivated a sense of ownership in the business among all the employees. For example, in the operations room, where company employees have lunch together, a dashboard on the wall gives the workforce a quick picture of how they are doing for the month. Sales comparisons are made to the previous year's levels. Also posted are the number of clients served for that day, the number of days since the last mistake, the cost of mistakes year to date in the amount of money refunded to clients, and the current cash index. Once the company reaches its sales target for the month, an announcement is made that everyone will be awarded a bonus based on the sales beyond that month's goal.

We asked Tom Walter, "Why would a truck driver get a bonus for a sales increase when that increase results from the efforts of the sales department?" He replied: "We do not have truck drivers; we have 'customer service specialists.' They are the key face to the customer. What they do can be a very big factor in repeat customers. They are just as important as food preparers in supporting future sales. They are all part of the team, so they all get a part of the bonus."

The Results of a Culture of Individual Discipline

The company's and the leaders' focus on employees has yielded tremendous results in employee-customer relations. Ubiquitous passion for superior customer loyalty and continuous improvement is evident in the way employees confront the truth throughout all facets of company operations. On a daily basis, all functional areas extract data from Caterease, the company's unique knowledge management system, to prepare meals, create delivery and staffing schedules, assess inventory, and order supplies. This information is critical for producing, obtaining, recording, and sharing customer feedback through which actual performance on each delivery can be assessed. The operations staff has direct, daily interface with customers and clients from whom employees learn about what's going well as well as areas that require additional attention. In essence, these are the data needed to support the culture of individual discipline and discretionary thinking.

Employees garner customer feedback through "pros and cons" reports on each special event catered by the company as well as daily callback reports on each scheduled corporate event. Team leaders use the pros and cons reports as immediate feedback to assess on-site success with customers, data on food and beverage consumption, the most popular food items on the menu, the volume of leftovers by food item, what went well from an operational standpoint, any complications with providing service, and the performance of the service crew and leader for the event. Reports also include suggestions for improving processes for specific clients. Each report constitutes an "after action review" through which employees learn and improve.

Similarly, corporate sales members follow up with every fourth client through callback reports within twenty-four hours of service to assess customer satisfaction and product sufficiency. Team members post callback and pro-con reports on the company intranet and distribute reports via e-mail to key personnel for corrective actions and follow-up, if necessary. Calling or e-mailing every fourth client every single day, recording and distributing related comments to the entire company, and in return, reading each pro and con e-mail could be seen as tedious, especially when the company serves as many as eighty clients in a single day, fulfilling orders for between 12 and 5,000 meals. However, the entire Tasty Catering staff embraces this practice as a chance for improving service to future customers as well as time to give praise for a job well done and to assess the quality of their personal efforts within their scope of freedom and responsibility.

All the gestures noted above reflect a deep commitment to quality and consistency in service and food product across the spectrum of venues in which the company serves. Likewise, all actions stem from the company's core values and culture statements as well as the character of individual workers who exercise discipline and responsibility. Because the leaders in the company are so committed to taking care of employees, the employees feel a similar responsibility to take care of the company. Because the leaders in the company practice loyalty to their employees, the employees practice loyalty to the company's clients. The loyalty extends from the client back to Tasty Catering's brand image, which results from how employees care for their clients.

Company culture extends beyond internal satisfaction and commitment. A positive brand image in a highly competitive environment is critical. A simple series of actions in developing and promoting a culture statement that says "We care about each other" has broad implications for customer service and buying decisions. The results of employee efforts can be best summed up in this comment made by a corporate client: "They just gave me exactly what I was looking for. They did such a good job that I wish I could afford to do more events with them . . . The quality of what they were able to give us was impeccable. I would use them again, and whatever they're doing to make this happen, they should keep doing it."

Tasty Catering's company culture has been a key differentiator not only in the marketplace as far as sales are concerned but also on the supplier end; companies work hard to keep Tasty Catering as their client. Supplier Michael Mocogni noted how Tasty Catering "employs the right people and makes the right decisions. From Tom and Larry and Kevin all the way down to the person who receives the product, everyone is treated the same in the company. It doesn't matter who it is."

In one case, a college-age on-site coordinator of an event made the decision, when lots of things did not go right, to go to the event organizer and say there would be no charge for the whole event. The client could not believe it and called Tasty; COO Larry Walter backed the decision. He said to the customer, "If that is her decision, we will stand by it, and we are very sorry that our performance was not up to our own expectations." They had a customer for life just because this young coordinator had the freedom to make the decision, knew it was in her area of responsibility; she knew the event did not meet the company's high customer-service standards, nor was it "quality in what they do," which are two core values. The right decision was made because she based the decision on the company's core values.

Longtime customer Janet Wandler noted how caring and respect make such a difference when she selects a caterer. "With Tasty, it's like they are part of our business . . . We give them business, they give us great service, and it's wonderful. We had a big fund-raiser, so they left two people with us who worked like crazy . . . They have always given us what we needed and have done last-minute things for me . . . They have never said 'no' to my requests." Respect and caring are the foundation for customer intimacy, which is one reason why customers remain loyal to Tasty Catering and the employees who serve them.

What We Learned from Tasty Catering

Much like what we found with the other companies we investigated, company culture has a direct influence on employee behaviors, which drive decisions and hence performance. In Tasty Catering's case, we focused on two aspects of their value system: an enduring culture of individual discipline, and freedom and responsibility within the culture of discipline. These two values have had a major impact on the company's quality, quantity, and service, and they are an important part of the puzzle of building an entangled organization. Here are five steps you can take to focus on giving employees freedom and responsibility within a culture of discipline.

1. **Begin with shared values.** Shared values are critically important for company success since employees naturally align with organizations in which they feel comfortable and know what is expected from their performance. Having a clearly defined and visible set of values that constantly remind employees about performance expectations helps keep everyone—from the CEO to the newest employee—accountable for behaviors that lead to outcomes. Peter Drucker taught that every organization is perfectly designed to achieve the results it gets, and leaders of exceptional companies know that the success of their design hinges first on the values that align and achieve routine displays of desired behaviors.

2. **Adopt an employee-first mentality.** Placing employees first does not mean turning the business into a democracy but rather adopting the mentality that company success depends heavily on dedicated frontline employees who continually impress customers through consistently demonstrated behaviors. Operational leaders bridge the gap between senior, strategic-thinking leaders and frontline leaders who face customers. Operational leaders must ensure that employees are trained, developed, and allowed to act as

confidently and autonomously as their responsibilities permit. Customers are best served by employees who personally accept responsibility for organizational performance and well-being. Building a broad circle of discipline that allows flexibility and freedom and defines responsibility helps to solidify a quality- and performance-centered culture of respect among customers, employees, and leadership. Customers respect quality performance; employees and leadership respect each other and work together to support the needs of the customer.

3. **Work to define the culture of individual discipline.** At Tasty Catering, we saw some of this "defining" through the expectations that were set for individuals. Defining jobs and performance goals that cover the full responsibilities of the individual is a critical part of this process. However, these responsibilities have to be carefully defined so they articulate the broad area of one's actions rather than limited goals. For example, focusing on the short-range profits of each transaction will overlook customer satisfaction or long-term goodwill. At Tasty Catering, that could lead to an employee not wanting to make allowances if something is wrong with the customer's experience of the catered event. Defining the circle of discipline must be broad enough to encompass the overall goals of the organization and to give the individual the discretion to use judgment in responding to events. So being able to compensate for a bad experience immediately when it happens in the field serves the long-term interests of Tasty. Can it be capriciously done for all events? Of course not. However, the defined circle of individual discipline does help specify the limits of the behavior of the individual. These are defined by precedent, training, experience, policy, and performance goals.

4. **Define freedom, responsibility, and discipline around the full organization.** Tasty Catering employees built customer loyalty and their reputation for service excellence through customer

intimacy, which became a key differentiator with competitors. Tasty's senior leaders realized that being strong in customer intimacy also required building operational excellence. Company leaders upheld their commitment to service excellence and customer intimacy by emphasizing the hiring and retention of employees with the right character for the culture. They also made the investment in equipment and processes to support the employees' efforts. But most important is defining a key role for each employee to work for the benefit of the organization. What led Hugo Rios-Tellez to feel compelled to call out the supervisor who was berating the summer worker? Hugo did what he did because he had moral authority—it was his company too! His bonus and his satisfaction with the job were based on how everyone worked together as a family, as a unit, as people who respected and cared for one another.

5. **Emphasize and build teamwork and knowledge sharing throughout the enterprise.** The rapid speed of external change demands organizational flexibility that hierarchical structures cannot deliver. Keeping the organizational structure simple can increase speed of responsiveness while engaging frontline employees with the best knowledge and experience for resolving customer concerns, as Tasty did with their intra-organizational online program. Leaders should develop teams that center on core values; provide freedom and flexibility to act within a culture of discipline; empower team members to act within defined authorities; encourage building a team where members work to support and teach each other; and encourage risk taking and innovation. This structure requires senior leader commitment and resources to build, maintain, and sustain a supportive infrastructure that includes training and development as well as information technology that makes large volumes of data available to all employees within a well-defined knowledge management system. There needs to be transparency in financial data through which employees can

better understand the impact of their actions on customer outcomes and organizational performance. We have seen this time and time again in the high-performance organizations we have studied. It is one more piece of the puzzle in building the entangled organization.

Selected Resources

Here are some additional sources you might find useful as you give employees in your organization freedom and responsibility within a culture of discipline to fully engage and entangle them.

1. Since reading Jim Collins's *Good to Great* (New York: HarperCollins, 2001) had such a significant impact on Tasty Catering's culture and performance, we suggest reading this text to gain an understanding of an effective performance-excellence framework from a strategic perspective. Yet the story does not end there since some of the companies Collins's research team studied are no longer considered top performers, which is why we also recommend Collins's sequel, *How the Mighty Fall* (New York: HarperCollins, 2009), to ensure your organization does not fall into traps that can derail high performance.

2. By placing employees first and emphasizing their ability to lead customers through intimacy and service excellence, Tasty Catering's founders have built a virtuous cycle for business similar to that of Southwest Airlines, but on a smaller scale. We recommend Mike Treacy and Fred Wiersema's classic article "Customer Intimacy and Other Value Disciplines," *Harvard Business Review* 71, no. 1 (1993): 84–93, to gain a better perspective on creating distinctive competence that brings greater value to customers. We also recommend Jody Hoffer Gittell's *The Southwest Airlines Way* (New York: McGraw-Hill, 2003), which discusses the power of relationships and relational competence in achieving high performance.

3. Although there are numerous leadership books on the market, Jim Kouzes and Barry Posner's classic, *The Leadership Challenge* (San Francisco: Jossey-Bass, 2008) is in its fourth edition because it effectively addresses the five practices of exemplary leadership and the commitments leaders must fulfill to be effective. We highly recommend Daniel Goleman's work on emotionally intelligent leadership, especially "Leadership That Gets Results," *Harvard Business Review* 78, no. 2 (March–April 2000): 78–90. We found such practices and preferred leadership styles, such as coaching and affiliation, visible within Tasty Catering and other high performers.

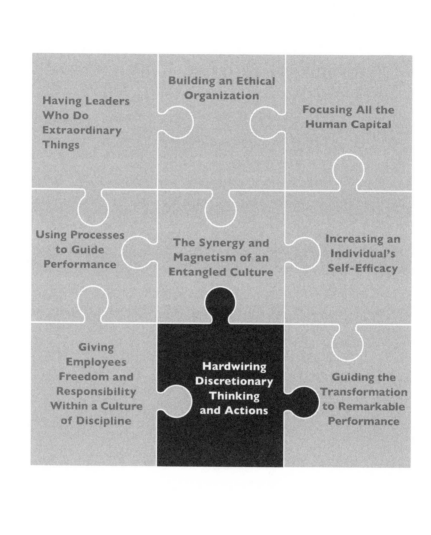

CHAPTER 7

HARDWIRING DISCRETIONARY THINKING AND ACTIONS:
Mike's Carwash

Senior leaders at Mike's Carwash want each member of the team to think and act in the best interest of the customer and the company. Leaders begin this process by referring to others in the company as team members rather than employees. To engage critical thinking on the part of their team members, leaders ask them to consider the following story during team member orientation.

> An older couple, in an even older convertible, rolls up to the carwash. Covering the top of the car is a soft, black, ragged roof possessing hints of what it used to look like back when it was a pure black, sleek, streamlined cloth cap for the automobile. The carwash is new, complete with high-powered water jets to better clean the automobiles. Once through the bay, the convertible looks pretty good. However, approaching the carwash window are the driver and his wife, both looking unhappy. They ask to see the manager. The carwash took years off the car's appearance, he says to himself; what more could they want? Apparently, water dripped onto the woman's head and ruined her new perm, and the couple demanded that the carwash pay for her to get a new one. The convertible top, clearly old and tattered, obviously had a leak. Was this really the fault of Mike's Carwash?

If team members have the right values and embody the company's culture, they will make the right call in this situation. They do not have to get permission from corporate; they are empowered to do what they believe is necessary to delight the customer, and that is to pay for the woman's new perm. And, in the process, Mike's Carwash hopes to gain a delighted and engaged customer. This is what hardwiring discretionary thinking and action are all about.

We have chosen Mike's Carwash as an organization that has done a good job in making discretionary thinking a permanent (or hardwired) part of the everyday culture at each of its widely dispersed retail outlets. Mike's is in a challenging, fragmented industry, one in which it is extremely difficult to gain attention for being unique because the service is very basic indeed: washing a vehicle. The technology involved is similar across all options—be it self-service, drive-through units or high-end businesses that offer, among other luxuries, hand waxing and detailing—and marketing is genuinely limited. The desire to earn a trusted, well-respected brand name that people go out of their way to visit is certainly uncommon.

That is the market that Mike's Carwash faces. The company's first unit was founded in Fort Wayne, Indiana, in 1948, and it was called Mike's MINIT Man Carwash. It was only one of eighteen carwashes in the United States at that time. It is currently in its sixty-third year in a $23.4 billion-a-year industry, carving out a niche with units throughout Indiana and Ohio, with three more opening this year and plans to grow by 10 percent each year thereafter. With revenues of $55 million in 2008, the privately owned subchapter S corporation, headquartered in Indianapolis, has more than six hundred team members. These statistics alone make Mike's a unique organization in the carwash industry. However, there is more to Mike's unique way of operating than just the end results.

Mike's Carwash is a second-generation family-owned company, with the addition of two main partners to help finance operations.

Their slow but stable growth over the years has been funded through operations. They have a solid business model that has supported revenue growth of about 3 percent over the past several years, including new units added into the mix. At the same time, the labor force increased by nearly 20 percent.

From the start, Mike's owners and managers had the vision that they were going to be a service industry leader, not a carwash. Consequently, shortly after Billy Schaming became COO, he and HR Director Joe Rice attended a prestigious weeklong workshop organized by a company known for providing highly rated customer service. After the workshop, Billy and Joe realized that great customer service originates with a workforce-centric culture. Since then, Mike's has focused its senior leadership team (SLT) on building a workplace that is responsive both to its customers and to the needs of its workforce. The end result: Mike's Carwash earned the *Wall Street Journal*'s 2009 Top Small Workplace award; the 2009 Best Place to Work in Indiana award, given by the Indiana Chamber of Commerce; the American Society for Training and Development's 2010 "Best Award," and the 2011 Torch Award for Marketplace Ethics, presented by the Better Business Bureau. Mike's has been featured in articles in *Auto Services Operator Magazine* (2001) and *Modern Car Care* (2008).

Mike's vision is simple, yet complex in its execution: "We will be the service industry leader by embracing innovation and providing opportunities for our team members to reach their full potential while ensuring profitable growth." The complexity comes in understanding what needs to be done to make the vision a reality, given the dynamics of the industry and of Mike's operations.

- Mike's has *many dispersed units* that are located a long way from senior management's oversight. How does an organization manage outposts that are far from the lines of control of its executive staff?

- A key part of the organization's profits come from *getting customers to go beyond a simple carwash* to pay for such additional services as "the works," with wheel cleaning, waxing, and other elements that boost the company's income. It can be done, but it takes knowledgeable and energetic team members who let customers know of the benefits of enhancing Mike's basic product.

- The workforce must go beyond just meeting customer needs to *engage the customer.* This is difficult if your employees treat the work as just a job. The challenge is to motivate a noncareer, part-time employee to take an interest in the customer and in the success of the organization. Add to this the young age of most of its employees, and Mike's faces quite a challenge.

- What do you do when *the employee is the face of the organization?* When how the employee dresses, speaks, and behaves will affect whether the customer returns or not? How can a leader design a system to ensure such consistent superior treatment of each customer that the individual will return even if the product (vehicle washing) is rather undifferentiated? This goes beyond the treatment of the customer to also include keeping the facilities clean and inviting.

- The *average team member at a Mike's location is a high school or college age student.* These are employees who, by nature, tend to have less of a sense of the importance of meeting customers' needs or a sense of valuing the organization. It is difficult for management to instill in these young employees a sense of satisfying the customer, serving the organization, or taking ownership in what they do.

- How do you *manage turnover?* Using youthful employees as part-timers is a recipe for high turnover, as most high school and college students aren't focused on a long-term job quite yet. A challenge for Mike's is keeping turnover low so there is a stable workforce trained to offer the quality services addressed above.

Mike's senior leadership realized that the team member is the core of their success. They wanted to provide personal service, not just an automatic coin-operated carwash, and that meant they had to get team members using their brains to engage and delight the customer, to create a positive experience, and to manage their own behaviors to maintain a positive face on the organization. When personal service is the keystone of what you have to offer, each team member must focus on making it happen. One disappointing experience with one team member may be the reason a customer does not return.

Creating the Structure to Support Discretionary Thinking

To keep the whole team in the game, leaders at Mike's Carwash used a balanced scorecard to set the organization's direction. The finished product (see the following Mike's Carwash Strategy Map) integrates the company's vision and values along with more specific directions for the organization; both elements are crucial in handling the many dispersed units. Robert Kaplan and David Norton created the Balanced Scorecard in 1992,[1] and they updated their scorecard in 2000.[2] That updated version is what Mike's used to develop their own proprietary scorecard. In the updated Kaplan and Norton model, *learning and growth* activities are directly focused toward improving *internal process performance*, which is directed toward improving *customer satisfaction*. Customer satisfaction leads to increased business from returning customers and to customers telling others about the quality of service. Increased business leads to the desired *financial outcomes*. We would advocate another category of outcomes, *employee engagement*, as keeping employees engaged and entangled to reach the other four desired goals.

A major part of Mike's scorecard is related to managing internal processes. Mike's senior leadership uses process design and management to provide direction for the organization. As the strategy map

Mike's Carwash Strategy Map

Our Vision: We will be the service industry leader by embracing innovation, and providing opportunities for our team members to reach their full potential, while ensuring profitable growth.

Financial Perspective

Return on assets

Conservative debt to net equity ratio

Revenue growth
(Average customer count/store and increased revenue/customer)

Customer Perspective

- We care about the community and environment
- We meticulously maintain a clean, bright and vibrant property
- Team members provide a friendly, feel-good experience
- We offer safe, convenient locations with fast service
- Customers drive away with a clean, dry, shiny vehicle
- We see our business through the eyes of the customer; we listen to our customers
- Customers see great value for dollars spent

Internal Process Perspective

- Develop and execute on lower cost building and equipment
- Utilize technology to maximize the efficiency of our key success factors
- Cost-effectively use/reuse and dispose of materials and resources in a sustainable manner
- Ensure continuity of human and information capital
- Minimize all non-mission-critical expenses
- Attract, hire, retain, and promote the right people, at the right time... in the right roles
- Utilize site selection metrics to expand and grow in new markets
- Enhance operational excellence and processes to protect the customer experience
- Explore and test new business models and strategic partnerships
- Innovate marketing strategy to connect with new customers/increase frequency of existing customers
- Develop new products and services

Learning and Growth Perspective

- Enable team members to reach their full potential
- Engage team members in our culture
- Develop the next generation of leaders
- Innovate by learning and incorporating external best practices
- Listen to preferences; know demographic information about customers/non-customers

While ensuring our profitable growth

← **We will be the service industry leader**

← **And by embracing innovation**

← **By providing opportunities for our team members**

demonstrates, Mike's senior leadership team has focused on several key aspects of processes: cost management in buildings and equipment, use of materials, use of technology to improve service, and minimizing all non-mission-critical expenses. Mike's executives stay focused on managing costs in order to make a reasonable profit because volumes are somewhat seasonal, alternative sources are plentiful, and the price pressure is intense from the gasoline chains with drive-through services. To be the service industry leader, Mike's Senior Leadership Team (SLT) knew they had to differentiate through human resource acquisition and development. Thus, much of the learning and development section of the scorecard focuses on team members.

Hardwiring Discretionary Thinking: Developing the Team Member and the Organizational Structure

The learning and growth dimension on the scorecard (the last row on the map graphic) links directly to developing internal processes in the organization. This category is where hardwiring of discretionary thinking occurs. It starts with developing processes in the organization that ensure hiring the right employees and creating processes that provide the framework to build and encourage the independent judgment of its employees. This includes orientation and training, leadership development, incentive and recognition approaches, policies and practices that support employee engagement, and aligning approaches to support the hardwiring of discretionary thinking and acting.

Hiring for Discretionary Thinking

The hiring process was one of the first aspects Mike's SLT addressed. The company hires roughly one out of a hundred applicants. Each candidate is interviewed by at least two people and takes a battery of tests that include attitude and basic math skills. It is imperative that team members have a good personality to interact with customers and make them feel welcome. "We can train the job, but it is more difficult to train for the attitude that is necessary," Schaming said. "We have learned over the years that there are some common denominators among the successful workers that you can spot. A lot of it has to do with the way they feel about themselves. Are they happy, do they make eye contact, are they outgoing?"

Perhaps it is this type of hiring process that makes qualifying for a job at Mike's such a plum for high school and college-age students. The more we spoke with the young employees, the more we learned about Mike's reputation as an employer and the reputation that team members of Mike's warrant simply by working there. Several told us it was considered "cool" if you had a Mike's Carwash hat displayed in the back window of your car. That meant not only that you worked there but also that you were good enough to work there.

These team members all spoke very highly of the organization and what it did for their development as young adults. For example, a one-year sales team member who has since returned to college full time told us that "the confidence Mike's SLT shows in me gives me confidence." She passed a Mike's sales course, which can take up to three months to complete, in just four days. She was able to excel because she knew Mike's leaders believed in her. She liked working at Mike's because the team members shared her values. This former employee learned permanent lessons she applies in other parts of her life, like the mnemonic LAST that is used when dealing with customer concerns: listen, apologize, solve, and thank. She said she practices LAST with her parents.

Orientation and Training

Orientation and training are relatively significant expenditures for Mike's, with about four percent of revenue reinvested in learning on an annual basis, which equates to about twenty-eight hours of training per year per full-time equivalent employee. The training focuses on three critical business needs: Increase revenues, preserve and develop the culture, and increase the retention rate of team members—all critical parts of Mike's balanced scorecard. The training focuses on improving the internal processes, and the internal processes lead to desired customer satisfaction and financial outcomes.

The Need to Increase Revenues

To address the need to increase revenues, organizational leaders developed two five-hour workshops for all team members to provide them with the knowledge and skills needed for selling to customers. Mike's has developed an additional online training module to reinforce what team members learned in the workshops. In addition, mystery shoppers[3] are used to further guide team members on what they are doing that works and what could be improved.

Training tools are not only for operational team members. Mike's developed a training module for managers to teach them how to coach their team members better and to help them improve their up-sell efforts (the process of encouraging customers to purchase more premium services). This multipronged approach does much to improve the effectiveness of the primary training because team members know they will be reviewed in the field and that they can receive support from their manager to improve their efforts, their reviews, and their contributions to the bottom line. This entire program demonstrates for team members the seriousness of the training effort by the organization and how the company supports each of them.

The Need to Preserve and Develop the Culture

One of the more difficult challenges for Mike's has been building and maintaining a culture that encourages discretionary thinking. When there are many different locations across multiple states, it is hard to guarantee that a consistent message and image are being presented to customers and team members alike. Most of the training takes place at each remote location, which is both cost-effective and productive regarding on-site reinforcement of the corporate culture.

The unit manager is one of the key players in keeping the unit team members focused on discretionary thinking. Mike's senior leaders developed a training guide to help each manager coach his or her team at their weekly meetings. They also created an "in field" assessment tool called the Station Observation Checklist, or S.O.C., which aligns with the mystery shopper's checklist and helps managers discover opportunities for their teams to improve in serving the customer.

To improve the impact of the training, senior leadership is involved in presenting values and ethics in some of the online training modules. In addition, Mike's uses a weekly online video called "In the Loop," which provides training elements and acknowledges the excellent work of top individuals and teams for the week. The ten-minute video also shares company news items throughout the organization. According to Rice, Mike's SLT considers this one of their most effective tools to reinforce the culture of discretionary thinking. "By providing examples of what other team members have done and having opportunities for the rest of the team members to share ideas, it builds a culture of engagement and idea contributions, an important part of what we want to happen at Mike's."

As effective as the weekly videos are in reinforcing the culture, face time is also important to leaders. Schaming is well respected by the field staff. He is known to join in spraying cars if he pulls up at one of the units and notices they are extremely busy. "It means a lot when the COO is there working with you," said one female team member.

The Need to Increase the Retention Rate of Team Members

Mike's conducts extensive employee development, including an eight-hour, face-to-face workshop titled "Hire the Best" that uses post-training online videos to reinforce key lessons from the workshop. Online training mostly focuses on the quality of team members, the organization's commitment to their development, and the importance of discretionary thinking. In addition, encouraging competition between units related to up-selling has helped build more of a team mentality and a focus on performance. But there is more. The field staff definitely like Schaming's leadership style. "He helps us out as a team member, not as someone over us," according to a team member. The culture also includes incentives and recognition for good performance, as outlined in a following section titled "Uncentive and Recognition Approaches.

The result of the training, orientation, and the culture of Mike's was a dramatic decrease in Mike's Carwash turnover, which was reduced by 25 percent with the introduction of the online training and the new approach to leading teams. Overall, the organization has turnover of less than 30 percent, which is outstanding for this type of industry.

Leadership Development Approaches

Mike's SLT includes team members in many of their deliberations to build more responsible leaders for the future, regardless if they stay with Mike's or move on in their careers. In addition, teams are encouraged to communicate with other units to learn "best practices" in the industry in terms of improving productivity, reducing costs, and serving customers better. As CFO David Zapp explained, "We make sure in our strategic planning process that we have team input into the process. We want to show them that we not only do the talking, we do the walking as well to integrate them into the process and into a culture of transparency; we drive home that everyone is a member of the team and we want their opinions." This is part of the overall learning and development of the organization, as indicated on the balanced scorecard.

Bill Dahm, son of founder Joe Dahm, echoed the importance for the company and for individual team members that Mike's has a positive approach to develop each person's professionalism.

We encourage the input of the team in the meetings at corporate or at the local unit. Most of those meetings end up being a lot of listening on the part of the senior management team. It really means a lot to the team; it helps them to mature as future decision makers, knowing that their views are valued by leadership.

One of the major growth and development features in our strategic plan relates to developing our team members into future leaders. We want to give them responsibility and decision-making capacity so they mature into more responsible adults. Everyone knows how they like to be treated. We want the team member to focus on the customer and be ready to create a positive experience. That means using your head and your heart. That comes from caring about the customer and caring about the company. By getting the team member engaged in the organization, we build that sort of internal direction. We want them to take responsibility to please the customer.

"For example," as Dahm explained further, "if someone gets their car 'egged,' that stuff will not come off with a regular carwash. A special compound and car wax is needed. In those cases, we would like one of our team members to speak up and encourage the customer to pull aside so the team member can clean it off for the customer." Seeing these special cases and acting to help the customer is part of discretionary thinking.

Mike's hardwires discretionary thinking in other ways. There is a process in place for the team members to send their ideas to Billy Schaming as president. He gets back to those participants and tells them they have been heard and then gives them honest feedback. Most of the major ideas to improve operations that have been implemented over the past two to three years came from a cross-section team and individual team members. Their input has affected how customers are greeted and has led to the addition of new pieces of equipment in the carwash tunnels. When asked why he includes his team members in the improvement process, Schaming replied, "You are going to make much better decisions when you get more people involved in the decision-making process, provided the people are engaged in the culture and have the same end-zone [goals and values]."

Incentives and Recognition Approaches

Mike's approach to using incentives and recognition to reinforce discretionary thinking are an important part of hardwiring that values team members. One of the first incentives is to encourage a team member to stay with the organization. Mike's SLT contributes to the tuition of qualifying student team members. This incentive works two ways. First and most obvious, it encourages team members to stay with Mike's longer, but additionally, right from the start it attracts hardworking prospects who are interested in continuing their educations.

Incentives that focus on job performance can do much to increase the quality and quantity of customer service. One approach is profit sharing. To counter the downside within profit sharing—that is, as a company gets larger, one person's efforts do not seem to matter—Mike's senior leadership team provides a "localized gain share" program that sets targets for labor costs at each unit. Based on beating targets at a location, the profit sharing program is translated into sharing the gains among managers and team members based on the number of hours each team member has worked over the time period. As Rice put it:

> It is important to develop an incentive plan that gets everyone involved, not just the manager. Also the full range of incentive systems has to balance the different goals of the organization. For example, if we only reward lowering labor costs, we may reach that goal at the expense of not serving the customer promptly and customer satisfaction will suffer. So it is always a balancing act. We try to balance the team members' ideas with demonstrated

involvement in productivity, customer treatment, keeping the facility clean and good looking, and improving their skills through the various training opportunities. We rely on the location general managers involved in the assessment process. However, we use mystery shoppers as well.

One way the organization improves the effectiveness of using those mystery shoppers is by broadening the effect of the visit. For example, Brandon Mitchell, general manager of one unit, believes that the evaluation of a transaction, which most probably involves a single team member, affects the whole team. This is an interesting concept and one that, at first blush, would seem unfair to the rest of the team. However, on further review, it is a good way for the culture to really "kick in." If each member of the team can affect the outcome for everyone else, team members become responsible for each other. This leads to more self-policing. "If part of my incentive is affected by how any of my team members treat customers, then I am more likely to get involved to make sure that person knows what to do and how to do it and when to do it," said one team member we asked. The "we're all in this together" mentality takes over, and team members learn to act with the organization's goals at top of mind. "Team members need to keep 'their heads in the game' and focus on what will be a plus for the customer and a plus for Mike's," another team member reported.

Mike's teams have found that competition can be a fun way to get everybody working toward a common goal. One supervisor, a college student, told us that his unit will contact another unit in the chain and challenge them to see which unit can sell the most extras on a specific shift. Because metrics are always current system-wide at Mike's, the winner can quickly be determined at the end of the shift. The losing team has to order pizza for the winning team from its favorite pizza place. That particular supervisor's unit hadn't lost in over eight months. The obvious next question was why do you do it? We anticipated an explanation involving leadership and motivation based on theories the supervisor was learning in his business courses. His answer, however, was beautiful in its simplicity. "That's easy. Most of the team members on my shift are young guys. There's nothing like competition. It gets us thinking and acting so we can win."

Mike's Carwash also employs a "Wow" program. Every time the company receives a customer letter praising one of the team members for going beyond expectations, that person is rewarded financially and receives recognition with a plaque at the annual awards banquet. It is a big deal to receive this honor, and the young team members strive for this company-wide recognition.

Schaming is also known for calling team members who have received a "Wow" card for exceptional performance and personally thanking them. His junior team members treasure those phone calls. Many told us how much it means, in such a large company, to have the COO call them up specifically and say: "You are awesome. Thanks for taking such good care of our customers! Have a great day." It encourages them to try harder and contribute ideas to further please Mike's customers.

Recognition for quality work, by the way, is not just limited to the units; it also applies to the staff at the home office. The managers of all the units are surveyed to assess the quality of the staff at the corporate offices. Questions are asked, such as How quickly are e-mails and phone calls returned? Do they seem happy to help you? Are they knowledgeable? Do they communicate in a respectful manner? As Mitchell stated: "Developing a company culture involves everyone. If you state that we assess quality customer care at one level and then at corporate we do not measure the quality of interaction that the staff has with its customers [the unit managers], then the culture seems to ring hollow. We want all our team members engaged in serving each other and doing the job right."

These systems are the hardwiring necessary to build a culture of empowerment that leads to discretionary thinking. The organization, according to Rice, tries to keep the assessment system, the incentive system, and the procedures simple so they are very clear to all team members. "We want it to be a clear and transparent process so the team members know it is an objective process, not a political process, as we evaluate and recognize people for good work."

The End Result: Hardwiring Discretionary Thinking

Our interviews with team members all revealed that this is an organization with an engaged workforce that knows it can not only make suggestions and utilize discretionary thinking but also exercise its right to do what will delight the customers without micromanagers assessing and berating every move that wastes time or resources. Quality team members know they don't have to subject themselves to a workplace in which management does nothing for their personal improvement. As a result, Mike's workforce is an energized and entangled workforce.

While we have not been to all the units that Mike's operates, we have been to some more remote locations such as South Bend, Indiana, which is about three hours from corporate headquarters. There we found a team that was helpful and eager to please. This was not an act; we did not tell corporate we were going there. We merely drove a dirty car through the carwash, acting as regular customers would, and asked a few simple questions.

In fact, to illustrate the responsiveness of the organization, when the South Bend facility had newly opened, we tried it and found that drivers had to make some tight turns in order to be on the right track for the cable to pull the car through the wash. We commented on that to Mike's SLT. The very next time we went to that location, the problem was fixed. That is typical of the culture you find at any Mike's Carwash unit and at its headquarters, and typical of any organization with a dedicated and entangled workforce.

Mike's Carwash also works with community groups on fund-raising events and provides veterans and police officers with free carwashes as part of the goal of being considered a good member of the community. In addition, Mike's uses environmentally friendly products and processes whenever they can. They work to keep each facility clean and inviting to demonstrate they care about maintaining the community's value. According to the COO, "This meets many of the values of our team members and gets them engaged and supportive of what we are trying to do as an organization."

Indeed, team members feel good about the place, the people, the leadership, the job they are doing, and their ability to contribute. Team member Gretchen Koch said, "The culture is the most important thing about Mike's." The culture is the differentiator that eventually attracts customers because the staff is so courteous.

Other team members agree. In fact, one of Mike's managers faced a tough choice: studying at an area university or staying on at Mike's. She couldn't fit them both into her daily routine. Instead of quitting Mike's, she stepped down as manager to become a part-time team member. She would rather reduce her pay than work somewhere other than Mike's. Perhaps that is the best example of the importance of Mike's work culture to its team members.

This organization knows how to hardwire the elements together to support discretionary thinking. As a result, customer and team member satisfaction levels are high, turnover is low, and the organization is a benchmark of financial and good incremental market-share growth.

What We Learned from Mike's Carwash

Mike's Carwash is an interesting case study because it has so much going against it. They have youthful, non-career team members who may not have developed good work habits and are working part time. This makes it hard to build much affinity for the organization or for serving the customers well. In addition, the multiple locations, which span in excess of a hundred miles from corporate, make coordination of a consistent product and customer experience very difficult. How did they make it happen, and what does that mean for other leaders who want to hardwire their organization to improve discretionary thinking?

1. **Create a scorecard** to guide each and every staff member. The scorecard is a vision statement to guide the direction of the organization. The vision statement focuses on being an industry leader by, in part, providing opportunities for team members (employees) to reach their full potential while ensuring profitable growth. A key statement of what the organization wants to do is to develop team members. What a great way to start developing a culture—by appealing to the workforce to work with the organization because its leaders are committed to each team member's own development. When an organization supports values that team members embrace, the team members are motivated, in turn, to contribute ideas to improve the organization, thus strengthening discretionary thinking.

    Previous research supports the notion of building an emotional attachment with the organization, the organization's goals, or personal bonds with the leaders of the organization, which leads to greater commitment than just monetary reinforcements alone.[4] The emotional attachments will lead to greater commitment of the workers to their job and to helping the organization succeed.

2. **Create aligned metrics of performance** to assess all key processes in the organization and the effectiveness of each unit. These metrics are tracked over time and are compared across units to help the organization manage the effectiveness of their teams and their marketing efforts. If you do not have measures, it is hard to know what is going on in the organization. If you do not have the right

measures, you may not have a good understanding of what is going on. Through the measures they use through their scorecard, Mike's leaders have designed a set of metrics that align different levels of scorecard performance and include the right metrics to effectively manage various parts of the organization.

3. **Train and develop team members and leaders.** This is a major part of Mike's hardwiring a culture of discretionary thinking. By having an understanding of the organization, the team member can make more reasoned contributions to its growth and success. However, Mike's goes beyond training workers simply about the carwash business; they are committed to developing leadership abilities in each team member. Even if the team member does not stay at Mike's in a leadership position, Mike's philosophy is that they want to strengthen the qualities of each team member so they contribute on a higher level to the success of the business and society.

4. **Recognize team members for outstanding performance.** Incentives and recognition for performance provide a clear direction for a team member or a team. Senior leadership is saying, "Hey, this is what is important to us and this is what we want you to do." There is a clear body of evidence that supports incentives whether they are monetary or non-monetary.[5] Even verbal commendation or the celebration of successes with acknowledgment of performance can be an important motivator.[6] However, a leader must make sure the incentives lead to the desired behaviors[7] and are of sufficient magnitude to encourage team member action.[8] In a symbolic sense, incentives demonstrate to team members that leaders care about them and what they do and consider their specific actions and behaviors important enough to reward. That message, in itself, would help support a performance-centered culture. Reinforcing discretionary thinking is an important behavior to reinforce as part of hardwiring a culture that supports innovation and idea generation.

5. **Be a supportive leader.** Leadership is the lifeblood of the culture. The culture will fail if the leader is not out there day-to-day to support it.[9] As we talked with Mike's Carwash teams in the field, we heard repeatedly that "leaders ask us how to improve things and they listen to our ideas," meaning they were out there each day visiting units in person, providing the ten-minute weekly videos to all the units to support the culture and values of the organization, and receiving feedback from the teams on how to do things better. They relied on weekly "5-15" reports, so named because they should take no longer than fifteen minutes and are filled out the fifth day of the week. They list the accomplishments of the previous week, goals for the next, and what the team needs to do to be better at their job. By simply listening, learning, and reacting to the teams' input, senior leaders demonstrate how important each team is to them.[10] What a splendid, inexpensive way to build a positive culture in the organization, in addition to learning stuff from a team that is out in the field and knows the customers and the processes better than the leadership.

6. **Design and develop a culture that supports discretionary thinking.** This was done by Mike's senior leadership team with a lot of forethought about the end product in mind. The organization's culture is directed by the scorecard, training, incentives, and leadership actions to create a profitable organization that is customer focused, employee focused, and performance focused. These dimensions are contained in much of the Baldrige criteria for what an organization needs to do to be a world-class organization.[11]

Mike's growth and positive consumer response is a function of building the culture, and this was done in an environment where many managers would say it could not be done. How do you motivate high school students? Most would say you cannot. "They don't care about the job; it won't be their career and they are only at it part-time." Senior leadership at Mike's has proven naysayers wrong. They have a committed set of teams that care about the organization and go out of their way to treat each customer as someone special. Team members also participate in generating new ideas—a rare commodity even in organizations with a more mature workforce. Culture trumps strategy all the time.[12] Senior leadership has designed and developed the culture (hardwired it) to meet the strategy, and it has worked. They practice many of the elements that research has shown to be essential in building a performance-based, positive organizational culture.[13]

Selected Resources

Here are some additional sources you might find useful as you hardwire discretionary thinking and action in your organization to create a culture of engaged and entangled men and women.

1. The importance of a strong and aligned organization to an enterprise cannot be emphasized enough. Most organizations look only at financial outcomes rather than at those things that got the organization to those outcomes. That is why Kaplan and Norton's Balanced Scorecard can be so helpful. We recommend the first article, which explains the concept (Robert Kaplan and David Norton, "The Balanced Scorecard: Measures That Drive Performance," *Harvard Business Review* 70, no. 1 [January–February 1992]: 71–79), then their modification of that model, which clearly shows the hierarchical relationship between variables ("Having Trouble with Your Strategy? Then Map It," *Harvard Business Review* 78, no. 5 [September–October 2000]: 167–176). Another article goes further to ensure there is alignment between outcomes and process performance: Kenneth Thompson and Nicholas Mathys, "The Aligned Balanced Scorecard: An

Improved Tool for Building High Performance Organizations," *Organizational Dynamics* 37, no. 4 (2008): 378–393.

2. Culture will occur whether or not you are an active force in directing attitudes and behaviors. Kenneth R. Thompson and Fred Luthans developed a good understanding of how to create and manage a culture in "Organizational Culture: A Behaviors Perspective," which appeared in a major treatise on culture and organization climate edited by Ben Schneider, *Organizational Climate and Culture* (San Francisco: Jossey-Bass, 1990).

3. Hardwiring applied to building a high-performance culture is an interesting concept. The first time we came across this concept was in a book authored by Quint Studer, CEO of the Studer Group, in *Hardwiring Excellence* (Gulf Breeze, FL: Fire Starter Publishing, 2004).

4. We refer to the role of the leader in building the culture. Two self-help leadership books you might find of value because they are behaviorally based (they focus on behavior rather than attitudes) are Bruce J. Avolio and Fred Luthans, *The High Impact Leader* (New York: McGraw-Hill, 2006) and Christopher P. Neck and Charles C. Manz, *Mastering Self-Leadership: Empowering Yourself for Personal Excitement*, 4th ed. (Upper Saddle River, NJ: Pearson, 2007).

5. Steven Kerr wrote a classic article several years ago that was recently reprinted. It describes the bane of many leaders and is a good read for those wanting to better understand the importance of rewarding the right outcomes in the organization. Steven Kerr, "On the Folly of Rewarding A, Hoping For B," *Academy of Management Executive* 9, no.1 (1995): 7–14. Fred Luthans and Alexander Stajkovic advocated the importance of going beyond just incentives in "Reinforce for Performance: The Need to Go Beyond Pay and Even Rewards," *Academy of Management Executive* 12, no. 2 (1999): 49–57.

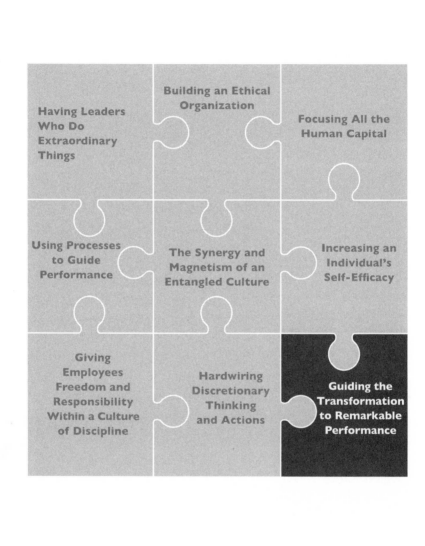

CHAPTER 8

GUIDING THE TRANSFORMATION TO REMARKABLE PERFORMANCE:
Advocate Good Samaritan Hospital

When Dave Fox took the helm of Advocate Good Samaritan Hospital (Good Sam) in Downers Grove, Illinois, in late 2003, he knew he had a good hospital. Yet as he oriented himself to the hospital's performance, it was clear Good Samaritan was not realizing its potential. According to Fox, the quality of care was perceived as generally good, but other measures of quality were mediocre at best. Physician relationships were strained, and the hospital sat in the middle of a highly competitive environment where six other hospitals within a ten-mile radius vied for Good Samaritan's physicians, patients, workforce, and business. Good Samaritan's 950 affiliated physicians were independent and "splitters," which meant they were on staff at other area hospitals and could choose where to send their patients.

Within his 333-bed hospital Fox needed to enroll the 950 physicians, 2,700 associates, and more than 500 volunteers in a vision to improve performance to ensure Good Samaritan's long-term sustainability. Unlike some CEOs who might make radical and/or incremental operational changes to address the challenges, Fox knew that what Good Samaritan needed was a transformation of both its operations and its culture. *Transformation*, according to Fox, means creating something that currently is not possible unless or until there's a shift in how people think and act. On the other hand, *change* is about doing or having something better, different, or more with what is already possible or already exists.

Having a Level I trauma center and a Level III neonatal intensive care unit meant that patients with the most serious injuries and mothers with at-risk pregnancies were routinely sent to Good Sam for treatment and care. Despite this highest level of care designation, physician reviews about nursing care at Good Samaritan were mixed; some units or shifts great, others less desirable. This caused physicians to choose to split their practices with other hospitals. Satisfaction of associates was not exceptional either. The hospital's facilities and technological infrastructure were perceived as falling behind financial investments made by competitive hospitals. One hospital to the east of Good Sam launched a $480 million expansion, and two hospitals to the west were completing a merger. These actions could easily draw more patients away from Good Samaritan.

It was during his first strategic planning session in early 2004 when Fox and his senior leaders had questions about just how effectively the hospital was fulfilling its mission. Fox noted: "Outpatient satisfaction was at the seventh percentile, while inpatient satisfaction was at the twenty-sixth percentile . . . so we were clearly not a place [that was] meeting the needs of our patients. We needed to do something different, and we knew we could not outspend our competitors to do it." To Fox and the senior leadership team at Good Samaritan, things had to change for the hospital to fulfill its responsibilities to the community to provide the highest quality health care.

Redefining the Operating Paradigm

Marjorie Maurer, vice president of operations for patient care services and the chief nurse executive since 1997, noted that Fox's approach to reshaping leadership was not like that of others. He did not "clean house and bring in his own team," as some CEOs intent on turnarounds are known to do. To break the trend of past performance, Fox knew he needed a different approach, an approach to get people to voluntarily commit to creating a different future. Fox's philosophy is *leaders go first.* So his first step was a deliberate effort to enroll his leaders across all disciplines. He spent several months listening to physicians in one-on-one meetings, rounding on all shifts, conducting associate forums, and engaging with leaders in dialogue about what was working and what wasn't. He began painting a compelling picture of a different future that resonated with physicians and leaders.

Like many hospitals, a silo mentality was evident at Good Sam, as was skepticism within the medical staff.[1] As a result of their training, development, and practice, physicians are dedicated scientists who rely on empirical data for proof. Dr. Donald Steiner, who had been a Good Sam Emergency Department physician for thirty years, was a veteran of "countless, various consultants of the week or month or year" and many "flavor of the month" programs over the hospital's thirty-five-year history. When Fox came on board, he found himself thinking, "Here we go again."

"People talk about culture, and you understand that there is a culture in every organization," Steiner began, "but how people actually *change* the culture is hard to get your arms around." Yet through Fox's countless hallway conversations and visits to the physician lounge and units as well as his deliberate actions, many doctors began to warm to the possibility of a true organizational change. Steiner stated, "Dave shared some compelling ideas, such as we have values, and as physicians, we're not just doing a job. There was a return to a feeling about having a mission. Dave did not say we weren't *good*; he said we were not being *great* consistently. In short, we could do much better."

Dr. Stephen Crouch, medical director of the Emergency Department, noted that although the transformation began with Dave Fox, physicians and leaders in other disciplines began to see health care delivery in a different light. According to Crouch, the belief that medicine is a *service* as well as a *science* was embraced.

Fox summarized the core understanding that emerged from that 2004 strategic planning session this way: "At the entrance of Good Samaritan Hospital is a sign that reads: 'Welcome All to This Place of Healing.' Good Samaritan was not fulfilling its promise to our customers to be a place of healing. So for everything else we wanted to accomplish in creating a new and different future, we wanted to make sure foundationally that we made good on that promise." The leaders at Good Sam decided they needed to adopt a philosophy and a culture that would differentiate them from their competitors, build trust with their constituents, and boost the hospital's reputation as a place of healing. Fox and his colleagues decided to pursue a strategy based on the values of the organization that would make the competition irrelevant. That strategy was a journey, and that journey was called "*Moving from Good to Great*" (G2G).

That journey meant changing the culture and the way care was delivered; the patient had to be at the center, and relationships had to be paramount. Staff perceptions of, attitudes about, and actions toward physicians needed to change; physician perceptions, attitudes, and actions about the staff who served them, as well as their relationships with hospital administrators, would also need to change. According to Fox, moving from good to great meant transforming the hospital so that everyone coming through Good Sam's main entrance would sincerely believe the statement that greeted them. "Welcome All to This Place of Healing" had to be reflected by every administrator, physician, associate, and volunteer in *every* interaction.

By 2010 Advocate Good Samaritan Hospital was achieving some of the best health-care outcomes in America, which were validated by numerous awards including the Malcolm Baldrige National Quality Award (see the box that follows). Fox noted that Good Sam's best in class performance has been the result of the collective efforts of all leaders, physicians, associates, and volunteers and a very intentional transformational plan. The following sections focus on some critical steps through which the entire organization became *entangled* in the journey of moving Good Sam from *Good to Great* (G2G).

MAJOR RECOGNITIONS OF EXCELLENCE IN HEALTH CARE, 2006–2012	
2012	**100 Top Hospital® for Overall Excellence** (Thompson Reuters)—Also 2009 and 2011
	100 Great Hospitals (*Becker's Hospital Review* Magazine)
2011	**50 Top Cardiovascular Hospitals** (Thompson Reuters)
	Partner for Change Award (Practice GreenHealth)
2010	**Malcom Baldrige National Quality Award** (National Institute of Standards and Technology, U.S. Department of Commerce)
	Lincoln Gold Award for Achievement of Excellence (Lincoln Foundation, State of Illinois)
	Get with the Guidelines Gold Award (American Heart Association)—Good Sam has received this award since 2006
	Get with the Guidelines Gold Award Stroke (American Heart Association)
2009	**Magnet Recognition for Nursing Excellence** (American Nursing Credentialing Center)
	America's Best Hospitals Digestive Disorders (*U.S. News & World Report*)
2008	**Blue Cross "10 Star" Award** (only one of three in Illinois)
	Most Innovative Mental Health Program (National Alliance on Mental Health Illinois)

Transforming from Good to World Class

We introduced entangled organizations as those in which tensions between internal expectations for excellence drive continually better performance, outcomes, and sustainability. Entangled employees focus on gaining the best possible result in the moment; they live and breathe the company purpose, and devote more of their discretionary thinking and mental energies to solving vexing problems and overcoming organizational challenges. Entangled employees go beyond being engaged because their values and efforts are so deeply entwined with the organization's purpose that the continual drive for maximal performance, customer satisfaction, and exceptional outcomes become second nature.

Within Good Sam, we found that entangled employees have so closely fused their personal values and attitudes with the hospital's purpose that employees and physicians move as one rather than as individuals. Being entangled also means directing one's discretionary thinking toward improvement efforts as a pleasurable and challenging endeavor. We saw subtle handoffs and integration of effort within Good Sam that reflected entanglement akin to a well-oiled machine operating at peak efficiency.

Good Sam's transformation from an ordinary to a world-class entangled organization took Dave Fox and his team seven years to accomplish. Fox noted that in a county where excellent health care was the norm, Good Sam had to begin with the basics—clinical, operational, and service. "First and foremost, we're a clinical enterprise. While some hospitals 'talk' quality, we determined we were going to be all about quality, with measures to demonstrate our quality. We believed that advancing performance excellence, quality, and safety would be the gateway to much greater accomplishments."

Sandy Churchill, vice president of operations for professional services, described how the transformation started in 2004. "It began with the inspiring vision to be the best we could be for patients, physicians,

GOOD SAMARITAN'S FOUNDATIONAL PRINCIPLES	
Core Competency:	Building loyal relationships with patients and families, physicians, associates, and volunteers
Vision:	To provide an exceptional patient experience marked by superior health outcomes, service, and value
Core Values:	Compassion, equality, partnership, excellence, and stewardship
Key Result Areas (Pillars):	Health Outcomes Patient Satisfaction Physician Engagement Associate Engagement Growth, and Funding for Our Future
Behaviors of Excellence:	Always ... Be Responsive Be Respectful Be Professional Be Accountable Be Collaborative

and associates." Pattie Skriba, vice president of learning and organizational effectiveness, explained that the next step was to "enroll" leaders and then the workforce in that vision. Compliance was not enough; ownership and commitment were the goals. According to Fox, ownership will make it happen, be generative, and inspire others through both their actions and their speech. Fox and his team fully employed a principle of change management noted by John Kotter in his book *The Heart of Change.* "Changing behavior is less a matter of giving people analysis to influence their thoughts than helping them to see a truth to influence their feelings...The heart of change is the emotions. The executive team did not just explain the vision but set a context that connected it to the values our workforce already had as health-care professionals." Churchill added, "The platform established by the executive team struck a chord in our hearts." According to Skriba, Churchill, and others, building the right culture began with getting back to basics, which meant reaffirming the foundational principles on which, and toward which, all hospital activity had to be directed (see table on previous page).

Fox and the senior leadership team created a rationale for and framed the G2G transformation in a context of becoming the best— the best place for physicians to practice, for associates to work, and for patients to receive care. (See the following table for details.)

GOOD SAMARITAN'S TRANSFORMATIONAL RATIONALE	
Mission:	To make good on our promise to be "a place of healing."
Operational:	To create a framework to advance quality and safety by building loyal relationships with physicians and associates.
Strategic:	To ensure future success by becoming the best place for physicians to practice, associates to work, and patients to receive care.

Clinical Outcomes and Safety as a Critical Foundation

The initial, central focus of the transformation effort was to improve clinical outcomes, patient safety, and service. This focus reconnected physicians and the workforce to their personal reasons for choosing health care as a career. In addition, senior leaders believed that improvement in the quality of health care provided would strongly correlate with physician, patient, and workforce satisfaction levels.

With the organization enrolled in a journey to create a different future, the next step was to align goals from the top of the organization to the bottom. This was accomplished through organizational goals being created across six pillars: health outcomes, associate engagement, patient satisfaction, physician engagement, growth, and funding for the future. Some of these goals were linked with publicly reported data, and others were linked to Good Sam's areas for improvement. Then specific, individual leader goals that aligned with the organizational goals were developed and cascaded to every leader. Progress on these goals was tracked, and leaders' performance reviews depended on performance.

With the goals defined, the focus was then to get cross-team involvement in developing ways to improve the quality of care. Using a defined performance improvement approach, teams of physicians, leaders, and frontline associates collaborated to improve clinical outcomes and patient safety. Data review and transparency were key. The intent was to make changes to processes to achieve higher levels of quality and to change the process so that errors would be less apt to happen—what quality professionals call *poka yoke*, a Japanese term that means mistake-proofing.

Skriba indicated that multidisciplinary clinical teams provided physician champions and frontline associates a structured forum to articulate opportunities for improvement while holding themselves and others mutually accountable for results. The trust that evolved from this honesty inspired employees to raise the bar to improve and innovate in new directions. Fox's low-key approach and the transparency of the results supported ongoing discussion of opportunities for improvement into the hospital's culture.

Dr. Chuck Derus, vice president of medical management, commented: "The hardest change that accompanied the cultural journey was learning how to open the door, turn on the light, and say 'Wow, we need to fix this place.' " Acknowledging imperfections and less-than-optimal practices or processes required an equally strong commitment to taking corrective actions that would ensure permanent change and continuous improvement. For Derus, Fox, and other senior leaders, delivering on the promise to facilitate excellence meant benchmarking against the best organizations even if they were businesses outside health-care institutions. For example, one measure of assessing the quality of a process or activity is the Six Sigma approach popularized by Motorola in the 1980s. Six Sigma quality can be translated into an error rate of 3.4 errors per million products produced in a manufacturing organization or procedures in a hospital.

Derus noted the health-care industry is nowhere near Six Sigma quality. Health care needs to be more demanding in terms of quality and safety. Since 2004 HealthGrades has released the annual Patient Safety in American Hospitals study, which identifies common errors that cost lives and dollars.[2] Their first study supported the Institute of Medicine's conclusion that medical errors cause up to 100,000 deaths annually, and subsequent reports have shown more can be done to reduce error-related deaths in hospitals.

Nationally, this was a number that doctors had a hard time believing. However, this data with its supporting research methodology was a driver of change at Good Samaritan. As Dr. Steiner said, "Doctors had become comfortable with the procedures they used following industry standards [provided through The Joint Commission[3]—the main hospital accreditation organization]. However, the 100,000 lives lost nationwide challenged us to think about a possible quantum leap, doing something really different, rather than simply making incremental changes." At Good Samaritan, the feeling among the staff and the administration was that there needed to be a stronger emphasis on the precision of how things were done, called the protocols or step-by-step ways of doing a particular clinical procedure.

The imperative to create a culture of patient safety required that everyone reexamine the premise of quality care. Steiner cited a study where doctors who trained in advanced cardiac life-support protocols had better results with cardiac arrests than did attending doctors who followed their own ideas or training. Other research supported similar findings. It took some time for doctors and nurses to accept the value of protocols, but the improvement in clinical outcomes was difficult to ignore, and they soon accepted the benefits of the approach. They began to look at patient care differently, realizing that having established parameters and boundaries helped them follow rules as well as break them when necessary.

Aeran Garcia, director of women's and children's services, noted how patient care can improve with a continual focus on individual and team behaviors. Across Advocate Health Care, the parent organization for Good Samaritan Hospital, specific behavioral and communication tools that foster a culture of patient safety were developed. These tools are taught to every employee and physician and are integrated into operations. "Near misses" are often caught because of how the workforce uses these tools. (See the box below for a list of those practices.)

GOOD SAMARITAN'S CORE PRACTICES FOR CREATING A CULTURE OF PATIENT SAFETY

1. Never leave your wingman.
2. Pay attention to detail.
3. Communicate clearly.
4. Execute effective handoffs.
5. Maintain a questioning attitude.

One former president of the medical staff gave an example of the culture of patient safety that is evolving at Good Sam. "A patient care technician was transporting a patient when she found a disconnected oxygen tube. She took care of the problem without having to go up a chain of command or through a burdensome bureaucracy. We encourage staff to look for problems and use critical thinking, and then we reward and recognize those who make 'good catches' as life savers."

Another example was a nurse who was doing a predischarge

physical on a newborn during the midnight shift. She discovered that the infant had a dislocated hip, which occasionally occurs in vaginal births. Rather than waiting for morning, she immediately called and awakened the attending physician at home and expressed her concerns based on her examination. Trusting the nurse's judgment, the physician ordered an immediate X-ray that confirmed the nurse's assessment; immediate corrective action ensued. The nurse received meaningful recognition from her superiors for her questioning attitude, critical thinking, and good judgment.

Moving Beyond Engaged to Entangled Through Working Together

As the G2G journey continued, a major paradigm shift was taking place: Individuals were managing more by data, work became more process driven, developing "standard work" was the norm, and protocols were created and adopted collaboratively. These systematic approaches improved efficiency and effectiveness while fostering collaborative, innovative thinking. For example, clinical protocols did not eliminate the need for discretionary thinking but rather encouraged it through improved diagnostics that resulted from more systematic reviews of patients' symptoms. Although physicians were ultimately responsible for the care patients received, they realized they needed to listen to other associates to get different perspectives or to learn about issues that might affect a patient's treatment or care. The culture shift toward shared responsibility for the highest level of clinical outcomes and patient safety helped physicians and employees see more opportunities to keep patients safe and to improve in all areas of practice.

The cultural shift took a lot of time and hard work by dedicated leaders, including Marj Maurer, who had initiated changes several years earlier to strengthen the quality of nursing care. (See the section titled "Developing the Quality of the Nursing Staff to Become Partners" later in the chapter.)

Realizing clinical care could not improve without having advanced clinical experts help nurses improve their competence in each clinical area, Maurer and Fox were convinced of the merits of a shared leadership model, also known as a dyad model. In that model, a nurse manager oversees nursing unit operations and a clinical nurse specialist oversees clinical outcomes and professional practice standards within a unit. The hospital hired eighteen clinical nurse specialists who were deployed to each unit throughout the hospital. The direct cost was approximately $2 million, but the return on this investment has been priceless in terms of clinical outcomes, saved lives, and significant improvements in patient, nurse, and physician satisfaction.

The observable trust between nurses and physicians that evolved within Good Sam is both remarkable and replicable. While on an executive retreat, Maurer asked one of the medical directors for ideas on how to improve collaboration between physicians and nurses. A multidisciplinary mentoring program was created, which the leaders called Collaboration, Communication, and Critical Thinking Equals Quality Patient Outcomes (CCC = QO). The program is a forum designed by physicians and nurses to teach others. A real Good Sam case study is presented by both physicians and nurses; they then challenge the attendees to identify the diagnosis or diagnoses and steps of treatment. As the case unfolds, the learners' critical thinking and medical knowledge expand while the partnership role between the physician and nursing staff is clearly highlighted. CCC began with medical-surgical cases and subsequently expanded to other types of patients and departments. Today more than one hundred professionals attend, and the case studies include multiple views from medicine, nursing, dietetics, rehabilitation, and others. Everyone learns how to provide better holistic care to obtain the best possible outcome.

CCC has resulted in a more collegial environment where doctors and nurses candidly and respectfully discuss challenges in delivering care more effectively. They show a deeper appreciation for one

another's roles and responsibilities as well as their partnership imperative. Although this effort was initiated in the name of clinical outcomes
and safety, it has had a very positive impact on staff relationships
throughout the entire hospital.

Maurer noted, "In 2004 physicians felt nurses were not timely in
their follow-through and were not knowledgeable on specific patients.
Physician satisfaction was at the sixty-second percentile several years
ago, but doctors now consistently show a ninety-sixth percentile satisfaction rating with hospital performance. Physician satisfaction with
overall nursing is at the ninety-first percentile."

According to Dr. Vibhaben Thaker, medical director for neona-
tology and chairman of pediatrics, nursing satisfaction with physicians
is also very high, as seen in the number of doctors that nurses have
nominated for quarterly hospital MVP (mission, values, and philosophy) awards. Similarly, physicians have nominated nurses and associates
for recognition. "Physicians commonly receive thank-you notes from
nurses," said Thaker, "for teaching them or spending more time with
them, and many physicians do the same." The paradigm shift throughout the hospital culture represents the entangled efforts of leaders and
staff in all disciplines and at all levels to fulfill the mission and live the
values that define organizational performance.

In our observations and interviews, we didn't just see physicians
and associates simply "engaged" in their work. We saw associates and
physicians who were fully entangled with their mission of being a place
of healing, actively engaged in looking for ways to keep elevating the
quality of care and the quality of interactions among staff, physicians,
and patients.

Developing the Quality of the Nursing Staff to Become Partners

One of the key drivers of physician loyalty is the quality of nursing. As
noted earlier, Marj Maurer had set in motion initiatives to strengthen

Good Sam's nursing staff prior to Dave Fox's arrival on the scene. When she assumed her chief nursing executive role, the physicians who were her primary customers did not rate the nurses very highly. She also needed to address low patient satisfaction scores and show better patient clinical outcomes. She recognized that gaining physician trust was the critical path toward increasing both physician and patient satisfaction. Maurer believed "nursing needed to clean up its own act." Doing so meant nurses needed to see themselves differently. To achieve this goal, Maurer knew radical changes were necessary in the way nurses approached their profession and their daily work.

As a starting point, Maurer used the ANCC Magnet status criteria[4] to conduct a gap analysis and determine which nursing practices needed to change to achieve a world-class, nursing professional practice at Good Samaritan.

Maurer and her team of directors established a nursing Shared Governance model through which nursing leaders leveraged the education and experience of frontline nurses and gave them a voice and presence in the creation of practice standards, policies, and procedures for which they bore execution responsibilities. To ensure that this professional practice structure would be embedded in the organization long-term, Maurer and her nursing staff established bylaws—a legal, binding document. Shared Governance at Good Samaritan Hospital will stand the test of time.

Physicians are self-governed through a peer-review process; Maurer decided to mirror the nursing peer-review process after the medical staff process. This allowed nurses to assess individual performance against standards of evidence-based nursing practice found in the latest research literature. Since nurses are hospital employees with mandated annual performance reviews, expert clinical nurse specialists facilitated the peer-review process, which served as the foundation for assessing individual effectiveness in the domains of nursing practice. From this foundation, peer-review panels would give feedback to improve individual performance, which informed the annual performance review at the next review cycle administered by the manager. "This approach," noted Maurer, "helped nurses think, 'I'm a professional and need to own my nursing practice.' " This enabled nurses to improve critical thinking skills and become more competent. Shared Governance and practices such as peer review helped nurses define their circles of discipline and articulate the freedoms they had in fulfilling responsibilities to their team, patients, and the organization.

To foster more effective communication and personal development, nursing leaders established what they called Nursing Outcomes Councils as a part of the Shared Governance structure. The council is populated and chaired by staff nurses, with representatives from leadership. Patterned after the medical model, each council has a dedicated focus: clinical excellence, professional development, nursing research, and operations.

The metamorphosis of nursing care within Good Samaritan stemmed from the basic premise that nurse managers, supervisors, and directors needed to be exemplary leaders. In 2004 Good Samaritan established quarterly Leadership Development Institutes for all leaders—frontline supervisors through the executives. During these development events, nurse leaders learned tools for success, such as how to run a meeting or deal with conflict, while increasing their knowledge about the other departments. As nursing leadership was strengthened, the voice of frontline nurses through The Shared Governance model was captured, and the level of nurse competency contributed to Good Samaritan's mission to provide exceptional patient experiences, which were marked by superior health outcomes and patient safety. It was a giant leap for quality, a giant leap for the nursing staff, and a significant step on the G2G journey of quality at Good Samaritan Hospital.

Creating Transformational Partnerships

Many movies and TV shows have played up the battle between doctors and nurses, both humorously and seriously. But what happens when nurses and doctors don't see eye to eye in real life? Good Samaritan may have known what that was like before the cultural shift, but today nothing but respect exists between the disciplines and among these practitioners.

Physicians and nurses focused on developing a team mentality toward serving the patient. For example, Thaker played a key role in the long, laborious process of transforming the neonatal intensive care unit (NICU) from a Level II to a Level III unit, especially in teaching nurses how to care for really sick babies. Although she spent a lot of time educating, lecturing, and writing new policies, she also worked side by side with nurses at patient bedsides. Doing so allowed her to teach nurses one-on-one and build their confidence to the point where NICU nurses, according to Thaker, "can now take care of anything."

Some of the innovative, collaborative programs created by physicians and nurses—such as grand rounds, which involve physicians and nurses who have a unique medical case they present to their professional colleagues—have caught the attention of the Joint Commission. This concept expanded into quarterly CCCs (collaboration, communication, and critical thinking) discussed previously.

Throughout Good Samaritan, we found extensive evidence of the personal commitment physicians have made in sharing their knowledge and further fostering a physician/nurse partnership. Dr. Jeffrey Oken claims that when he arrives at a nursing unit to see his patients, the nursing staff routinely ask him, "Is there anything we can be doing better, Dr. Oken?" He believes the inquisitiveness and sincere desire of nurses and associates to make things better has a synergistic, motivating effect on physicians to shift into "knowledge sharing" mode rather than simply dictating what needs to be done.

Director of Oncology Services Paula Timmerman, RN, believes Dr. Oken "invites collegiality just by who he is. He is willing to teach, and by sharing his passion for making the hospital the best place where patients can receive their care, he has brought patient care forward."

The partnership between physicians and nurses at Good Sam reflects the entanglement of dedicated professionals who constantly blend their talents to provide top-level care while seeking the best possible solutions to new challenges. As Marj Maurer noted, laughing, "The medical staff will now take me on if I do anything to the nursing staff; they love their nurses here."

Entangled Teams Working for World-Class Clinical Outcomes

The major differences within Good Sam's culture today, as compared to that of the past, are:

- Clearly defined expectations and accountabilities through the Behaviors of Excellence,
- Clarity of performance goals and behaviors for every leader,
- Openness and constancy of critical conversations essential to moving from good to great,
- Shared belief that everyone is on the team working for the patient, and
- Unwavering commitment to and passion for a shared purpose to serve the patient.

Good Sam's leaders have continually set their sights on performance excellence, to move from good to great; first through a focus on clinical and service outcomes, and then through the adoption of the Baldrige criteria to create a more process-driven culture.

Dr. Oken noted, "Everyone is thinking about hardwiring processes organizationally so if leadership changes, we can sustain the journey to excellence and the delivery of the highest-quality care." He noted how senior leaders who preceded Dave Fox each had "their thing," but "they did not build the culture. In contrast, everybody here 'buys into the culture'; it isn't just a leadership thing. Nurses, aides, everybody— we have a lot of people doing important patient care that requires they understand their role and how it fits in the bigger picture of Good Sam and all the good work being done here."

Understanding the big picture includes seeing how important the handoffs are to the integration of care, as well as the staff's ability to anticipate and attend to clinical outcomes and safety, especially where effective patient care could fall through the cracks and safety issues could arise. Improving the integration of care includes systematic collection, review, and analysis of critical data and timely knowledge sharing along with recognition systems that reinforce the culture and best practices.

Monthly, Fox distributes Good Samaritan's "report card" to more than 300 leaders, including the Governing Council and Advocate Health Care senior leadership. Individual departments track and post key metrics, including annual goal performance and performance-improvement indicators. The nursing staff track sensitive nursing indicators, which has resulted in competition between nursing units to improve care. A little competition among high performers is a healthy way to encourage continuous improvement, regardless of the industry. As a result of better patient outcomes and shared learning gained through CCC=QO and unit-level collaborations, advanced practice nurses now serve on medical staff peer-review committees because physicians want collaborative input from nurses as to what is reasonable to expect for nursing practice when they review cases.

Trust between physicians and nurses has grown. When a patient appears to be turning for the worse, nurses now call for a "rapid response," which has significantly reduced the number of code blue[5] incidents outside the Critical Care Unit and has raised the quality of patient care. The Chief Nurse Executive is now a permanent member of the Medical Staff Executive Committee to provide input and perspective. Many doctors and their families have chosen Good Samaritan as their hospital for their own or family member's care. This type of collaborative environment has inspired excellence and excitement on the part of the staff and doctors, elevating the level of practice to the highest level.

Peggy Farrell, RN, manager of the NICU and pediatrics, noted that thirteen years ago in her first three months of employment, she never saw a write-up for a clinical near miss. She knew 'bad' things could have occurred if not for luck. "We had to develop the culture where it's okay to talk about these events and write about them. Being able to talk about 'near misses' allows us to change processes before something regrettable happens." A culture to report, discuss, and correct "near misses" now permeates Good Samaritan. Within nursing, new associates are assigned mentors. "Unlike other nursing cultures that have been known to 'eat their young,' we appreciate our new nurses as well as the seasoned ones," Farrell said. She claims this transformation was the result of constant communication, role modeling, mutual respect, and a commitment to constant learning.

At Good Sam, recognition and reward go hand-in-hand, further raising the focus on performance. For example, high-performing leaders across all areas are recognized as "pillar leaders" at the quarterly Leadership Development Institutes. Associates who make "good catches" are recognized as "Life Savers." Physicians, associates, and volunteers can be nominated for an MVP award when they demonstrate the five organizational values. A wall at Good Sam is dedicated to recognizing physicians; monthly comments about physicians from the patient satisfaction surveys are selected and the physicians' photos and patient's comment are posted. This wall is a highlight for physicians; some have been seen bringing their own family members to see the display.

In addition, several years ago, the medical staff executive committee established six nursing excellence awards that recognize nurses who have had the most impact on patient outcomes and serve as exceptional models of professional nursing. Each award carries a $500 honorarium for the recipient, but the greater impact is that each recipient is nominated by peers who want to acknowledge top performers. Dave Fox noted that loyal relationships have created the breakthrough accomplishments that have led to the number of quality awards Good Samaritan has received.

What We Learned from Advocate Good Samaritan Hospital

Although Good Samaritan was the most complex of all the organizations we studied, the lessons we learned paralleled those of other high-performing organizations. Most of all, Good Samaritan showed us how leaders throughout a very complex organization dealt with organizational transformation through a commitment to quality, structure, reliability, and a transcendent purpose that permeates every operational and strategic aspect of the organization.

1. **A well-defined transformational leadership system, coupled with a strong change model, is critical for executing large-scale, systemic culture change.** In Good Sam's culture, leaders go first. An intentional investment and focus on leaders was key to transformation. Good Sam's Leadership System was created by senior leaders and clearly defines what leaders must accomplish and the behaviors they cannot delegate. Good Sam leaders use an eight-stage change model for guiding the organizational transformation. All Good Sam leaders are also taught how to lead using this system. The commitment to and proliferation of ongoing leadership development programs tied to the Leadership System reinforces the message that culture change is an imperative for sustainability.[6]

2. **Long-lasting transformation requires an approach that captures the souls as well as the minds of the workforce.** Good Samaritan's journey of *Moving from Good to Great* began with an inspiring vision to be the best—the best place for physicians to practice, associates to work, and patients to receive care. A context for the future was set by senior leadership, and leaders were

enrolled first, which allowed all leadership to enroll the entire work-force. The focus was on creating a context for meaningful work. The intent was not compliance, but ownership. Culture is key, and culture cannot change without the hearts of the workforce.

3. **Relationships are the key to accomplishment.** A narrow breadth of relationships creates a small window of what can be accomplished; but a broad, deep base of relationships will allow for the achievement of extraordinary results. Dave Fox and other leaders cite the *building of relationships* as the first step to world-class results. They are the first to admit Good Samaritan is not perfect, yet patients, physicians, and associates agree that they would not want to receive care or work anyplace else, in large part because of the partnerships that have evolved through deep respect for each member of the team and concerted behaviors and practices that have built relationships.

4. **You're only as good as your people.** World-class results can-not be bought; they occur when high-performing employees collab-orate in a culture where both world-class aspirations are embraced and structures support them. This type of culture is perpetuated through current employees selecting new employees. It is also per-petuated through ongoing assessment of and conversations about high, solid, and low performance. It is also perpetuated through leadership connecting with the workforce through systematic prac-tices such as rounding, 30/90 day conversations, and ongoing rec-ognition and appreciation such as hand-written thank-you notes.

5. **Defined, aligned goals keep the commitment to world-class performance excellence at the heart of the culture.** If going back to basics and focusing on a culture of excellent clinical outcomes and safety are the building blocks and prepara-tion for the quality journey, then improvements to service, care, and outcomes are the routine practices that support building and reinforcing an entangled culture. Goals for every leader and

transparency of progress toward those goals focuses leadership action and work, and it drives collaboration. Director of Radiology Dina Loughlin noted: "As leaders, we have to position ourselves so that everything in health care is nothing but positive. The only negative in health care is when we are not successful in saving a patient's life. But everything we do is very positive, and if it's not approached in that manner, we have every opportunity to lose that success." This optimistic view also carries a warning that is shared throughout Good Samaritan. The hospital's leaders are preoccupied with clinical and operational excellence, they pay attention to details and are sensitive to operations, and they routinely defer to internal expertise, regardless of where that expertise resides. Leaders constantly turn to those around them for firsthand knowledge and other views that can improve a decision, regardless of whether the topic is a patient's care or a practice or process that should be revised.

Selected Resources

Here are some additional sources you might find useful as you guide the transformation process to remarkable performance in your organization to create a culture of engaged and entangled men and women.

1. Two works by John Kotter, Professor Emeritus at the Harvard Business School, head the recommended readings about leading and transforming organizations. His article, "Leading Change: Why Transformation Efforts Fail," *Harvard Business Review* 73, no. 2 (March–April 1995): 59–69, is an excellent introduction to his longer but very readable book, *Leading Change* (Boston: Harvard Business School Press, 1996). Both address the eight-stage change model; we suggest leaders have both items available for ready reference.

2. Another classic *Harvard Business Review* article by Ikujiro Nonaka, "The Knowledge-Creating Company" (originally published in vol. 69, no. 6 [November–December 1991]: 96–104, and re-released in vol. 85, nos.7/8 [July–August 2007]: 162–171) is a must-read for understanding a leader's responsibility for knowledge creation rather than mere knowledge management. To gain a deeper understanding of how effective leaders create and nurture a collaborative, creative culture, we recommend several sources, beginning with Ikujiro Nonaka and Toshihiro Nishiguchi's *Knowledge Emergence: Social, Technical, and Evolutionary Dimensions of Knowledge Creation* (New York: Oxford University Press, 2001). Nonaka and Nishiguchi discuss creating the fertile ground for innovation by generating spirals of knowledge that continuously feed the growth of new ideas.

3. The July–August 2011 edition of *Harvard Business Review* (vol. 89, nos. 7/8) provides four critical articles every leader should read to understand how to build a collaborative culture. The first two articles focus on individual perspectives, while the last two address collaboration from an organizational view. Herminia Ibarra and Morten Hansen's "Are You a Collaborative Leader?" (pp. 69–74) compares collaborative leadership to traditional command-and-control and consensus styles, which are less than effective in the rapidly changing environments and situations leaders face today. In "The Unselfish Gene" (pp. 77–85), Yochai Benkler clarifies the natural propensity toward cooperation rather than competition and describes how to build cooperative systems that encourage communication, ensure authenticity, and foster empathy. John Abele discusses building a collaborative culture in "Bringing Minds Together" (pp. 86–93), while Paul Adler, Charles Heckscher, and Laurence Prusak address four keys to creating a culture of trust and teamwork in "Building a Collaborative Enterprise" (pp. 95–101). Although you probably will not be surprised by the four keys Adler et al. describe, you will learn about large, well-known organizations

that have gained by applying techniques similar to those used within Good Samaritan.

4. Finally, Karl Weick and Kathy Sutcliffe's *Managing the Unexpected: Assuring High Performance in an Age of Complexity* (San Francisco: Jossey-Bass, 2001) is a must-read for anyone interested in learning about high-reliability organizations (HROs).

Building an Ethical Organization

Having Leaders Who Do Extraordinary Things

Focusing All the Human Capital

Using Processes to Guide Performance

The Synergy and Magnetism of an Entangled Culture

Increasing an Individual's Self-Efficacy

Giving Employees Freedom and Responsibility Within a Culture of Discipline

Hardwiring Discretionary Thinking and Actions

Guiding the Transformation to Remarkable Performance

CHAPTER 9

THE SYNERGY AND MAGNETISM OF AN ENTANGLED CULTURE

When we began our journey of discovery, we had no idea whether there would be any elements common to the organizations we studied. All we knew was that we had identified several award-winning companies, and we were curious to find out what made them so special. We purposely selected organizations in a variety of industries, regions, and markets, and with a variety of goals. We found that several universal principles underlie the results achieved by exceptional organizations. And we found much more.

This chapter links the elements the organizations held in common and puts the pieces of the puzzle together into a whole for leaders to follow in building a culture where employees own what they do and take responsibility for the quality of their performance. During our field visits, this oft-cited quotation kept coming to mind: "All organizations are perfectly designed to get the results they are now getting. If we want different results, we must change the way we do things."[1] Across the board, the leaders who observed dramatic improvement in performance, attitudes, and aptitudes among their employees discovered that these outcomes resulted from the ways in which they treated, respected, encouraged, and honored those workers. Despite their differences, these eight organizations were uniformly committed to innovation, growth, and better quality in how the organization functioned. The organizations' leaders were all striving for even a better work environment and better results. They felt they were on a quality journey rather than settling for the current state of things as a destination. What we found was a winning formula that other leaders could and should learn about in order to achieve performance excellence.

Putting the Pieces Together to Create the Entangled Culture

The preceding chapters highlighted the elements in that winning formula, each representing a unique thread within a given organization. What we learned was that, as several of nine puzzle pieces evolved in an organization, a synergy was created that made the organization stronger as the different pieces of the puzzle came together. It seemed, as we explored further, that each of the puzzle pieces was not so much a stand-alone concept but part of something larger; a synergy occurred that created what we refer to as the entangled organization.

However, each organization's journey to excellence resulted from something more than that synergy. The structural and behavioral elements within each organization connected in a way that we could only describe as compelling, magnetic forces that wound and tightened individual, collective, and organizational efforts into an integrated whole through which many people contributed to achieving exceptional results.

Of the puzzle's nine pieces, eight reflect the key elements that integrate to create the synergy that melds the entangled organization. We used the ninth element to demonstrate the synergy among the elements; this synergy creates a magnetism that draws people to do extraordinary things and organizations that are extraordinary places to work and do business. The elements alone cannot sustain a superior work culture that leads to high performance; it is the powerful combination of leadership, structure, and supportive behaviors that create the truly magical environment where employees say, "It's my company too!"

Entangled organizations are places where people *want* to get involved in helping the organization exceed everyone's expectations—where the employees want to feel they and their coworkers are part of an exceptional place that gets the best out of people because the culture creates the efficacy and esteem in each person that helps them believe they can go on to do exceptional things. And, if you believe you can achieve greatness, you are only a step or two away from being able to do so.

In this chapter we examine how the organizations we studied use the elements in the puzzle to greater and lesser degrees and how you can use the total puzzle to develop your organization.

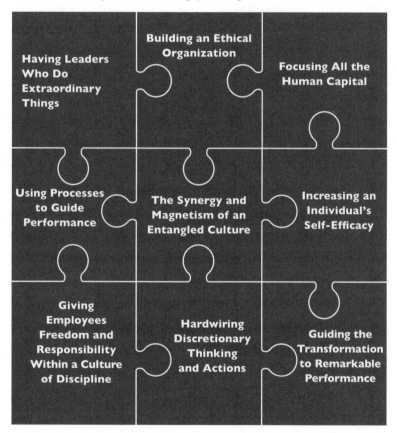

Having Leaders Who Do Extraordinary Things

Springfield Remanufacturing Corporation (SRC) serves as an example of the primacy of leadership in shaping a performance-excellence culture where discretionary thinking and grassroots leadership are the norm. The metamorphosis within SRC involved three critical structural components: visionary leadership, transformational leadership at all levels, and organizational alignment on a transcendent purpose.

Visionary leadership existed in every organization we studied, not merely at the top of the organization but throughout the fibers that comprised each organization's muscles. Although some may perceive vision as the domain of a company's CEO or president, we found shared visions that extended well beyond the most senior leaders. Senior leaders accepted responsibility for guiding the change process[2] within their organizations and for modeling the way,[3] but followers equally accepted their responsibility to help the organization to achieve the vision.[4]

Transformational leadership at all levels is a leadership theory that has emerged over the last thirty years.[5] A key element of this theory is that leaders operate on a continuum between transactional leadership, in which they focus heavily on getting a task done, and transformational leadership, in which they focus on building trust, asking critical questions, and developing *relationships* with others, through which everyone achieves more. We found the relationship-building aspect of transformational leadership prevalent in all organizations we studied.[6]

Remarkably, transformational leadership was not confined to strategic leaders or the top of the organization. Within an entangled culture—with the focus on freedom and responsibility in a culture of discipline and an emphasis on discretionary thinking and action—each employee had leadership responsibility. The ability to influence buying decisions was evident within frontline staff at Tasty Catering and MidwayUSA who interacted directly with customers and clients; the same frontline staff influenced operational leaders who were responsible for smooth operations throughout each enterprise. Within very small organizations like Sweet Beginnings, we found peer-to-peer leadership critically important in helping new entrants in programs like U-Turn Permitted, but we also found this practice consistent within our sample organizations. The confidence senior SRC leaders had in grassroots leaders' abilities deepened trust within the organization and employees as a whole and created a stronger sense of ownership for all the employees.[7]

Organizational alignment on a transcendent purpose was possible because leaders engaged others to dream about a future that was above and beyond anything any one individual or group could accomplish alone.[8] This visioning process included connecting each person to something greater than personal concerns and integrating the unique identities and traits of individuals with organizational values and a coherent, congruent belief system. Through development efforts, leaders helped followers at each level realize their aspirations and potential. In effect, the shared vision became embedded in followers' minds and got them thinking about a new reality. The vision connected to what they did each day, to what really mattered both to them and to the people they serve. This created a meaningful work environment that supported the employees' involvement in decision making and shared governance.[9] In part, having everyone aligned on a transcendent purpose helped to create the entangled organization culture.

Building an Ethical Organization

Our initial discussion on building an ethical foundation focused on the Integrated Project Management Company, Inc. (IPM) because their business is based entirely on leading and guiding the knowledge and actions of others. The twenty-first century is the age of the knowledge worker,[10] and as such, it demands leaders to approach their businesses differently from the past. Rather than being told what to do, employees need and want to be appreciated for the knowledge, unique talents, and gifts for which they were hired. Leaders of entangled organizations embrace this view while also aligning everyone on core values that define the ethical rules underpinning daily actions. A major part of building a high-performing culture rests in the development of a clear mission, a vision, and a set of values that make clear where the organization is going and how it plans to get there.[11]

Explicit core values that focused on respect, trust, ethical conduct, and a customer focus formed the clarion call employees could personally rally behind. Shared values are a differentiating distinction of cultures with high levels of discretionary thinking; value statements invariably addressed how everyone in the organization would show respect for others.[12] Whether the values were hanging on wall charts or printed on pocket-sized laminated cards, everyone in the organizations we studied knew the structure through which they and their organization would treat fellow employees as well as their customers.

Daily actions in support of the values made the set of core values a meaningful pronouncement of what the organization holds dear.[13] For example, personal character stood out as a critical determinant in hiring decisions. Simply said, character is values put into action; thus, hiring people with the right character means ensuring personal values align with core organizational values.[14] Emphasizing this dimension in the hiring process and making it well known to existing employees, customers, and communities, as well as potential candidates, helps attract the right kind of applicants and sends signals that the organization wants the best employees who will fit the culture while serving the community.

Doing what you say you are going to do builds a foundation of trust, which is the foundation for building a relationship between suppliers and customers. Customers trust a supplier to deliver goods or services that meet or exceed their needs and expectations, while the supplier trusts that a customer will pay for those goods and services on time and in full.[15] Without trust, the capitalistic free-market system suffers. Trust stems from the character of individuals who demonstrate trustworthiness by taking responsibility and being accountable for their actions.

Yet building trust takes time. Leaders of entangled organizations understand how trust is built on a *pattern of leadership that demonstrates good character*, such as consistent and continuous acts of responsibility, accountability, fulfilling commitments, caring about their work and those being served, and insisting that each member of the workforce demonstrate the same behaviors. Within entangled organizations, we found caring is a core value for building trust, from which long-term relationships and continuing business evolve.[16]

The loyal relationships that IPM and other companies built with their clientele were possible because of the caring and trust that permeated company philosophies, value sets, and performance. In short, the synergy between personal and organizational values created organizational character, which served as the ethical foundation on which individual and corporate decisions were made.[17]

Focusing All the Human Capital

MidwayUSA was our leading example of an entangled organization that created a focus on defining and setting individual work expectations throughout the organization to create world-class status. By engaging the employees to develop a visionary strategic plan, Larry Potterfield created an outstanding culture of people working together. The senior leaders at MidwayUSA and other companies we studied had inspiring visions about the future of their organizations. In addition, these were shared visions, where cross-functional teams[18] actually worked as equals with the senior leadership team to develop the mission, visions, performance goals, and strategic plans that guided the development and execution of more detailed action plans for processes, units, and individual performance plans.[19]

Engaging cross-functional teams helped eliminate silo thinking, reduce internal conflict and tension, provide better focus on desired outcomes, and elevate thinking about potential solutions. Teams responsible for aligning strategic and operational goals with the organization's vision, mission, and core values had a deeper awareness of the entire organization, which improved decision making and results.[20] Showing support for and confidence in employees' abilities were key components in building trust and extending organizational learning. Employees were encouraged to think critically about their work and the consequences of their decisions, and frontline workers had wide latitude in how they met customer needs.

Setting metrics of performance was a key activity to support organizational focus.[21] In most of the organizations we studied, leadership and cross-functional teams were engaged in setting the primary direction of the organization through the mission, vision, and values and the metrics that assessed progress. For example, Good Samaritan Hospital developed its six pillars and developed goals covering those six pillars. Specific metrics were set for product outcomes (clinical and safety outcomes) and financial outcomes for the organization (to support sustainability). In addition, satisfaction outcomes were articulated for patients, physicians, and the workforce—nurses, staff, and volunteers. MidwayUSA, Mike's Carwash, and Tarlton used similar performance objectives to track their success related to internal and external performance dimensions. The strategic plan evolved from these measures, and the strategic plan needed to be aligned with these measures to keep everyone focused on achieving their key goals.

Linking the action plans to strategic plans and to individual performance metrics was a major preoccupation of the senior leadership team to support the organization focus. The strategic plan provided the framework for growth and innovation for the total organization. The action plans for unit and process improvements were aligned with the overall strategic plan. Mike's Carwash used a balanced scorecard[22] to help employees visualize at all levels how their goals contributed to organizational success. Linking the action plans to individual performance plans is a process consistent with the value of respect. In this process, leaders served as coaches and partners rather than overseers, and they used the aligned set of performance goals as a tool for educating as well as guiding others. MidwayUSA charted unit and individual performance in their call center and order fulfillment center as a way to provide performance feedback to employees.

Having this set of *cascading performance metrics that align with the main objectives of the organization* is a necessary element to create the entangled organization. In this process, each member of the organization understands the importance of his or her role in helping the organization reach its goals. This creates the intimacy of experience where a call-center employee at Midway can say, "I made a difference in my customer's satisfaction" or, in order fulfillment, an employee can say, "I helped this organization serve the customer because I did my job well today."[23] This clarity in understanding one's role in organizational and performance expectations helped to guide performance and provide a benchmark for employees to assess the quality of their own behaviors.[24]

Using Processes to Guide Performance

Many organizations face geographic dispersion as a fact of life. Tarlton Construction served as our primary example of dispersed work teams with managers and construction workers operating wherever construction projects exist. Integrated Project Management faces a similar challenge. Managers in geographically dispersed units use process maps to define and delineate step-by-step processes for delivering results. These tools helped managers ensure consistency in actions and achieve specific goals, regardless of the physical location of those responsible for getting the job done.

However, process maps are not just used for organizations with dispersed work groups; MidwayUSA has 1,500 defined processes to help them better meet the needs of customers. Process mapping and management are a central part of understanding and focusing on the key things an organization does. They help guide performance of individuals and groups and provide greater assurance that the activity will be completely done as each step in the process is followed.

Defining the key processes in the organization is a first step in understanding the key things the organization does. The Baldrige approach is focused primarily on the notion that the organization should be viewed as an integrated set of processes and the only way to effectively manage the organization.[25] Only by defining itself can the organization effectively improve performance.

Managing and improving processes is a second step to a fuller understanding of what the organization is all about. Once processes are defined, it becomes clearer to existing and new members of the organization what the big picture is and what their role is in contributing to that picture. In addition, performance metrics can be constructed for each step in each process; these metrics help staff assess items such as error rate (process reliability), cycle time, cost, process capacity and potential bottlenecks, and measures of satisfaction for either internal or external customers. Having these measures makes it easier to understand each person's role in the process and their performance expectations. Because these are well defined and aligned to organization performance, an employee may be engaged to look for ways to improve both the process and the performance measures if a culture exists that supports discretionary thinking and employee involvement in innovation. So defining processes and setting metrics of performance for these processes is another part of focusing the organization.

Increasing an Individual's Self-Efficacy

North Lawndale Employment Network and Sweet Beginnings added another important element to creating an entangled organization—namely, the importance of the person and increasing his or her self-efficacy.[26] Individuals need to be confident and perceive that they have the ability to succeed at what they are doing. For an organization to develop entangled employees, *the focus must begin with the individual.* This is

consistent with the principle of building a set of values in the organization that stresses the respect due the dignity of each person. As Vince
Lombardi said: "The spirit, the will to win, and the will to excel are the
things that endure. These qualities are so much more important than
the events that occur."[27] The will to excel is there; it just takes support
from leaders, the team, or friends to help the person find that will. This
begins with building trust, which comes with a pattern of behaviors that
demonstrate to the person and to others that one deserves to be trusted.
Leaders support people, encourage them, and lead by example.

How are self-confidence and esteem developed? Leaders
who want to nurture self-confidence and self-efficacy in the workforce
must begin by creating reachable goals for their employees, then boldly
recognizing and rewarding them when they achieve those goals. As a pattern of reaching basic goals emerges, the bar gets higher—with praise for
achievement, not just for reaching the goal but progress toward the goal
and so on. Self-efficacy and esteem are developed over time from patterns
of success.[28] A leader can support that pattern of success through systematic goal setting, counseling, mentoring, and training on how to reach the
goals, as well as acknowledgment of performance improvement.

Creating this sort of culture builds the spirit to win and the will to
excel. The desire is to create the internal mind-set that Walter Payton
had when he stated, "I want to be remembered as the guy who gave his
all whenever he was on the field."[29] The entangled culture creates self-
efficacy and esteem and encourages employees to give their all through
personal encouragement, training, realistic goal setting, and clear performance expectations, all while creating an ethical culture of respect
and of valuing the employee.

Giving Employees Freedom and Responsibility Within a Culture of Discipline

Another common feature within entangled organizations that emerged
in our study was that all employees had freedom to exercise their

individual responsibilities within a culture of discipline that was understood, appreciated, nurtured, and protected. Although entangled leaders defined their cultures of discipline differently, the culture set boundaries within which each person could contribute ideas freely.

The culture of discipline comes from knowing expectations and what needs to be done—goal setting, processes, and performance metrics—and an allegiance to the team and the organization. Leaders throughout an organization share responsibility for defining, building, nurturing, and protecting the unique culture that emerges over time. Leaders throughout the entangled organizations we examined enacted the culture through a well-defined purpose and value set; built the culture by hiring the right people with the right character, desire, talents, and skills; nurtured the culture through training and development; protected the culture by strengthening and developing quality leadership; and advanced the legacy of the culture through long-term, trustful relationships. In short, entangled employees live their lives more fully because their work and the environment in which they choose to work align closely with their personal values and identity.

But how are freedom and responsibility within a culture of discipline systematically created? It starts with defining each employee's role and performance expectations, which establish the area of responsibility. This is what we emphasized in the chapter about Tasty Catering. Discipline relates to the culture of what is appropriate conduct. Ethical conduct and appropriate treatment of customers, peers, suppliers, leaders, and subordinates help to define what is meant by personal discipline.[30]

Freedom may be the more difficult element. By freedom we mean that the individual is free to exhibit discretionary thinking, act to best reach his or her performance goals, and help the organization excel.

To build the discipline of freedom and responsibility, the organization must hire not just on skills and technical competence, but on attitudes and character as well. Leaders work to develop and encourage employees' viewpoints to show how leaders value and engage different perspectives. Leaders also acknowledge behaviors that demonstrate the "will to excel." This is an essential part of creating the entangled organization.

Hardwiring Discretionary Thinking and Actions

A 2011 Gallup poll of "engaged" employees indicated that about one-third of employees in most organizations are engaged, while the remaining two-thirds are either not engaged (51–53 percent) or are actively (19 percent) disengaged.[31] Actively disengaged employees undermine the organization with the capability of destroying it if left unchecked, much as a cancer attacks and eats away at the human body. The 2011 poll also showed how highly educated and middle-aged workers are less likely to be engaged in their work.[32] Numerous articles and recent books have addressed the engaged employee, but entangled organizations go well beyond engagement.

By hardwiring we mean that we create the structures and behaviors in the organization to support the kind of culture that will result in employee commitment and engagement that ultimately yield the entangled organization. The goal is to make discretionary thinking and action an established part of everyday thinking so that the entangled culture will transcend the change in leaders and employees over time. We have already covered many of the elements, but in order to hardwire them, the organization needs to define them as policies and practices and write them down. This is similar to what many of the organizations that we studied, such as Mike's Carwash, have done. They make it clear to everyone the importance of building the kind of culture that supports employees' active involvement in quality service and innovations to improve the organization. This structure was evident in the Good to Great Council at Tasty Catering, the use of huddles at SRC, and the Process Improvement Teams at MidwayUSA.

The structure is also in the policies. For example, many organizations include a policy that staff conduct a postmortem after successful as well as unsuccessful major events to determine what went right and what needs to be improved.[33] As was done at Good Samaritan and IPM, a need exists to encourage workers to report mistakes so that processes can be changed and be less prone to error. The goal is to hardwire each process while encouraging open discussions on how structures and behaviors can be changed to improve the organization.[34]

A process to acknowledge and celebrate individual successes, adopted ideas, or unit improvements needs to be made permanent and "hardwired" to encourage further improvements and keep ideas flowing. Leaders must make clear to all that they value each person's contribution to improve the organization and that they desire to support discretionary thinking and actions. Encouragement is a day-to-day process throughout any entangled organization.[35]

Guiding the Transformation Process to Remarkable Performance

The transformational process from being a good organization to one that is great required the encouragement to "rework" failures while celebrating successes. For example, Good Samaritan Hospital moved from being a quality hospital to a world-class hospital through a series of progressive improvements over several years. Good Samaritan's leaders applied several process improvement and strategic planning approaches, most recently focusing on an integrative management systems approach using the Baldrige criteria—the same criteria that MidwayUSA and others embraced.[36]

The transformation process begins with the end in mind. The senior leadership team needs to have both an understanding of and an agreement about where they want to go. From knowing where they want to go and the metrics they will use to know how they are progressing, leaders can articulate strategies to get there, along with resultant action plans to help focus the efforts. Some of the strategies would focus on developing the structures and behaviors to support the change, including the need for new hires who would contribute to the transformation, how to develop and train workers in the new approach, and the actions leaders would take to support the needed changed behaviors.

The transformation process is incremental in most cases, so the culture must change with the transformation because "culture trumps strategy" all the time.[37] Creating the entangled organization will take time because building trust, self-efficacy, and discretionary thinking and action involves continual and dedicated effort, as we saw in the organizations we studied. While transformation may not be a quick fix, it nevertheless leads to a fantastic return to the leaders, employees, and customers as well as the sustainability of the organization.

The Synergyism and Magnetism of an Entangled Culture

This section connects the "what we can learn" section that concluded each chapter into an inclusive web. We might even suggest that you turn the following pages into a plan for managing your career and life perspectives since what you do within a profession, career, or job is elemental to your well-being. Whether you are a CEO, an owner, a department manager, or a project team leader, you must acknowledge that change starts with a single step.

We should all work to create enriching experiences that bring joy and delight rather than boredom or dissatisfaction to those who depend on our leadership. Although controlling the external environment is impossible given uncertain futures, as leaders we can ensure that our lives have a positive impact on others with whom we share the journey. The following recommendations should help you do just that.

1. **Strive to become an extraordinary leader.** Regardless of your area of responsibility, treat everyone with respect, encourage input in decisions, take time to listen to others' ideas, and help

others develop their critical thinking skills, which will improve their confidence and personal efficacy. You will learn more by listening than by telling others what to do. In the long run, your efforts in building disciplined teams will solve more issues and improve the quality of decisions and actions. Managing your own behavior as a leader, such as being patient and consistent, is the first priority for obtaining desired outcomes.

2. **Build an ethical organization.** Being honest and transparent are critical traits for building trust with employees and customers. To engage greater discretionary thinking and action, leaders must first show they sincerely care for followers; uncaring leaders lose the trust and credibility they need in order to lead. An ethical organization begins with shared core values that must include respect and an unwavering commitment to ethical conduct. Leaders and followers alike must live those values, reinforce good conduct, and immediately correct behaviors that violate standards. Ethical codes alone are insufficient; periodic customer audits must validate that everyone is fulfilling commitments for doing the right things.

3. **Align efforts through a well-defined organizational purpose and strategic direction.** Vision, mission, and core values statements focus employee efforts and increase commitment when these elements of organizational purpose are inseparable from daily practices. A living strategic plan provides direction, and supporting action plans guide individual and team performances toward goals. Well-defined metrics help employees measure and gauge their progress toward those goals. Incentives and compensation systems that reinforce positive gains and desired performance further clarify the actions that employees at all levels need to support. Recognizing discretionary thinking and actions through timely feedback leads to innovative ideas and more demonstrations of discretionary thinking, which strengthens a growth climate.

4. **Use process mapping to guide performance.** There is a dearth of understanding about the importance of organizational processes, which contributes to the waste and inefficiencies within the majority of American businesses. Process management is a critical building block for innovation, continuous improvement, and company growth. Leaders can build a more collaborative culture by recognizing, defining, and communicating the unit processes critical for fulfilling the organization's mission. Managers must pay close attention to time, cost, errors, capacity, and customer responsiveness, but it is the employees executing those processes who have a direct impact on customer satisfaction and future buying decisions.

5. **Build self-efficacy and confidence.** Employee confidence is critical for building discretionary thinking. Confidence begins with one-on-one leadership that sets and communicates SMART goals,[38] solicits input for improving organizational practices, and consistently develops employee competences through which they will be able to accept greater responsibility for outcomes. Greater participation leads to improved engagement and commitment, which lead to the entangled organization. Leaders who complain that building self-efficacy is not their job don't deserve to lead. Leaders have the responsibility to teach and guide the next generation of leaders and create a learning culture that supports high performance.

6. **Foster individual freedom and responsibility within the culture of discipline.** The whole notion of the entangled organization, one that values high discretionary thinking and actions, depends on an environment in which individual employees understand their roles and the behavioral expectations of their circle of discipline. Defining job scope, responsibilities, and performance expectations through individual performance and action plans creates the circle of discipline. With this clarity, each employee has the freedom to make discretionary choices on how work will be done to meet his or her responsibilities and performance expectations.

7. **Hardwire discretionary thinking throughout the culture.**
Leaders cannot mandate or demand discretionary thinking; it stems from the personal decisions employees make through their perceptions of their culture and leadership. Hardwired discretionary thinking occurs in collaborative cultures with supportive structures and leaders who welcome new ideas, share decision making, recognize efforts publicly, and emphasize the value of contributions from employees at all levels. Embedding discretionary thinking in organizational culture requires leaders who know that no one person has all the answers. Public recognition of the results of discretionary thinking supports the importance of this behavior to the organization. Making it a policy hardwires the approach.

8. **Guide the transformation process.** Transformation occurs through iterative actions of continuous change and growth. Building trust, focusing efforts, and defining processes and process performance should be developed in parallel as a concerted strategy to develop an entangled culture. Creating and nurturing the right culture and developing others as capable contributors require actions on multiple fronts. Moving from clear purpose to well-defined processes, a comprehensive planning and execution system, alignment of goals with strategy, effective deployment of capabilities, and incentive/recognition programs that reward behaviors effectively requires dedicated effort and unwavering commitment to positive change. In short, transformation requires coming full circle to the demand for extraordinary personal leadership followed by extraordinary leadership throughout the organization. Transformation takes time and patience, but it has significant benefits for the organization and its stakeholders.

A Story of Entanglement to End On

Steve Schwartz is a seventeen-year veteran of the cardiac catheterization team at Good Samaritan Hospital, where he plays a critical role in saving lives of heart attack victims. When a heart attack patient arrives in the hospital, doctors and their teams must rush the patient to the cardiac cath lab to restore heart rhythm and blood flow, which many times means getting a clogged cardiac artery open with a balloon the size of a pencil head. How quickly the doctor inflates the balloon determines how fast blood flow returns to a weakened heart and how much permanent damage the heart muscle sustains—if the patient lives, that is. Reducing the minutes it takes to get a patient from the emergency room door to an inflated balloon is critical in saving lives.

When Steve suffered a shoulder injury that disabled him for three months, he could not sit back and relax. Although physically separated from his team—his closest friends and the pride of his life—Steve was constantly thinking about ways he could still be part of the team. Limited in what he could do, Steve spent hours at the computer each day researching the latest advances in cardiac catheterization.

He came across the trans-radial approach, which was being used extensively in Europe. The U.S. standard at the time was the femoral approach in which a catheter was inserted through the femoral artery in the groin area and inched up to the clogged artery. Unfortunately, this process has several potential complications, such as femoral aneurysms or arterial bleeds, which can be fatal. The trans-radial approach uses the wrist as the catheter's entry point instead; it is faster and more effective because complications from radial artery insertions are less serious, the most prominent being loss of a radial artery pulse in less than four percent of reported cases.

When he returned to work, Steve shared his research with his supervisor, Stacey Prentis, who encouraged him to bring his ideas forward. Convincing doctors—especially those entrenched with past successes from the femoral artery process—to accept the viability of this newer, radical technique would not be easy. Steve had to present an ironclad, scientific slideshow with lots of data and examples of real-life success.

According to Dr. Stephen Rowley, chief of cardiology at Good Samaritan, some physicians can be skeptical and prone to say, "We're the doctors, you're not, and we'll let you know if this is a good idea." Yet Rowley, who had been using femoral artery catheterizations with success as standard practice for twenty years, appreciated Steve's application of discretionary thinking as a fellow scientist. Rowley's view reflected Good Samaritan's culture, where openness to new ideas for improving the quality of patient care trumps a staff member's position, seniority, job title, or professional background. Good Samaritan's door-to-balloon time with the femoral approach was less than an hour, which was already lower than other hospitals in the area and the state. The new process would reduce this time further while also reducing patient risks, thanks to the dedication of a fully entangled employee who kept thinking about a challenge even when "off the job." The result of Steve's research, the culture that supported the notion that each person is a member of the team, and the physicians who were focused on improving quality led to a procedural change that saves lives.

The impact of Steve's dedication is telling, and in Good Samaritan's case, it's a matter of human life. The accepted risk-adjusted mortality rate for Illinois hospitals is 1.0. Seven years ago, Good Samaritan's rate was an acceptable .91, but today's rate of .31[39] is so far below the national average that fellow professionals are noting the quality of Good Samaritan's clinical outcomes.

Based on our research to date, the entangled organization is not a destination but rather a continuous journey toward performance excellence. As each milestone is met and each goal is achieved, entangled employees set their sights on new horizons and greater achievements in such a way that the vision is never fully achieved. In short, entangled organizations, much like the employees entangled within their webs of influence, such as Steve Schwartz, never fully self-actualize because "something better" is always in the distance as they strive to give their all while embracing the attitude, "It's my company too!"

We learned that entangled organizations come in all shapes and sizes and are in different states of evolution. For MidwayUSA and Advocate Good Samaritan Hospital, the journey has taken employees to an envied level of performance excellence, but their position is relative. Dave Fox shared how Good Samaritan has gone through only two iterations of excellence; the next level will seek to eliminate all forms of negativity that detract from running at their highest levels of efficiency and effectiveness.[40] But how much better can they be? Only time and their efforts will tell. What we do know with certainty is that entangled organizations are high performers and that we can all learn from them.[41]

Within these pages, we have shared a limited number of stories from the hundreds we have heard. In sharing these stories, we've attempted to describe how entangled organizations, regardless of their size, have harnessed the power of discretionary thinking and, in that process, have created their unique competitive advantage. These are world-class organizations with respect to the quality of the product or service, financial performance, customer satisfaction, and employee satisfaction and engagement. It was an exciting experience for us to research these organizations and offer their success stories to you in the pages of *It's My Company Too!* We hope you gain as much as we did through this process.

OVERVIEW OF ORGANIZATIONS INCLUDED IN THIS STUDY

Advocate Health Care: Good Samaritan Hospital

Good Samaritan Hospital is part of Advocate Health Care, the largest health system in the state of Illinois. It is an acute-care medical facility in Downers Grove, Illinois, that has evolved during the past thirty-five years from a midsized community hospital to a nationally recognized leader in health care. Good Samaritan Hospital features DuPage County's only Level I trauma center and certified Level III neonatal intensive care unit.

Noted for cancer care, women and children's services, and surgical services, Good Samaritan Hospital received the American Nurses Credentialing Center Magnet® designation, the highest level of recognition awarded to nursing excellence in national and international health care. With a workforce of 2,700 associates, 500 volunteers, and 950 independent physicians representing 59 specialties, this 333-bed facility is only one of a few health-care organizations in the nation to receive the Malcolm Baldrige National Quality Award.

Contributors from Advocate Good Samaritan Hospital and its affiliates included David Fox, Leslie Allgeyer, Mitch Ashcroft, Janet Belinski, Jim Christian, Sandy Churchill, Dr. Stephen Crouch, Dr. Charles Derus, Usha Dunn, Teri Evans, Peggy Farrell (RN), Kathleen Forner, Aeran Garcia, Annette Goetz, Gail Gotsis, Donna Iverson, Marie Levy (RN),

Dr. Barbara Loeb, Dina Loughlin, Marjorie Maurer (RN), Mickey Nottoli (RN), Dr. Jeffrey Oken, Kim Osinaike, Jodi Overbeck, Stacey Prentis, Dr. Stephen Rowley, Stephen Schwartz, Joseph Sibu, Jim Silvestri, Pattie Skriba, Marian Sorce, Dr. Donald Steiner, Dory Stipetic, Laura Taylor, Dr. Vibhaben Thaker, Paula Timmerman (RN), and Mary Ann Zabel.

IPM (Integrated Project Management Company, Inc.)

C. Richard Panico, the founder, president, and CEO of Integrated Project Management Company, Inc. (IPM), established the firm in 1988 with the goal of building a company based on honesty, integrity, and ethical precepts. With this foundation, Rich envisioned a service-focused company that would execute projects reliably and efficiently—a quality he felt was sorely lacking in the industry. Today IPM's application of process, discipline, and leadership in the project management framework assures execution of the organization's most critical initiatives.

Beyond its project management expertise, IPM's real competitive advantage comes from values-driven, self-motivated, and highly skilled employees, the company's most important asset. The award-winning culture sets the company apart from others through values-based leadership, honesty, integrity, courage, and the ability to inspire. These same principles are apparent as the company has contributed to, and continues to engage in, programs that positively influence the world in which we live.

Contributors from IPM included C. Richard Panico, Karen Heiting, Jill Cochrane, Scott Grzesiak, Joann Jackson, Mike McLeod, Larry Meyer, Mike Moody, Andy Myslicki, Jeff Mumford, Rob Neufelder, and Adam Wojcik.

MidwayUSA

MidwayUSA is a "brick and mortar" catalog and Internet retailer of sporting goods, carrying merchandise related to shooting and hunting and other outdoor products. Established in 1977, this family-owned and -operated company employs more than four hundred individuals and has its headquarters in Columbia, Missouri. The company's vision—"To be the best-run business in America, for the benefit of our customers, by systematically applying the modern leadership and management principles from the Baldrige Criteria for Performance Excellence"—provides a great insight into the organization's DNA.

MidwayUSA constantly strives to achieve its goals of customer satisfaction, employee satisfaction, vendor satisfaction, and shareholder satisfaction, and the accompanying key stakeholder requirements. These goals, along with the results from their key measures, are key components of MidwayUSA's strategic planning process. MidwayUSA is ISO certified 9001:2008, a 2008 recipient of the Missouri Quality Award, and a 2009 recipient of the Baldrige National Quality Award.

Contributors from MidwayUSA included Larry Potterfield, Brenda Potterfield, Sara Potterfield, Linda Bounds, Stephanie Buckner, William Burke, Jared Carlow, Josh Costello, Jake Dablemont, Erin Evans, Joel Felten, Matt Fleming, John Franklin, Stan Frink, Jim Golden, Delilah Griffin, Stacey Hargrove, Deanna Herwald, Krystal Higgins, Scott Keel, Nic Klein, Kevin Kleindienst, Carson Lepper, Dave Loucks, Courtney Lybarger, Bob McNulty, Aaron Oelger, Andrew Owenby, Doug Ragland, Adam Ray, Kerri Ross, Brett Russell, Patrick Shay, Katie Smith, Jim Swofford, Stacey Uptegrove, Bridget Whetstine, and Eddie Wirths.

Mike's Carwash

Founded by Joe Dahm, Mike's Carwash is a private, family-owned business. Mike's Carwash specializes in exterior-only automated carwashes complete with self-serve car care products and other services available for the interior. The first Mike's opened in 1948 in Fort Wayne, Indiana, and today allows customers to get their cars clean, dry, and shiny, at any of their forty locations.

No matter the location, Mike's Carwash utilizes two essential components that have been proven to fuel their success. First, customers will consistently get clean, dry, and shiny vehicles on each visit, courtesy of state-of-the-art equipment and technology. Second, and most important, Mike's Carwash hires and trains only the best candidates for employment, creating team members who embody professionalism and personality on a daily basis. Customers frequently tell Mike's Carwash that they keep coming back because of the way they are treated by the six hundred caring team members.

Contributors from Mike's Carwash included Bill Dahm, Mike Burleson, James Flett, Mike Heidenreich, Sarah Keller, Gretchen Koch, Brandon Mitchell, Christine Peacock, Joe Rice, Billy Schaming, Drew Schmutte, and David Zapp.

North Lawndale Employment Network (NLEN)/Sweet Beginnings

The North Lawndale Employment Network (NLEN) has one goal: to aid North Lawndale residents in gaining economic advancement and an improved quality of life through innovative employment. Founded in 1999 through an eighteen-month community planning effort led by the Steans Family Foundation, NLEN aims to serve the unmet employment needs of individuals with significant barriers to employment in the North Lawndale community. NLEN addresses extremely high rates of unemployment and underemployment by offering employment services and transitional jobs to residents, many of whom are formerly incarcerated persons and others with barriers to employment. NLEN is committed to assisting those with these barriers—especially former offenders—in securing jobs with family-supporting wages, partnering with employers in recruiting and retaining workers, advocating on behalf of low-income job-seekers, empowering job seekers with access to financial tools and literacy, and creating a thriving and sustainable community.

Contributors from NLEN included Brenda Palms Barber, Holly Blackwell, Dr. Dennis Deer, John Hansen, Felicia Griffin, Dr. Richard

Kordesh, Michael Malacek, Coretta Rivers, Pauline Sylvain, Ron Tonn, Jose Wilson, Elesha W., and Sterling G.

Springfield Remanufacturing Corporation (SRC)

In 1983 Jack Stack and twelve business partners scraped together $100,000 and borrowed another $8.9 million to buy one of International Harvester's divisions. The future looked bleak for the Springfield, Missouri–based engine-rebuilding plant they called Springfield Remanufacturing Corporation (SRC). With hundreds of jobs on the line and morale at an all-time low, Stack knew he had to do something drastic to keep the business afloat: He turned the business into a game based on open-book management, a concept that Stack later described as "The Great Game of Business" (GGOB). Through GGOB, SRC has become a thriving company of over 1,200 employees in more than 17 business units across a variety of industries. For thirty-one years, SRC has been remanufacturing products for the agricultural, industrial, construction, truck, marine, and automotive markets, with success after success as the oldest employee-owned remanufacturer to original equipment manufacturers (OEMs) in North America. SRC is known worldwide for an open-book culture that espouses transparency, integrity, and economic literacy, which is the way all areas of the company do business and prefer to do business with others.

Contributors from SRC included Jack Stack, Rich Armstrong, Neil Chambers, Jeff DeCarlis, Jeremy Dodd, Ron Guinn, Becky Lane, Mike Lofton, and Rodney Swope.

Tarlton Corporation

Tarlton Corporation is a St. Louis–based, privately held business providing general contracting and construction management services. Formed in 1946, this WBENC-certified Women's Business Enterprise serves a wide range of clients in the institutional, life sciences, federal government, power, industrial, and commercial markets, as well as concrete repair and restoration. Tarlton's projects range from $10,000 to $150 million in both new construction and complex renovations, led by teams that thrive on meeting unique construction challenges. Tarlton is consistently recognized not only for its award-winning projects, outstanding safety record, and top-notch reputation in the subcontractor community, but also for its industry leadership and civic involvement. The firm is ranked in *Engineering News–Record*'s Top 400 Contractors, and has been named a "Winning Workplace" for its demonstrated commitment to employee education, health, and well-being. Tarlton's expertise in sustainable construction and operations is showcased in its LEED Silver headquarters.

Contributors from Tarlton Corporation included Tracy Hart, Bryce Cooper, John Doerr, Dirk Elsperman, Bob Elsperman, Dan Fahey, Rick Finnerty, Scott Green, Ted Guhr, Wanda Hill, Chris Kestner, Andy Kovarik, Angela Lovatto, Jeff Moore, Steve Moore, Kevin Oakley, Matt Pfund, Staci Piasecki, Donny Provance, and Sondra Rotty.

Tasty Catering

Tasty Catering is more than the typical catering company; it is really a service company that specializes in corporate catering, event planning, and event production. The company has been serving the needs of suburban Chicago organizations for more than twenty years. With a strong, company-wide foundation in core values, all 250 full-time, part-time, and seasonal employees are committed to the same goals and morals.

A growing reputation for quality food and quality people has given Tasty Catering a set of very important market differentiators. Tasty Catering is the whole package, from delivering coffee and tea in the morning for a breakfast meeting, all the way up to planning and executing a thousand-person, grilled, on-site picnic. They populate each and every event they perform with exceptional food and exceptional staff, from the initial order all the way to the cleanup, exceeding expectations of clients and guests alike.

Contributors from Tasty Catering included Tom Walter, Larry Walter, Kevin Walter, Kristen Banks, Shari Brown, Chris Buczkowski, Fabiola Cerecero, Devonne Coleman, Molly Evans, Ricardo Gervacio, Julie Goosetree, Kornel Grygo, Ellen Harte, Karen Holden, Jim Mullen, Patrick Pankiw, Jamie Pritscher, Raul Ramirez, Eddie Rios, Eugene Rios, Dan Rogers, Katie Rynott, Kari Sobaski, Jesse Vazquez, Alfredo Velazquez, Delia Velazquez-Castro, Effrian Velazquez, Mike Walter, Tim Walter, Anna Wollin, and advisers Julie Baron, Chef Joe D'Alessandro, Sheri Kagan, John Pankau, and John Rudy.

ACKNOWLEDGMENTS

Ken Thompson, PhD, Acknowledgments

I dedicate this book to my loving wife, Ann, and my two children, Tracey and Wesley, for all the love and joy they bring into my life. I also thank my mentor, teacher, and friend, Fred Luthans, who believed in me and continues to believe in me.

Ray Benedetto, DM, Acknowledgments

When I began the research journey several years ago that served as the genesis for this book, little did I realize how far or how broad the concept of "character" was that would lead me and eventually my fellow authors, Tom, Ken, and Molly, to this point. Inspiration comes in many ways, and over the years God put remarkable people in my path at the right moment; to say this journey has been a test or lesson in faith is an understatement.

Most important, I am grateful for the many leaders God put before me and us to reinforce the importance of ethical leadership, especially Tom Walter and his brothers Larry and Kevin, who welcomed my research proposal because of their own beliefs in the power of character within organizations. I thank Ken Thompson and Molly Meyer for their patience, dedication, and fortitude as we moved to the book phase. I continue to learn from them and more recent entrants into my circle of influence, like Rich Panico, Dave Fox, Jack Stack, Fred Luthans, and Bo Burlingham.

My bride of forty-one years has been my steadfast support through years of study and research; Joan's love, patience, and understanding—especially with my weird work hours and passion—have been the sustaining power behind my portion of this project. I also thank our children and their spouses—Andrea and Luke, Jason and Brandy, Julie and Russ, and our dearly missed Stacey—as well as our grandchildren Lauren, Abby, Nick, Victoria, Anthony, Gigi, and Jayce for the love and joy with which they fill my life. I dedicate this book to all of them, but especially to the memory of Stacey, who was always interested in the impact of my work.

I must also thank Dr. Linda Wing, my mentor and friend, for without her influence I would not have developed into the ethnographer I have become. Similarly, the Greenleaf Book Group Press team is another great blessing; without the support and shared belief in this book from Lari Bishop, Bryan Carroll, Linda O'Doughda, and Hobbs Allison, our message would not be in print.

May God bless each and every one of you abundantly for the gifts you have shared to make *It's My Company Too!* a reality rather than simply a dream.

Tom Walter Acknowledgments

I am extremely grateful and indebted to my precious bride Bobbi, who has endured with my entrepreneurial craziness for more than forty years. No other person has had a greater influence in my life. I am a proud parent of two children, Erin and Tim (and his wife Peggy), who must have listened to the dinner table discussions because they have both become entrepreneurs. I also am deeply grateful to my brothers/partners, Larry and Kevin, who have been with me for the long ride of both failure and success.

Every day at work is enjoyable because I am surrounded by incredible associates whose brilliance and teamwork never cease to amaze me.

The members of the Small Giants Community have been a recent source of inspiration. These are worldwide business owners who choose to be great, not necessarily big. Bo Burlingham's book *Small Giants* validated why I felt our companies should remain small and intimate, yet be high performance. The authors from the Small Giants Community have written the most appropriate business books for small to midsized businesses and have had a profound impact on my approach to entrepreneurship.

Thank you also to the folks at Greenleaf Book Group: Hobbs Allison, Lari Bishop, Bryan Carroll, and so many more.

We appreciate the efforts exerted by Julie Baron of Communication Works, Sandra Diaz of Smith Publicity, and the folks at nuphoriq for creating the marketing and publicity for *It's My Company Too!*.

Crafting this book with Ken, Ray, and Molly has been an enriching experience: four authors, four approaches, one result—sometimes stressful, most of the time fun, but always enriching. We drilled deep into eight amazing companies led by some very inspirational leaders. Learning how these leaders engaged their employees and captured their discretionary thoughts was very inspiring.

Molly Meyer Acknowledgments

It would be silly for me not to begin by thanking the three authors of this book who not only took a chance on committing to a relatively raw, young person to this project, but made her such a large part of the process and result. To Ray and Ken, thank you for your intelligence, guidance, expertise, and constant communication over the past two years. To Tom, thank you for raising me in a culture of service leadership, for believing in the talents of my generation, and for voicing your beliefs loudly to all. I hope that all young people have someone to light their path as brightly as you have lit mine.

To my family, thank you for nurturing me to be a competitive, driven, hard-working being. I am grateful every day that you raised me with a sense of humor and the ability to see things through others' eyes.

To my coworkers at nuphoriq, you have given me an outlet in more ways than I can count. When I needed consulting, consoling, coaching, and more, you've given it to me willingly. Thank you for your support and understanding throughout this long process.

And finally, a girl is lucky to have met and continue to meet terrific people around the world that truly inspire. I happen to be one of the lucky ones who has collected and continues to collect precious life experiences that result in emotional and intellectual growth each and every day. To individually name everyone would be impossible, but to acknowledge their spirit and memory is necessary. Thank you.

NOTES

Introduction

1 See J. H. Fleming, C. Coffman, and J. K. Harter, "Manage Your Human Sigma," *Harvard Business Review* 83, no.7/8 (July–August 2005): 107–114, as well as R. M. Kanter, "How Great Companies Think Differently," *Harvard Business Review* 89, no.11 (November 2011): 66–78, and the discussion about Southwest Airlines' approach to labor relations in A. Beard, R. Hornik, H. Wang, M. Ennes, E. Rush, and S. Presnal, "It's Hard to Be Good," *Harvard Business Review* 89, no.11 (November 2011): 91–92.

2 The Institute for Health and Human Potential is a consulting organization that stated this claim, and several other sources have picked up the quote, but it is unclear if this claim is based on empirical evidence or just stated estimates.

3 See L. Buchanan, "Things They Do for Love," *Harvard Business Review* 82, no. 12 (December 2004): 19.

4 See K. Sheridan, *Building a Magnetic Culture: How to Attract and Retain Top Talent to Create an Engaged, Productive Workforce* (New York: McGraw Hill, 2012).

5 See W. E. Deming, *The New Economics for Industry, Government, Education* (Cambridge: Massachusetts Institute of Technology Center for Advanced Engineering Study, 1993).

Chapter 1

1   Jack Stack and Bo Burlingham, *A Stake in the Outcome* (New York: Currency-Random House, 2003).

2   For a full description, see the book by the same name: Jack Stack and Bo Burlingham, *The Great Game of Business* (New York: Currency-Doubleday, 1992).

3   Bo Burlingham, "America's Top 25 Most Fascinating Entrepreneurs," http://www.inc.com/magazine/20040401/25stack.html.

4   For more information, see the Great Game of Business website at: http://greatgame.com/.

5   For more information, see SRC's website at: http://srcreman.com/.

Chapter 2

1   The source for this data is the IPM 2009 Project Performance Client Survey and Evaluation (Leadership).

2   The source for this data is the IPM 2009 Project Performance Client Survey and Evaluation (Schedule).

3   For a broader discussion of freedom within a culture of discipline, see Jim Collins, *Good to Great: Why Some Companies Make the Leap . . . and Others Don't* (New York: HarperCollins, 2001).

4   For more insights on how everyday companies become extraordi-
     nary performers, see Keith McFarland's *The Breakthrough Company*
     (New York: Crown Business, 2008).

5   For a deeper discussion of organizational culture within the Ameri-
     can workplace, see the work of G. Neilson, B. A. Pasternack,
     and D. Mendes, "The Seven Types of Organizational DNA,"
     Strategy+business no.35 (Summer 2004): 95–103.

6   For more on corporate values, see R. Van Lee, L. Fabish, and N.
     McGaw, "The Value of Corporate Values," *Strategy+business* no.39
     (Summer 2005): 52–65.

7   For more on values in the workplace and ethical behavior, see
     A. Argandoña, "Fostering Values in Organizations," *Journal of
     Business Ethics* 45, no. 1/2, part 2 (2003): 15–28, and R. Chun,
     "Ethical Character and Virtue of Organizations: An Empirical
     Assessment and Strategic Implications," *Journal of Business Ethics*
     57, no. 3 (2005): 269–284.

8   For a deeper discussion and understanding of ethical leadership
     behaviors, see R. R. Sims and J. Brinkmann, "Leaders as Moral
     Role Models: The Case of John Gutfreund at Salomon Brothers,"
     Journal of Business Ethics 35, no. 4 (2002): 327–339.

9   For more on market leadership, see M. Treacy and F. Wiersema,
     "Customer Intimacy and Other Value Disciplines," *Harvard Business
     Review* 71, no.1 (January–February 1993): 84–93, and M. Treacy
     and F. Wiersema, *The Discipline of Market Leaders: Choose Your Custom-
     ers, Narrow Your Focus, Dominate Your Market* (Reading, MA: Addison-
     Wesley, 1995).

10   See Collins (2001) for additional details.

11   For more on codes of ethics, see M. S. Schwartz, "A Code of Ethics for Corporate Code of Ethics," *Journal of Business Ethics* 41, no. 1 (2002): 27–43.

12   See J. L. Badaracco, "The Discipline of Character," *Harvard Business Review* 76, no. 2 (March–April 1998): 114–124.

Chapter 3

1   See Malcolm Gladwell's *The Tipping Point: How Little Things Can Make a Big Difference* (Boston: Back Bay Books, 2002).

2   A Baldrige examiner acts as a reviewer of applications for organizations that have applied for Baldrige consideration. The training process involves forty hours of reviewing an application with thirty-three hours of training. Many organizations send their employees to obtain Baldrige training as examiners so that they better understand the Baldrige process and what examiners look for as they review applications and make site visits.

3   See Lawrence James, Lois James, and Donna Ashe, "The Role of Cognition and Values," in Benjamin Schneider, ed., *Organization Climate and Culture* (San Francisco: Jossey-Bass, 1990) 40–85.

4   See MidwayUSA's Baldrige Application at http://www.baldrige .nist.gov/PDF_files/MidwayUSA_Award_Application_Summary .pdf. The strategic planning process is described in section 2.1 on page 6.

5   A partner is any organization or individual working in concert with the organization, such as a supplier.

6   For a good discussion on this relationship see Mark Blazey, *Insights to Performance Excellence 2011–2012: Understanding the Integrated Management System and Baldrige* (Milwaukee, WI: ASQ Press, 2011) 12–296.

7   *Shooting sports* refers to target, skeet, and clay shooting as well as hunting with rifles.

8   See Section 7.5 of MidwayUSA's Baldrige Application Summary for levels and trends of key measures and indicators related to operational performance of work systems within the company.

9   See Mark Blazey, *Insights to Performance Excellence 2011–2012*, pp. 12–29.

Chapter 4

1   LEED (Leadership in Energy and Environmental Design) is a United States Green Building Council system for rating sustainable projects. A project is "registered" during the design phase to initiate the submittal process. Following construction completion and some period of operation, the final LEED application is evaluated and a level of certification (Certified, Silver, Gold, or Platinum) is awarded. LEED certification provides independent, third-party verification that a building, home, or community was designed and built using strategies aimed at achieving high performance in key areas of human and environmental health: sustainable site development, water savings, energy efficiency, materials selection,

and indoor environmental quality. See http://www.usgbc.org /DisplayPage.aspx?CategoryID=19.

Chapter 5

1   Self-efficacy is defined as the individual's perception that she or he has the ability to do a certain activity.

2   Albert Bandura, *Social Foundations of Thought and Action* (Upper Saddle River, NJ: Prentice Hall, 1990).

3   http://www.uicni.org/page.php?section=neighborhoods&subsecti on=northlawndale

4   http://www.nlen.org/documents/cir_report.pdf.

5   Richard S. Kordesh, *Restoring Power to Parents and Places* (Lincoln, NE: Universe, 2006).

6   A good book that demonstrates this research is Fred Luthans, Carolyn M. Youssef, and Bruce J. Avolio, *Psychological Capital* (Oxford: Oxford University Press, 2007).

Chapter 6

1   See Paul Guyer, *Kant's System of Nature and Freedom* (New York: Oxford University Press, 2005), particularly chapters 6, "Kant on the Theory and Practice of Antonomy," and 11, "The Unity of Nature and Freedom," for detailed discussions of Kant's philosophy.

2   Jim Collins, *Good to Great: Why Some Companies Make the Leap—and*

Others Don't (New York: HarperBusiness, 2001).

3   The concept of KASH (knowledge, abilities, skills, and habits) might be attributable to several sources; one of the authors was first introduced to this acronym by the late Rod Winkle, former director of organizational learning for the Cooper Tire Company, Findlay, Ohio. KASH is an excellent way to remember the critical human capital that each employee brings to work and invests within the organization each day.

Chapter 7

1   Robert S. Kaplan and David P. Norton, "The Balanced Scorecard: Measures that Drive Performance," *Harvard Business Review* 70, no. 1 (January–February 1992): 71–79.

2   Robert S. Kaplan and David P. Norton, "Having Trouble with Your Strategy? Then Map It," *Harvard Business Review* 78, no. 5 (September–October 2000): 167–176.

3   A mystery shopper is a reviewer paid by an organization to rate its employees' interaction with customers; the rating is based on what the raters experienced and what behaviors the organization indicated the raters should expect.

4   For example, see Kenneth R. Thompson and Fred Luthans, "Organizational Culture: A Behavioral Perspective," in B. Schneider, ed., *Organizational Climate and Culture* (San Francisco: Jossey-Bass, 1990): 319–344.

5   Jacqueline Coyle-Shapiro, Paula C. Morrow, Ray Richardson, and

Stephen R. Dunn, "Using Profit Sharing to Enhance Employee Attitudes," *Human Resource Management* 41, no. 4 (2002): 423–439.

6   Fred Luthans and Alexander D. Stajkovic, "Reinforce for Performance: The Need to Go Beyond Pay and Even Rewards," *Academy of Management Executive* 13, no. 2 (May 1999): 49–57.

7   Steven Kerr, "On the Folly of Rewarding A, Hoping For B," *Academy of Management Executive* 9, no. 1 (1995): 7–14.

8   Alexander D. Stajkovic and Fred Luthans, "A Meta-Analysis of the Effects of Organizational Behavior Modification on Task Performance, 1975–1995," *Academy of Management Journal* 40, no. 5 (October 1997): 1122–1149.

9   For several examples, see B. Schneider, ed., *Organizational Climate and Culture* (San Francisco: Jossey-Bass, 1990).

10 The classic in the area of leadership is Bernard M. Bass, *Bass and Stogdill's Handbook of Leadership: Theory, Research, and Managerial Applications*, 3rd ed. (New York: Free Press, 1990).

11 The Baldrige Core Values and Criteria reflect the importance of these dimensions. See http://www.nist.gov/baldrige/ and the Baldrige criteria books under current publications, particularly the core values and leadership criteria (cat. 1.1) and workforce focus (cats. 5.1 and 5.2).

12 Many have used this quote, including the authors of this book. We could not find its original source; it has been cited by many over the past decade.

13 Carolyn Youssef and Fred Luthans, "Positive Organizational Behavior in the Workplace: The Impact of Hope, Optimism, and Resilience," *Journal of Management* 33, no. 5 (2007): 774–800.

Chapter 8

1 A functional silo condition exists when units operate independently, with little copperative effort.

2 Since 1998, HealthGrades has analyzed risk-adjusted mortality and complication rates in nearly 5,000 American hospitals; in 2004, it began issuing an annual study in patient safety. For detailed discussion and a downloadable document with more details, see http://www.healthgrades.com/business/img/PatientSafetyIn AmericanHospitalsReport2004.pdf. HealthGrades recognized Advocate Good Samaritan Hospital in its 2012 "America's Best Hospitals" report as one of the top 50 hospitals in the United States, and as one of six in the Chicago area that year after year ranks in the top 5 percent of American hospitals for clinical excellence. For more details, see http://www.healthgrades.com /business/img/HealthGradesAmericasBestHospitals Report2012.pdf.

3 The Joint Commission on the Accreditation of Healthcare Organizations (JCAHO) is the primary accrediting body for health-care facilities within the United States. An independent, not-for-profit organization, JCAHO accredits and certifies more than 19,000 health-care organizations and programs. JCAHO accreditation and certification is recognized nationwide as a symbol of quality that reflects an organization's commitment to meeting certain performance standards. JCAHO serves the accreditation needs of several types of health-care-related facilities; among the most prominent are hospitals,

ambulatory health care, office-based surgery, long-term care, behavioral health care, and laboratory services. For more information about how to obtain JCAHO standards, see http://www.jointcommission .org/standards_information/standards.aspx; for general information about JCAHO, visit http://www.jointcommission.org/.

4   Magnet status is not easily gained. The American Nurses Credentialing Center (ANCC) administers the Magnet Recognition Program® Model, which "provides a framework for nursing practice and research" around fourteen forces of magnetism that operate in five areas: transformational leadership; structural empowerment; exemplary professional practice; new knowledge, innovation, and improvements; and empirical quality results. Good Samaritan Hospital received Magnet recognition in 2009. For more information, see http://www.nursecredentialing.org/Magnet/Program Overview/New-Magnet-Model.aspx.

5   "Code blue" is the standard internal hospital call for an emergency response to a life-threatening event, such as heart attack or respiratory arrest, when a patient's heart stops beating or the patient stops breathing, which means oxygen is not getting into the bloodstream to sustain life.

6   The hospital's Baldrige Award application summary (Section 1.1) states, "The GSAM Leadership System (GSLS) ensures that all leaders at every level of the organization understand what is expected of them . . . The GSLS aligns and integrates our leaders at all levels by providing them with the tools to model the GSAM values and lead consistently . . . Driven by our Mission, Values, and Philosophy (MVP), all leaders must understand stakeholder requirements . . . This focus on performance creates a *rhythm of accountability [that] leads to subsequent associate development* . . . and reward and recognition

of high performance. Development and recognition ensures associates feel acknowledged and motivated. . . . *As leaders review annual performance, scan the environment, and re-cast organizational challenges, communication mechanisms are used to inspire and raise the bar"* [italics added].

Chapter 9

1   See Tom Northup, *Five Hidden Mistakes CEOs Make: How to Unlock the Secrets That Drive Growth and Profitability* (Brisbane, Australia: Solutions Press, 2008).

2   See J. P. Kotter, "Leading Change: Why Transformation Efforts Fail," *Harvard Business Review* 73, no. 2 (March–April 1995): 59–69, and *Leading Change* (Boston: Harvard Business School Press, 1996).

3   J. M. Kouzes and B. Z. Posner, *The Five Practices of Exemplary Leadership* (San Francisco: Pfeiffer, 2003) identified five core practices of exemplary leaders: modeling the way, inspiring a shared vision, challenging the process, enabling others to act, and encouraging the heart.

4   See D. Moberg, "Role Models and Moral Exemplars: How Do Employees Acquire Virtues by Observing Others?" *Business Ethics Quarterly* 10, no. 3 (2000): 675–696.

5   James MacGregor Burns, author of *Leadership* (New York: HarperCollins, 1978) and *Transforming Leadership* (New York: Atlantic Monthly Press, 2003), is credited with defining transformational leadership, which transcends conflict and differences and "excites the previously bored and apathetic . . . recreates a political connection with the alienated . . . reaches to the wants and needs of the anomic and shapes

their motivation . . . and reaches out to the bored and disaffected" to give "new meanings to issues and causes" (2003, p. 137).

6   See Bernard Bass, "From Transactional to Transformational Leadership: Learning to Share the Vision," *Organizational Dynamics* 18, no. 3 (1990): 19–31, a classic discussion of the differences between leadership styles and the effectiveness of the transformational style.

7   See H. Bergmann, K. Hurson, and D. Russ-Eft, *Everyone a Leader: A Grassroots Model for the New Workplace* (New York: Wiley, 1999), for a good explanation of grassroots, front line leadership.

8   According to M. G. Pratt and B. E. Ashforth, "Fostering Meaningfulness in Working and at Work," in S. Srivastva and D. Cooperrider, *Appreciative Management and Leadership*, rev. ed. (Euclid, OH: Williams Custom Publishing, 2003): 309–327, the key to transcendence is a "comprehensive system of beliefs that connects and explains 'who one is' (identity) and who belongs (membership), what matters (values) and what is to be done (purpose), how and why things hang together. . . . to constitute 'reality' and 'truth' (ideology), [and] how one is embedded in that reality and connects to what matters and what is to be done (transcendence)."

9   Pratt and Ashforth (2003) discussed meaningfulness *in* work and *at* work. Meaningfulness *in* work focuses on the individual, specifically employee, involvement, and job redesign practices. Professions to which one appears to be "called," such as medicine, teaching, and public or military service, and which involve specific roles and identities, typify this category. The authors noted, "Organizations that focus only on enriching one's organizational membership—and not the work that one does" describe meaningfulness *at* work (p. 317). Based on the Pratt and Ashforth model, organizations that build

communities through visionary, charismatic, or transformational leadership, comprehensive ideologies, and collective-level identities would exemplify meaningfulness *at* work. From these definitions, we see entangled organizations providing meaningfulness both *in work* and *at work* rather than being mutually exclusive.

10 See P. Drucker, "Knowledge-Worker Productivity: The Biggest Challenge," *California Management Review* 41, no. 2 (Winter 1999): 79–94. Before his death in 2005, Drucker was recognized as one of the most prolific experts on organizational management. His work on innovation and the knowledge worker is "must reading" for every executive.

11 See R. Van Lee, L. Fabish, and N. McGaw, "The Value of Corporate Values," *Strategy+business* no. 39 (Summer 2005): 52–65. The authors noted that executives and governing boards were paying more attention to the central role of values in guiding behaviors within organizations.

12 Michael S. Schwartz, in "A Code of Ethics for Corporate Code of Ethics," *Journal of Business Ethics* 41, no. 1 (November–December 2002): 27–43, discussed how organizations across the globe have adopted codes of ethics that include trustworthiness, respect, responsibility, and fairness as core values.

13 See, in R. R. Sims and J. Brinkmann, "Leaders as Moral Role Models: The Case of John Gutfreund at Salomon Brothers," *Journal of Business Ethics* 35, no. 4 (2002): 327–339, a discussion on the impact and trickle-down effect of senior leader behaviors on employees throughout an organization.

14 T. Lickona and M. Davidson, in *Smart and Good High Schools: Integrating*

Excellence and Ethics for Success in School, Work, and Beyond (Cortland, NY: Center for the 4th and 5th Rs [Respect & Responsibility]/ Washington, DC: Character Education Partnership, 2005), identified two sides of individual character. *Performance character* is centered on intrapersonal competence related to doing the best job possible, with character traits such as conscientiousness, initiative, and dedication that relate to the emotional intelligence domains of self-awareness and self-management. *Moral character* focuses on interpersonal competences related to being the best person one can be toward others, with character traits of respect, dependability, and trustworthiness that relate to the emotional intelligence domains of social or organizational awareness and relationship management. S. A. Bowen, in "Organizational Factors Encouraging Ethical Decision Making: An Exploration into the Case of an Exemplar," *Journal of Business Ethics* 52, no. 4 (July 2004): 311–324, noted ethics and values are core to organizational culture since ethics and values affect how people treat others within the organization. J. Badaracco, in "The Discipline of Building Character," *Harvard Business Review* 76, no. 2 (March–April 1998): 114–124, noted how character formation flows continuously through life because tests of character arise every time a person chooses between two values; thus employees form and reinforce their individual character in organizational settings whenever they must choose between two actions or values.

15 S. Forbes and E. Ames, in *How Capitalism Will Save Us: Why Free People and Free Markets Are the Best Answer in Today's Economy* (New York: Crown Business, 2009), described how most people work within a "web of trust" in daily transactions (p. 34). According to Forbes and Ames, Bernard Madoff was able to dupe others not because of his greed but because of others' willingness to trust.

16 See J. Carlzon's *Moments of Truth* (New York: Ballinger, 1987) for

a discussion of how customers determine value and make judgments that affect their future interactions and decisions concerning suppliers.

17 R. Lukasova, "Organizational Culture: Relationship Between Organizational Character and Behaviour," *Management of Organizations: Systematic Research* 32 (December 2004): 95–103, defined the "corporate character of an organization . . . as the personality of the individual organization" (p. 96). We found especially pertinent the discussion of J. P. Birnholtz, M. D. Cohen, and S. V. Hoch in "Organizational Character: On the Regeneration of Camp Poplar Grove," *Organization Science* 18, no. 2 (March–April 2007): 315–332; they described organizational culture as "the coherent content of the ensemble of dispositions that generates the distinctive actions of the organization" (p. 317), and they argued that the "ensemble of dispositions" that represents organizational character "resides in the individual procedural memories of organizational participants, and is coherent, persistent, and regenerative" (p. 317). M. W. Grojean, C. J. Resick, M.W. Dickson, and D. B. Smith, in "Leaders, Values, and Organizational Climate: Examining Leadership Strategies for Establishing an Organizational Climate Regarding Ethics," *Journal of Business Ethics* 55, no. 3 (2004): 223–241, noted company success depends on how leaders understand the critical contribution of character education to the normative side of organizational culture.

18 See J. Katzenbach and D. Smith, "The Discipline of Teams," *Harvard Business Review* 71, no. 2 (1993): 111–120, a classic discussion of the differences between teams and groups.

19 A company's business plan should be a comprehensive set of plans that integrate long-term strategic plan perspectives for the next

three to five years with shorter-term plans focused on the immediate future—for example, the next six to twelve months. The business plan needs to address the integration of operations, financial,
marketing, infrastructure, and human resource efforts required to
execute actions. The development and execution of action plans
and individual performance plans represent near-term operational plans designed to help the organization achieve annual goals
through various tactics.

20 Robert Kaplan and David Norton, in "Mastering the Management
System," *Harvard Business Review* 86, no.1 (January 2008): 62–77,
noted that successful organizations create a closed-loop management
system that links strategy and operations. Strategy development and
effective execution stem from a well-defined organizational purpose
that includes mission, vision, and value statements.

21 See Robert Kaplan and David Norton, "The Balanced Scorecard:
Measures That Drive Performance," *Harvard Business Review* 83,
no.7/8 (July–August 2005): 172–180, and "Using the Balanced
Scorecard as a Strategic Management System," *Harvard Business
Review* 85, no.7/8 (July–August 2007): 150–161, for excellent intro-
ductory discussions on metrics and performance measurement.
Kaplan and Norton (2005) noted how employee behaviors are
strongly affected by measurements.

22 For a more detailed examination of the Balanced Scorecard, see
books by Kaplan and Norton: *The Balanced Scorecard: Translating
Strategy into Action* (Boston: Harvard Business School Press, 1996)
and *The Strategy-Focused Organization: How Balanced Scorecard Companies Thrive in the New Business Environment* (Boston: Harvard Business
School Press, 2001).

23 See M. Treacy and F. Wiersema's classic article, "Customer Intimacy and Other Value Disciplines," *Harvard Business Review* 71, no.1 (January–February 1993): 84–93, to understand the critical role value disciplines play in an organization's strategy, direction, and results. The intimacy of experience evident in MidwayUSA and other organizations within our research reflected a strong customer-intimacy value orientation.

24 See F. Luthans, C. M. Youssef, and B. J. Avolio, *Psychological Capital: Developing the Human Competitive Edge* (New York: Oxford University Press, 2007), for a deeper understanding of positive organizational behavior (POB). POB represents the "study and application of positively oriented human resource strengths and psychological capacities that can be measured, developed, and effectively managed for performance improvement in today's workplace."

25 See www.nist.gov/Baldrige for the set of criteria and specifically the scoring guidelines that focus on defining processes.

26 According to Stajkovic and Luthans (as cited in Luthans et al., 2007), self-efficacy is "an individual's conviction (or confidence) about his or her abilities to mobilize the motivation, cognitive resources, and courses of action needed to successfully execute a specific task within a given context" (p. 16).

27 Vince Lombardi's last speech was given in Dayton, Ohio, on June 22, 1970; he died three months later. A full transcript of the speech is available through http://www.conservativeforum.org/essaysform.asp?ID=12129.

28 Luthans et al. (2007) discussed the contagion effect of self-efficacy, through which the psychological capital of a leader's self-efficacy

can trickle down or spread laterally to others, such that "investments in authentic leadership" are "likely to yield exponential returns that far exceed conservative estimates" (p. 56).

29 See Walter Payton with Don Yeager, *Never Die Easy: The Autobiography of Walter Payton* (New York: Random House, 2011), p. 11.

30 E. Schein, *Organizational Culture and Leadership*, 3rd ed. (San Francisco: Jossey-Bass, 2004), noted that values are a foundational part of organizational culture. Thus, establishing a culture of discipline means operating within the values defined for the organization.

31 For additional details and insights, go to http://www.gallup.com /poll/150383/Majority-American-Workers-Not-Engaged-Jobs .aspx to review study results released on October 28, 2011.

32 The same Gallup study showed 26 percent of employees in world-class organizations were not engaged and 7 percent were actively disengaged.

33 For an excellent discussion and guidance on after-action reviews (AARs), see M. Darling, C. Parry, and J. Moore, "Learning in the Thick of It," *Harvard Business Review* 83, no.7 (2005): 84–92.

34 See the discussion about fully effective versus dysfunctional organizational designs in G. Neilson, B. A. Pasternack, and D. Mendes, "The Seven Types of Organizational DNA," *Strategy+business* no. 35 (Summer 2004): 95–103. Based on an ongoing study of several thousand companies across all industries and markets, approximately two-thirds of companies are ineffective in executing their missions. The roughly 25 percent of companies that effectively execute have cultures in which employees are empowered and

organizational learning is a priority, much as we saw within the organizations included within our study.

35 Encouraging the heart is the fifth practice of exemplary leaders (see note 3 for chapter 9). To assess your personal efficacy at executing the seven essential practices for encouraging others—e.g., setting clear standards, setting an example, personalizing recognition, and expecting the best—see J. M. Kouzes and B. Z. Posner, *The Encouraging the Heart Workbook* (San Francisco: Jossey-Bass, 2006).

36 The seven categories of the Baldrige design are presented in abbreviated form here. For more details, see J. Latham and J. Vinyard, *Baldrige User's Guide: Organization Diagnosis, Design, and Transformation* (New York: Wiley, 2005), as well as http://www.nist.gov/baldrige /publications/business_nonprofit_criteria.cfm.

37 See B. Jaruzelski, J. Loehr, and R. Holman, "Why Culture Is Key," *Strategy+business* no. 65 (Winter 2011): 30–45. In their Global Innovation 1000 study, Jaruzelski et al. found only 44 percent of companies had high alignment between culture and innovative strategies, which had direct impact on gross profits and enterprise value.

38 SMART stands for "Specific, Measurable, Attainable, Results-Oriented, and Time-Bound."

39 Advocate Good Samaritan Hospital Malcolm Baldrige National Quality Award Application Summary, which is available via http://www.baldrige.nist.gov/PDF_files/2010_Advocate_Good _Samaritan_Award_Application_Summary.pdf/.

40 See T. Peters and R. Waterman, *In Search of Excellence* (New York: Harper and Row, 1982). Like several subsequent studies, including Jim Collins's *Good to Great: Why Some Companies Make the Leap . . . and Others Don't* (New York: HarperCollins, 2001), many of the companies Peters and Waterman studied fell off their pedestals after appearing in *Excellence*. However, Collins, in *How the Mighty Fall and Why Some Companies Never Give In* (New York: HarperCollins, 2009), noted that hubris born of success is the first fault of company leaders who think too much of themselves. Collins (2001) emphasized the importance of humble Level 5 leaders at the top of organizations that sustain excellence over the long term. The leaders of the organizations highlighted within this book exemplified Level 5 leadership.

41 J. Kirby, in "Toward a Theory of High Performance," *Harvard Business Review* 83, no.7 (July–August 2005): 30–39, examined ten distinct analyses of high performance, including Peters and Waterman (1982) and Collins and Porras, *Built to Last* (New York: Harper Business, 1994). Kirby noted a single definition of a high-performing company does not exist because measurements of what constitutes "a winner" vary. Whereas Collins and Porras (1994) and Collins (2001) used comparative analyses of matched pairs of companies, other studies examined paths (J. Katzenbach, *Peak Performance: Aligning the Hearts and Minds of Your Employees*, Boston: Harvard Business School Press, 2000) or mindfulness within high-reliability organizations (K. E. Weick and K. M. Sutcliffe, *Managing the Unexpected: Assuring High Performance in an Age of Complexity*, San Francisco:

INDEX

ABOUT THE AUTHORS

Ken Thompson, Ph.D., is a professor and former chair of management at DePaul University. He has coauthored four textbooks and is the senior editor of the *Journal of Leadership and Organizational Studies*. Ken is past chair of the Management Education and Development Division of the Academy of Management. He was a Senior Examiner for the Baldrige National Quality Award Program and is a senior lead examiner for the Illinois Sate Performace Award.

Ray Benedetto, DM, is a retired USAF colonel. Ray founded a consulting firm that helps leaders build high-performing, character-based cultures. He teaches leadership and strategic planning for the University of Phoenix Chicago Campus MBA program. Ray is an active member of the Academy of Management and a Fellow of the American College of Healthcare Executives.

Tom Walter has been in the food and beverage service industry for over forty years as a partner, principal, president, or CEO of twenty-nine start-ups and three acquisitions. His focus on a moral and ethical workplace culture and the value of human capital has resulted in numerous awards such as "Best Places to Work." An active member of the Academy of Management and the Small Giants Community, Tom was inducted into the Chicago Entrepreneurship Hall of Fame.

Molly Meyer is a marketing professional and freelance writer. As the creative director for nuphoriq, a Chicago-based marketing group, Molly translates strategy into fresh and compelling creative for multiple mediums. Molly was an All-Atlantic 10 and Academic All-American student athlete at University of Dayton.